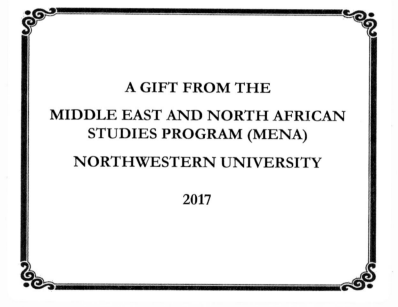

BRIAN T. EDWARDS

AFTER THE
AMERICAN CENTURY

The Ends of U.S. Culture in the Middle East

Columbia University Press / New York

Columbia University Press
Publishers Since 1893
New York   Chichester, West Sussex
cup.columbia.edu

Library of Congress Cataloging-in-Publication Data

Edwards, Brian T., 1968–
    After the American century : the ends of U.S. culture in the Middle East /
Brian T. Edwards.
        pages cm
    Includes bibliographical references and index.
    ISBN 978-0-231-17400-8 (cloth : acid-free paper)
    ISBN 978-0-231-54055-1 (e-book)
    1. United States—Relations—Middle East.   2. Middle East—Relations—
United States.   3. Popular culture—United States.   4. Popular culture—
Middle East.   5. Orientalism—United States.   6. Ethnic attitudes—Middle
East.   7. Culture diffusion—Middle East.   8. Globalization—Social aspects—
Middle East.   9. Middle East—Civilization—21st century.   I. Title.

DS63.2.U5E38 2016
303.48'256073—dc23

2015020790

COVER IMAGE: Mural in Isfahan, Iran, advertising a local
fruit-and-vegetable market. (Photograph by Brian Edwards)
COVER DESIGN: Archie Ferguson

For Kate Baldwin

and for our children

Oliver, Pia, Theo, and Charlotte

Neither . . . had asked her why, but she thinks now that if they had she might have told them she was weeping for her century, though whether the one past or the one present she doesn't know.

William Gibson, *Pattern Recognition*

CONTENTS

CONTENTS

EPILOGUE
Embracing Orientalism in the Homeland

199

PREFACE

W HEN I FIRST started this project in 2005, I expected that Beirut
would be one of the principal sites of my research and get its
own chapter. I have since traveled to Lebanon's capital seven
times. For about a year, I engaged a research assistant in Beirut, whom
I asked to track when and how American cultural artifacts appeared in
Lebanese media, including book and film reviews, popular culture, and
online postings. I didn't quite know what I was looking for, though we
gathered a great deal of interesting material. The amount was quickly overwhelming. And then Beirut was under attack by Israel again, and such a
project seemed incidental if not impracticable.

On one of those trips to Beirut, I happened across a little café called Café
Younes. The branch in Hamra is well known to those who live in or travel
to the city, around the corner from the famous Commodore hotel, where
Western journalists were based during the Lebanese civil war of the 1990s.
It remains a place I visit on each trip.

In 2005, Café Younes was not much bigger than a walk-in closet, with a
roasting machine squeezed in the corner and some stools pulled up to a shallow counter along the wall.[1] At first glance, this location gave off a certain
air of authenticity. Seventy years earlier, in 1935, Amin Younes had returned to Lebanon from Brazil to open a coffee shop in downtown Beirut

(the branch in Hamra opened in 1960 and was the second). When I visited, a man named Abou Anwar was celebrating a half-century as roaster. He had worked for Younes since 1955, when he was sixteen years old.

To be sure, multiple traditions and styles of coffee preparation were in evidence here, a palimpsest left behind by the numerous imperial powers with an interest in Beirut. At Younes, you could have Turkish coffee made to order or excellent espresso or café crème from the traditions learned during the French Mandate period. American-style filtered coffee, too, was on the menu.

My first visit to Café Younes came five years after a big Starbucks had opened on Hamra Street, just a few blocks away. In news coverage about the massive expansion of Starbucks in those years, journalists worried that the great café culture of the Arab Middle East would be lost or—worse—Americanized by the huge Seattle chain. Language similar to that which greeted the arrival of McDonald's in Moscow and Beijing during the previous decade was reemerging.

I myself wondered how a Starbucks around the corner would affect Café Younes. How could this place compete with the trademark frappuccinos, to say nothing of the spacious seating area, plush chairs, and sidewalk terrace, none of which Younes had here?

Posted on the wall were news clippings from the local press. There I found my answer. Amin Younes, the founder's thirty-something grandson, had been asked precisely the same question that was on my mind. He answered in a way that surprised me: the arrival of Starbucks had the potential to improve his business. Starbucks was changing how his own customers thought about coffee drinks and in turn provided him with the opportunity to expand his menu. As Younes told a journalist, "When Starbucks opened, we had fewer than 10 varieties of coffee drinks on offer. Weeks later, we had expanded the selection to more than 20, and sales were higher."[2]

Though I decided not to pursue research in Beirut for this book, Younes's comment stuck with me. In the face of a challenge that others (myself included) assumed would wipe out his business, Younes's response represented not only business acumen—the recognition that Starbucks was helping him expand his own menu—but also a form of creativity. Younes took the

American menu and, rather than replicating it, made it into one his own customers would cherish, responding to their own now altered sense of what a café might serve. There were the typical espresso drinks, but now he added drinks with Middle Eastern flavors and spices, such as a cardamom-flavored espresso, lattes laced with rose water, and smoothies that incorporated green bananas and mango.

On my most recent visit to Beirut in February 2015, I visited not only the small location in which I had first sat in 2005 but also the new, large-scale addition next door, complete with souvenirs, books, customized mugs, and T-shirts. Though there were now comfortable seating and a sidewalk terrace, the place was no replica of Starbucks but had retained its own personality. Café Younes had done well.

A few months earlier, in May 2014, as I was completing the manuscript of this book, the Middle East and North African Studies Program at Northwestern hosted the Tangier filmmaker Moumen Smihi. Smihi's visit was in connection with a film retrospective organized in Santa Cruz that we had brought to Evanston. Though I was working on this book when he came, I assumed Smihi was working in a different paradigm than the younger Moroccan filmmakers I discuss in chapter 4. After all, Smihi—born in 1945 and a former student of Roland Barthes—was more influenced by structuralist theory, I assumed, than by digital culture.

After one of his talks, I asked Smihi what he thought about what anthropologist Kevin Dwyer has called the paradox of Moroccan cinema, wherein the movie houses are closing even as a dynamic series of films is emerging from Morocco. The curator of the retrospective had gone to considerable expense to procure and screen 35-millimeter prints of Smihi's lush films, which were otherwise out of circulation.

Smihi responded to my question in a way that surprised me: "Actually," he said, "this crisis of [movie] theaters in Morocco is my chance." By "chance," he meant the French sense of the word, "my good luck." He went on to say, "It's the distributors who decide how many [in the] audience they must have, and then [the distributors don't] take films below a certain number." He paused. I reflected on how little known Smihi himself was in the United States precisely because of this dynamic. But then, again, he surprised me.

"In Morocco there is a real revolution that is not of the Arab Spring, of theaters collapsing, etcetera," he said. "The real revolution is that you can buy all the Bergman and Hitchcock films on the sidewalks, pirated films, for 10 cents a film."

Later that week I watched Smihi's film *Moroccan Chronicles*, which had been released in the last year of the twentieth century. The film is ostensibly the depiction of three tales told by a mother to her young son as he recovers from his circumcision. Each of the three tales is set in a different Moroccan city: Marrakech, Essaouira, and Tangier. But they are also in complex ways engaged with American cinematic forerunners—most explicitly *The Man Who Knew Too Much* (1956), which Alfred Hitchcock had filmed in Marrakech, and *Othello* (1952), which Orson Welles had filmed in Essaouira. I knew both of the forerunners quite well—I had written about the Hitchcock film in my first book—but I had not known about Smihi's reworking of them. As I watched Smihi's film now with great admiration, I thought about what I would have said about it a decade ago when I was finishing my book *Morocco Bound*. Back then, I was fascinated by Moroccan texts that "disoriented" American representations of Morocco. I had analyzed a film by another Moroccan director that recast the iconic *Casablanca* dramatically.

How had I missed this film, which reoriented Hitchcock and Welles in such interesting ways? I berated myself.

Hitchcock's film had made its way into Morocco on those cheap pirated copies, I realized, where a filmmaker such as Smihi or his followers could pick it up and do what they might with it. But the circulatory process works differently in the other direction. Smihi's 1999 film is still not distributed on DVD, and ten years ago you would have had to track it down in the director's private collection or the Moroccan film archive. No one had written about it seriously yet, so there was no record in the scholarship that it engaged Hitchcock.[3] And now, in 2014, it took a film retrospective in a museum to bring it to general attention. Anyone could see the Hitchcock film, but I could count the number of the people in the Chicago area who might see Smihi's film.

These are but two stories of the curious pathways along which American cultural products and forms—a Hitchcock film and a Starbucks menu—have traveled in recent years. These stories begin to suggest the creativity with which some individuals in the Middle East and North Africa have taken up American culture for their own projects. At the same time, they alert us to the ways in which some of the more interesting new products end up out of circulation and remain local (a café down a side street, a brilliant film barely known outside of Morocco). Though many have assumed that globalization in the cultural realm brings endless circulation, these new products are end points, perhaps even dead ends, and they do not return easily. But neither do they particularly want to, and that is what makes them perhaps crucial to understand in grasping what the world after the American century looks like.

AFTER THE AMERICAN CENTURY

1

AFTER THE AMERICAN CENTURY

Ends of Circulation

I N THIS BOOK, I argue that because of the ways in which culture circulates in the digital age *and* because of the changed geopolitical status of the United States in the twenty-first century, we have entered a period after the American century—meaning that American culture, long popular globally and assumed to have a positive message or benefit to U.S. politics, is generally taken up by individuals in ways that detach the cultural product from its American referent and thereby shatter the presumption of their close relationship. Focusing on a series of cases from three contexts in North Africa and the Middle East, I try to make sense of the fragmented meanings that American cultural objects and forms—with recognizably American sources but unfamiliar in their use or application—now take in new and frequently unpredicted locations. In so doing, I am trying to map out what the period after the American century looks like from the perspective of literature, film, and cultural production.

I have been researching this project for nearly a decade in multiple sites. On one of my more recent research trips for this book, something happened in Rabat, Morocco, that revealed more about my argument than I had expected so late in the process. So I want to begin by telling that story.

I had just given a talk to a group of students and faculty at Mohammed V University, the eminent state university in the Moroccan capital. My subject that day in November 2012 was the American autumn and its relationship to the Arab Spring. "American autumn" was my shorthand for the paradoxical situation we find ourselves in: U.S. hegemony is in decline economically and politically even while the products of American culture are ubiquitous.[1]

This paradox is especially apparent in Morocco, where I have lived, traveled, and done research over the past two decades. Moroccan culture more and more incorporates elements of American culture, whether in the hip-hop of popular artists such as Hoba Hoba Spirit or Fnaire, the dazzling commercial spaces of Casablanca's Morocco Mall and Rabat's Mega Mall, or the sophisticated look of movies by younger directors such as Faouzi Bensaidi and Laïla Marrakchi. Indeed, after the talk I would be on my way to the Marrakech International Film Festival, where many of the year's crop of Moroccan films seemed painted from a distinctly American palette. As one Moroccan director said to me about another, "He's watched a lot of *CSI* [the American television series *CSI: Crime Scene Investigation*], and it shows."

Yet if much of local culture looks increasingly American, I have witnessed a steady decline in attitudes toward the United States over the past dozen years. Back in the 1990s, when I first lived in the country, Moroccans I encountered in daily life would routinely remind me that theirs was the first nation to acknowledge the sovereignty of the United States (in December 1777); the two countries were the oldest of friends, they would proudly say. The Moroccan–American Treaty of Friendship, signed by John Adams, Thomas Jefferson, and Sultan Mohammed III in 1786, was the formal proof. A letter from George Washington to Mohammed III (also known as Mohammed ben Abdullah) written in 1789 and on display in the Tangier American Legation Museum—itself the first property owned by the United States overseas, a gift of Moulay Suleiman in 1821 and for 140 years the location of the U.S. Consulate—testifies to this historical relationship. The urban landscape was pocked by signs of the popularity of American culture—so many shops named after the television show *Dallas*, so many copies of U.S. clothing labels and T-shirts—and the classrooms at the universities were filled with young Moroccans eager to learn English, not only for the jobs they were hoping to be able to apply for but also out of fascination with the United States. It was American English that these young Moroccans wanted to learn, including the pronunciation and the slang that they could pick up from movies broadcast on TV or music. Bill Clinton was extremely popular here during the 1990s, and people laughed at the scandal about *"monika"*—a homonym of the Moroccan Arabic word for "toy"—and many claimed it was a Zionist conspiracy to bring down Clinton.

Since the 2003 invasion of Iraq, however, that enthusiasm has steadily waned, and the election of Barack Obama to the presidency helped only briefly. Arab satellite news provides a steady diet of American drone attacks and Florida ministers who threaten to burn the Qur'an. It is difficult to compete with the constant stream of negative images of racial profiling of Muslims on American airplanes and Tea Party anxieties about Islam. Although Moroccans have numerous points of contact with the United States—many people know someone who won the visa lottery and lives there or have met American Peace Corps workers—these news stories tend to overwhelm them. No amount of cultural products from the United States could make those politics less offensive or upsetting here. To make matters worse, coverage of Europe's poor treatment of North Africans often bleeds into Moroccans' impressions of the United States, which were already plummeting after the invasion and occupation of Afghanistan and Iraq. In Morocco, the Islamist Parti de la justice et du développement (PJD), long powerless, won a substantial number of seats in parliamentary elections in 2002 and 2007; then in 2011 it secured enough seats to usher the party leader, Abdelilah Benkirane, into the office of prime minister. Multiple factors were in play, of course, but certainly one that helped launch the PJD into power was increasing enmity to the Moroccan leadership, which had partnered with the United States during the early years of the so-called war on terror.

Nevertheless, Morocco has a long history of incorporating cultural elements from occupying or aggressive powers. The popularity of American cultural products can be seen both as part of the long official friendship between the two countries and as an alternative to French and Spanish culture, well known through colonial occupation of the country. In the 1940s, after the arrival of American GIs during World War II, Moroccan folksinger

Houcine Slaoui (1918–1951) sang, "Zin u l 'ain az-zarqa jana bkul khir" (The beautiful blue-eyed ones brought us all good things). The song "Al Miri-kan" (The American) became an anthem of the era, and Slaoui's references to "shwing" (chewing gum) and cosmetics provide evidence of the impact of the cultural commodities that followed the U.S. Army's landing in November 1942. American slang, too, arrived with the army; Slaoui's famous chorus repeats the new words now part of the Moroccan lexicon: "Okay, okay, come on, bye-bye."[2]

Slaoui's wonderful song also provides us with an early example of the ways that Moroccans adapted and remade these cultural imports. Americans who listen to the song frequently do not understand that the word *shwing* is *chewing gum* pronounced in the Moroccan dialect, nor are most able even to understand the chorus. These American words became Moroccanized in their pronunciation, just as the objects themselves took on new uses and meanings. We should not assume that the arrival of these cultural objects was treated with horror—some new cultural imperialism. Although the song is clearly sarcastic about the "blessings" that the Americans brought with them, Slaoui's generation did find the arrival of American culture something of a relief compared to that which came with the French colonial occupation (1912–1956).

In my talk in Rabat in 2012, I spent some time discussing a digital pirate artist named Hamada who had been active in Morocco during the middle years of the first decade of the 2000s (I discuss him further in chapter 4).

About twenty-five people were in attendance, most of them students but also a few faculty members. The conversation after my talk was good, if a bit academic. My host made some comments about Albert Hirschman's book *Exit, Voice, and Loyalty* (1970) and then contrasted my account of the connection between the Arab uprisings and the Occupy Wall Street movement with the account given by political theorists Antonio Negri and Michael Hardt.[3] (I had given some evidence that Occupy Wall Street may have been influenced by events in Tahrir Square rather than vice versa, which suggests that democratic movements in the West might be learning from the Arab world.) The host's colleague, a former chair of the English Department at Mohammed V, discussed a contemporary Moroccan artist she thought was relevant to my subject. The students asked some tentative questions, but they seemed not to have heard of Hamada. Five or six years earlier Hamada's work had been everywhere, but popular culture is constantly changing, and he was forgotten by the time a new generation came along.

Then someone made a comment—an intervention, it would be properly called—that raised the stakes dramatically. Hakim Belabbes, a Moroccan filmmaker splitting his time between Chicago and Rabat, had come into the room about ten minutes into my talk, but he had listened attentively throughout.

He had been an undergraduate in this department thirty years ago, Belabbes said, and he too had sat in this room in the same chairs. He knew what the students were thinking because he had thought the same things himself. Belabbes told them that he could read their body language. He knew they had things to say.

Belabbes spoke about Hamada and about Moroccan hip-hop. He asked the students if they knew the work of a few musicians from his generation whose names he recited. He was startled when they did not, but he made his point: Moroccan musicians had already been using spoken word before the arrival of American hip-hop. Belabbes told me he agreed with my argument, and he wanted young Moroccans to know that they need not rely on outside forms to make their own culture. The last suggestion was a familiar refrain, reminiscent of nationalist arguments about self-reliance in the cultural sphere. It reminded me of comments I had heard in Iran in my previous visits there.

But then Belabbes started talking about the Internet movie *Innocence of Muslims*. Students shifted uneasily in their chairs. Belabbes asked me half rhetorically whether this film was an example of culture exported by the United States to the Arab world.

Some of the students became visibly upset. This topic clearly mattered to them. "The film should be stopped," one said. "It should be taken down off the Internet." My first impulse was to defend the principle of freedom of speech, even the most offensive speech. I also began to explain that the exception that many had pointed to—France's so-called Gayssot Law of

1990, which forbids Holocaust denial and discrimination based on membership in an ethnic group, one of several such laws limiting free speech in Europe—was not in force in the United States, which had a much more capacious sense of protected speech. But I also knew that paeans to the First Amendment didn't matter to the majority of these students. They were unimpressed. Here was a vivid case where the unpredictable pathways that cultural forms travel in the digital age matter urgently. Here, at this moment at Mohammed V, the cherished First Amendment of the U.S. Constitution seemed to be part and parcel of American Empire.

Innocence of Muslims, a film hostile to Islam and offensive to most Muslims, was one of the most important cultural exports from the United States in 2012. A thirteen-minute, low-budget film made in southern California had arguably wiped out years of cultural programming and efforts by the U.S. State Department—all of the investment in cultural diplomacy, the hip-hop tours, the rock concerts, the newfound attention to Twitter and digital diplomacy—to persuade Muslim hearts and minds that the United States is tolerant of Islam. Despite atrocious production values and lack of artistry, the impact of *Innocence of Muslims* overwhelmed that of films produced in Hollywood with budgets in the tens of millions of dollars.

When the origins of the film eventually were revealed, the world learned that it had been produced by an Egyptian American Christian living in Los Angeles and directed by another American with a string of soft-core porn films to his name.[4] The actors in the film later claimed they had been deceived and had believed they were acting in an ancient Egyptian epic. Reporters dug up the original casting call, which bore out the actor's claims. Analysis showed that scenes were later dubbed over with hateful and absurd references to the history of Islam. (In March 2014, one of the actresses involved requested sanctions against Google for up to $128 million for failing to remove all copies of the film from YouTube in violation of the Ninth Circuit of Appeals ruling on February 28, 2014.[5] In September 2014, a second actor sued both the filmmaker and Google for "reproducing his performance without authorization."[6]

What can *Innocence of Muslims* tell us about the circulation of American culture in the Middle East and North Africa?

The short film was first posted on YouTube on July 1, 2012, when it attracted little attention. (It had been screened at the Vine Theater in Hollywood once in late June under the title *Innocence of Bin Laden* to an audience of ten people.) But when a version dubbed into Arabic was introduced on YouTube in September, it drew the notice of Egyptian media. On September 9, Egyptian station al-Nas broadcast a two-minute clip by host Sheikh Khaled Abdalla. Other Egyptian bloggers and Internet media outlets picked up the story, and in a single day it quickly moved from Egypt across the Arab world and from there to the rest of the planet. With the anniversary of the attacks on September 11, 2001, approaching and fueled by attention from such notorious figures as Terry Jones, a small-time Florida pastor who had already achieved global infamy for threatening to burn the Qur'an on a previous anniversary of September 11, large protests and demonstrations against the video took place across Muslim-majority countries.[7]

In Cairo, as protesters approached the U.S. Embassy, nervous diplomatic staff sent a message by Twitter that implicitly criticized the YouTube video or apologized for it, setting off a firestorm of critical media in the United States.[8] The following day an attack at the American consulate in Benghazi, Libya, resulted in the killing of the U.S. ambassador and another American diplomat. At the time, given massive media coverage of protests over the video at a range of U.S. embassies and consulates in Muslim-majority countries, the assumption was that the political assassination was linked to a reaction to the film. Later investigation put this initial assumption into question—the attack on the Benghazi consulate had apparently been planned before news of the film spread—but the debate affected the 2012 presidential campaign and impacted the political future of Secretary of State Hillary Clinton. All from a low-budget YouTube video.

Now two months later, two thousand miles to the west of Benghazi and twenty-seven hundred miles west of Cairo, Belabbes's comments electrified the room in Rabat. The wound was still fresh across the Arab and Muslim world.

In later chapters of this book, I discuss topics such as what impact Hollywood formulas and narrative techniques have had on Moroccan cinema, how Iranians dub and redub films using computer-generated imagery such as *Shrek* (Andrew Adamson and Vicky Jenson, 2001), and the ways Egyptian novelists take American fiction in directions that would be unimaginable to their authors. In such cases, there is a fracturing of the American original so that something from it jumps publics into a new sociocultural milieu. Looking backward, we can see the U.S. origin of the cultural form, but what matters more is the creative novelty that form has permitted to Arab and Iranian creators in the new context. Part of the pleasure in their play is, as we will see, the collision of a global culture with a local subject (the Iranian dubbings of *Shrek* are highly local, as are the details in the Egyptian graphic novel, with its American-influenced style). In the end, as these newer cultural forms and products make their way across the circulatory matrix, they may carry some Americanness with them, but they also shed the United States as their point of origin or their ultimate meaning. This is one of the premises of a world beyond the American century.

And yet *Innocence of Muslims* was a case in which the American origin of the cultural product seemed to matter deeply, in which there was little rupture between the cultural product *as* American and the presumed link to U.S. politics. Here, content (anti-Islam), form (pornography, or rather the look of soft-core porn without the sex scenes or nudity), and origin (the United States) seemed to align. As a result, the film had a vivid and powerful meaning in Moroccan, Egyptian, and Iranian society and in turn affected politics.[9] Was it an American century again, but now with only negative effects?

What did it mean that this film, offensive to so many, was made in the United States, included American actors, and was distributed via YouTube, an American website that otherwise was alleged to stand for freedom, innovation, and the democratizing potential of the Internet and that in many other contexts had allowed Arabs and Iranians to post videos that worked against state censorship or autocratic rule?[10] What did the widespread circulation of this film made in the United States, as one person in the room at Mohammed V University pointed out, mean to American cultural diplomacy? What was the difference between unofficial cultural products such as *Innocence of Muslims*, from which the Obama administration was trying to keep its distance even while defending the film's right to exist, and other American cultural products emerging from more respectable or established venues, such as Ben Affleck's blockbuster film *Argo* (2012), which provoked so much controversy in Iran, as I discuss in chapter 3?

These questions matter to public diplomacy and the ways in which the United States engages with the Arab world, Iran, and Muslim-majority countries in the Middle East and in Central, South, and Southeast Asia. But they also matter to the ways in which we understand how literature, film, and other products of culture function in the digital age.

I left the room at Mohammed V University unsettled, both recommitted to the importance of describing and analyzing the way that cultural products move through the world and aware that the changes in technology and the democratization of access to massive distribution lead always to unpredictable ends—as *Innocence of Muslims* demonstrated with the pain and violence that followed in its wake.

We are living through a remarkable period of change. The meanings attached to the United States in the world have shifted decisively, and there is widespread distrust of American intentions. During the exciting winter and spring of 2011, the wave of global protests for democracy in the Arab world did not look to American models for sustenance and inspiration— nor did the protests in Iran in 2009. As I indicated in my talk at Rabat, some of the people who participated in Occupy Wall Street and its many affiliates avowed that they had looked to the Middle East for their inspiration.[11] Many of the sustaining principles that Americans held dear through the last half of the twentieth century have been questioned—and no longer on the margins of the left, but at the heart of American public discourse.

There are important ways in which the massive political transformations of the past two or three decades have been affected by new media technologies; some analysts even contend that the new technologies have created some of the political change. In chapter 2, for example, I explore the way American media credited Facebook with the Egyptian revolution.

To be sure, the world is experiencing the most profound technological revolution since that which rocked the late eighteenth century, another time of global transformation. The digital age has affected individuals across the globe, from those born in the twenty-first century to those in generations who remember the days before the smart phone, the Internet, and even the microcomputer. The ability to connect with people via cell phones or social networking sites, one on one or tens of thousands at a time, has changed our very sense of what it means to be an individual connected to larger communities—whether local, national, or global and whether real or imagined. This change is more than practical; it is epistemological, altering our very way of knowing—how we know what we know. In Iran, a vibrant blogosphere has emerged among 46.8 million Internet users, over 57 percent of Iran's population in December 2014.[12] India had 243 million Internet users in June 2014 and is predicted to overtake the American presence on the Internet in just two or three years.[13] As with the technological revolution in the eighteenth century, the links between new tools and the spread of ideas are intimate. Acceleration is the rule.

American cultural products from Steinbeck to supermarkets have, of course, made their way around the world for at least a century. Historians have taught us to see that the United States became a global cultural power decades before it was a military superpower, the way paved by American commodities and cultural products, whether via the work of the Rotary Clubs abroad in the early twentieth century, the massive popularity of brands and products such as Coca-Cola and Nike, and of course the arrival of Hollywood cinema and jazz music (figure 1.1).[14] In the post–World War II period, when the U.S. military and political apparatus emerged as hegemonic, the overwhelming presence of American commodities provoked anxieties, expressed, for example, in the cry by the French Left against what they called "Coca-Colonization" in the late 1940s and 1950s, the quotas of national music imposed on French radio stations, and the limitations on the number of dubbed Hollywood films that could be shown in Spain in the 1990s.[15] But it is particularly interesting to examine what happens when American culture circulates to places that are politically opposed to or resistant to the United States.

Despite the waning U.S. political reputation, U.S. cinema, music, popular culture, and especially digital culture remain incredibly attractive in

FIGURE 1.1 Mural in Isfahan, Iran, advertising a local fruit-and-vegetable market. Paintings of Mickey Mouse are very common in Iranian kindergartens and on children's stationery. The Iranian Parliament recently debated replacing Disney imagery with Iranian designs and characters. (Photograph by Brian Edwards)

FIGURE 1.2 Graffiti in Tehran celebrating American hip-hop artist 50 Cent. (Photograph by Brian Edwards)

Morocco and elsewhere in the region (figure 1.2). This has not been lost on the U.S. Department of State, which has attempted in a variety of ways to leverage the better or at least more charismatic aspects of American culture, so the jazz tours to the Middle East during the Eisenhower administration have given way to state-sponsored hip-hop tours in the Arab world during the Bush and Obama administrations. As Secretary of State Hillary Clinton put it in 2011, commenting on the state-sponsored tour to Damascus of hip-hop artist Chen Lo and the Liberation Family, "Hip hop is America. . . . I think we have to use every tool at our disposal."[16] "You have to bet at the end of the day," Clinton commented about the hip-hop program organized by the State Department in Syria, "[that] people will choose freedom over tyranny if they're given a choice." She went on to call cultural diplomacy a complex game of "multidimensional chess."[17] Clinton's comments not only make visible the ways in which the U.S. state has mobilized American culture—especially African American culture—but also suggest also a papering-over of the more uncomfortable U.S. political acts. As Hishaam Aidi commented on news network al-Jazeera's website at the time, despite the fact that rap "provided a soundtrack to the North African revolts," the role of hip-hop "should not be exaggerated." Aidi pointed to the ways in which authoritarian states such as Tunisia under Ben Ali and Syria under Bashar al-Assad had mobilized hip-hop with Western support.[18]

Audiences from the region have frequently shown that they will not be duped. But do those who embrace U.S. cultural products but are critical of the United States as a geopolitical entity struggle with inner conflict? Was that immediate shift in affect in the Rabat classroom a rare moment when such a reckoning was made visible?

My interest has been in charting how individuals in the Middle East and North Africa reflect this paradox, how they pick up American cultural objects and forms and remake them as their own. In other words, I am interested in how the cultural product—and sometimes more importantly the form that it takes—detaches from the source culture from which it comes. In this way, that which might have an American origin ceases to be American; rather, its national origin is left behind as a trace, and as *frag-*

ment it is propelled into the world. The energy that draws these American cultural fragments into global circulation comes from their uptake by new publics—their consumption—rather than from their production. Although this circulation of fragments happens more easily and rapidly in the digital age, it is by no means limited to the present.

During the Cold War, as is well known, many American cultural products were quite popular in the Soviet Union even while forbidden or restricted. But it was harder for Soviets and those behind the Iron Curtain to separate American culture from American politics—thus, the perceptions on both sides of the Cold War that American jazz posed a threat to the Soviet system. As Kate Baldwin has shown, however, Soviets did know how to see beyond American statesmen's proclamations of the diversity represented by jazz musicians and American commodities.[19] Penny Von Eschen has presented a remarkably useful cultural history of the Cold War jazz tours that adds further nuance to this point.[20]

Too often in both policy circles and critical American studies, debates and discussion are focused on the production side of the equation—the Madison Avenue firms engaged by the Bush administration in the wake of September 11, 2001, is a notorious example—whereas the consumption of American cultural products is neglected or taken for granted. What is especially useful about Baldwin's and Von Eschen's work is that it goes beyond the discussion of what the organizers and funders of the jazz tours or exhibitions intended and picks up on the ways the performers themselves resisted the logics under which they traveled (Von Eschen) and what the Soviet audiences saw, heard, and said when they attended these performances or exhibitions (Baldwin). Although this book does not focus on audience studies or employ massive reception surveys, I do follow the ways in which American culture is taken up, the meanings it produces, and the meanings it occasions in response to it.[21]

In the decades since the Cold War, the popularity of American culture and its forms in the Arab world and Iran would seem to be analogues to the Soviet response to American culture during an earlier period (figure 1.3). In the wake of September 11, 2001, and the subsequent "war on terror," much of the binaristic logic of the Cold War seemed to be repeated, sometimes

FIGURE 1.3 Painting on the wall of the former U.S. Embassy in Tehran warning of dangers of culture broadcast by satellite from the United States. (Photograph by Brian Edwards)

quite explicitly. But if it is now much easier to separate American culture from U.S. politics in the Middle East and North Africa, what has changed?

Part of the answer is technological innovation: the arrival of the digital age not only created different conditions for daily life but also changed the way we engage with cultural production. I should clarify what I mean by the term *digital age* because it is coming into prominence, and both more technical and less technical uses of it are already in circulation. I mean that since the 1990s the ways in which individuals both obtain information and engage with each other has become increasingly and pervasively mediated by new technologies; these new technologies collapse distances and redraw certain kinds of spatial, political, and identity boundaries by nature of the way they rupture space and recast it as noncontinuous. Thus, although I would be the first to agree that both the technologies and the logics of the digital were present decades earlier—in fields such as cybernetics (invoked in Norbert Wiener's 1948 book with that title) and of course in science fiction—the term *digital age* in the way that I am using it as a cultural historian cannot truly be said to have arrived until the early 1990s in the United States and later in the decade in North Africa and the Middle East. The recasting of the ways we engage cultural production—uploading it, viewing it on pixelated screens, carrying it around on handheld devices—has a profound effect on how we understand even those productions that predate the digital age (most cultural productions do). Not only is reading in the digital age profoundly altered, as contributors to a recent forum in *PMLA* (the journal of the Modern Language Association) dedicated to "the changing profession" detailed in a variety of dire essays,[22] but also watching movies, looking at art, and even engaging with the Internet itself are changing at dizzying speed. This means, among other things, that representations themselves function differently—they carry meaning in different ways than they did during the analog age. The term *analog age*, as I use it, is another name for the American century, but not because these periods of time are organized primarily by centuries. Rather, I am interested in the way culture moves, the way it is encountered, read, and seen, and the logics by which it is interpreted. American studies as a disciplinary formation is therefore associated with the American century—and therefore with the analog age—because of the logics by which it has understood and interpreted the products of culture in terms of national origin and has missed their potential to circulate as fragments.[23]

Having watched this process close-up for two decades in Morocco and observed it for nearly a decade in Egypt and Iran, I have come to the conclusion that we have arrived at a period after the American century, and one of my projects in this book is to show what this period looks like and how to make sense of it.

The chapters that follow show places where this movement of fragmented cultural forms happens. Along the way, I pause to examine a number of controversies that mattered locally—the censorship of Magdy El Shafee's graphic novel *Metro* in Cairo, the vigorous debate about Laïla Marrakchi's scandalous film *Marock* in Casablanca, the outcry in Tehran about Ben

Affleck's Academy Award for *Argo,* and the illegal dubbings of Dream-Works' movie *Shrek,* among others—and show how the presence of an outside text, formula, or cultural form from the United States often underlies the anxiety around these works.

* * *

Why does it matter that we understand how cultural products circulate across borders and publics or that we see how in their consumption these products jump publics and leave behind many of the markers of the cultures where they originated? Let me list four reasons:

1. The U.S. Department of State has invested time and funding in propagating the circulation of American culture.
2. American media venues have a continuing interest in this topic, whether in the coverage of the Egyptian revolution or in the popular fascination with books such as *Reading* Lolita *in Tehran* (2003) that depict Americans or American culture displaced in the Middle East.
3. There is a history of popular and influential writers, from the developmentalist Daniel Lerner in the 1950s to Thomas Friedman in the 1990s and 2000s to media studies journalist Clay Shirky, who assume a technocentric or cyberutopian determinism. In other words, there is a direct link between access to new technologies and media, on the one hand, and modernization and freedom, on the other; this position still has its powerful defenders, despite vivid critiques by Evgeny Morozov and others.
4. In the fields of American literary studies and comparative literature, the ways in which the American culture and literature are taken up around the world puts pressures on the ways of doing things in those disciplines.

As the first three reasons suggest, there is an unresolved relationship between culture and politics that I hope to address, even while noting the rupture between these worlds. To clarify, by the term *culture* I mean "cultural production"—those forms of creative enterprise that are produced from within a national or diasporic or transnational culture, including films, books, music, visual material, and other less traditional works, such as the digital piracy art by Hamada. The word has long had multiple meanings, which go back to the English word *cultivate*—the raising of a crop or a child.[24] There is a deep relationship between what academics call "cultural production" and what anthropologists of an earlier generation called a "culture." For a long time, scholars of literature, film, and art have categorized cultural production by national cultures, as if noting these two otherwise divergent meanings of the word. Though scholars in literary studies in the 1990s levied numerous critiques of the porousness of the nation and the need for a postnational criticism, the categorization of cultural products by nation persists by and large. The linguistic challenges necessary to follow the movement of peoples who write books across languages have been enough to keep this category relatively stable. American literature, French painting, or Iranian cinema need to be understood in relationship to the history and society of its home country and in turn might be a window to understanding that national culture, the argument goes.

There is some truth to this assertion, of course, but the ways in which categorizing culture according to nation limits our understanding are overwhelming. This categorization has led to the ignorance of literatures produced in the United States in languages other than English—so many German, Chinese, and Arabic texts produced in the United States have been overlooked, even though novels written in English by expatriate writers including Henry James, Gertrude Stein, Paul Bowles, and James Baldwin are included in the lists of "American literature." And the insistence on the primacy of national literatures has reduced many texts from the Global South to national allegories, ciphers of cultural difference.[25]

More pernicious and delimiting, however, in the insistence on thinking of literatures and cinemas and cultures in national terms rather than more dynamically is that it allows intellectually weak arguments such as the one Samuel Huntington gives in his essay "The Clash of Civilizations?"—which famously carved the globe up into seven different world civilizations—to stand.[26] Transnational affiliations, the global movement of peoples and ideas, the role of diasporic populations have long fractured the idea of a discretely bound national community, and those who take the time to read Huntington's essay with a vivid sense of the way the world is today may find that it describes a fairy-tale world. To be sure, much of what I want to describe here about Morocco, Egypt, and Iran shows the cosmopolitanism and transnational attentions of young artists in these parts of the world. And these attentions are not confined to the digital age, which makes the consumption of American cultural products much more possible and rapid, but were apparent earlier.

Politics may be a word that requires less discussion than *culture*, though it is no less intricate on closer look. My understanding of the term *politics* has been influenced by the work of sociocultural anthropologists who pay attention to the way "things" are consumed, used, and understood as they move across spaces. The anthropologist Arjun Appadurai wrote the theoretical manifesto for this tradition some three decades ago in his long introduction to the now classic collection *The Social Life of Things*.[27] Within a complex critique of Marxian political economy, Appadurai argued for the importance of attending to the demand side of the economic equation if one wants to understand how *value* is constructed socially. Value is, after all, socially laden and a process laced through with politics; that which the social values in turn informs politics. Put this way, the connection seems a truism, but because Appadurai was focusing on the commodity, he was making a break from a production-dominated Marxist position—itself quite influential in cultural studies—that saw the trajectory of a commodity always from the perspective of its production. (Marx's famous interest in the fetishistic qualities of the commodity was based in the alienated labor present in the production of that commodity.) For Appadurai, turning Marx on his head, as it were, the consumption of commodities—not that which is squeezed out of the labor that produced them—is where the social life of things is to be found, and thus focusing on demand, consumption, and value is a surer route to the politics of culture. The creation of *value* in consumption is a politically mediated process and a fraught one at that because those in political power cannot control demand. There are many twists and turns in Appadurai's especially long essay, such as his interest in what he calls "tournaments of value" (21), moments when values ascribed to products are rearranged—imagine an art auction where van Gogh's sunflower paintings emerge as icons in Japan, as occurred in the 1980s, or the massive consumption of a cheap toy such as a Beanie Baby or an amateur video that goes viral internationally on YouTube. These complex events are not only where individual status and wealth are at stake but where the potential lies to reorganize aspects of "the central tokens of value in the society in question" (21). Though I abandon the term, I consider such "tournaments of value" to include periodic large public debates over cultural products and texts, as we will see in a number of cases in subsequent chapters. This approach is related to reception or audience studies but distinct in that the focus on rich and complex discussions of particular texts and on their subsequent uptake in the work of later writers and cultural producers requires the kind of detailed attention of an ethnographer or a literary critic. Thus, for the research for this book I have engaged in what I call fieldwork in literary and film studies, a procedure to which I at times draw attention.

Appadurai's related interest in the diversion of commodities from their specified and prescribed pathways is also especially crucial. The diversion of commodities, Appadurai writes, is always a sign of creativity or crisis. Politics, then, is the "constant tension between the existing frameworks . . . and the tendency of commodities to breach these frameworks" (57). He notes that because commodities always exceed or spill over the boundaries of cultures, "political control of demand is always threatened with disturbance" (57). In my own adaptation of Appadurai's major insight on what happens with commodities as they stray beyond their frameworks, I develop the concept of texts that jump publics when they are taken up elsewhere. I adapt these ideas in later chapters and call the interpretation of these diversions, with a bit of a pun, the "ends of circulation."

Thus, I argue for the importance of following cultural products when they find themselves diverted from their prescribed pathways (increasingly the case because of the technologies of the digital age) and of attempting to read those unexpected responses carefully for what they explain about "politics" more broadly understood. But before proceeding with the three extended cases that constitute the bulk of this book, I would like to consider the role of history and the major formulation that precedes this discussion.

In early 1941, on the verge of the U.S. entry into a major international conflict, the publisher Henry Luce published a massively influential essay he titled "The American Century."[28] Luce was not particularly original in his call for his readers to accept a sense of international responsibility that might match U.S. economic power.[29] He was also notoriously vague on when such a century might have begun and on when and under what conditions it might end. However, by connecting America's "responsib[ility] . . . for the world-environment in which she lives" to the international spread of American culture, Luce was a forerunner of U.S. diplomats and statesmen who, both in the aftermath of World War II and in the wake of September 11, 2001, would attempt to harness the popularity of American cultural products to the policies and prerogatives of the government.

Luce's essay provoked significant debate at the time, from both the Left and the Right.[30] But from both sides of the political spectrum and from beyond the realm of politics, the idea that American culture has an uncomplicated message of freedom to offer a world marked by tyranny—from jazz during the Cold War to hip-hop during the war on terror and from abstract expressionism during the 1950s to *Reading* Lolita *in Tehran* in the 2000s—has held sway. American cultural products from the realms of cinema, literature, comic books, and music as well as commodities identified with America, such as the fast-food restaurant, the carbonated soft drink, and the athletic shoe, have not only been popular around the world but have been allied with cherished American cultural values of freedom, choice, and independence. The sellers of these commodities have propagated this marriage of commerce and culture via marketing, further confusing American values with U.S. capitalism.[31] Less tangible but no less influential have been cultural forms that either have emerged directly from the United States or have been associated with it: American models of higher education, shopping malls, hip-hop's style of vocalizing lyrics and sampling the work of others, comic books and graphic novels, and social networking sites on the Internet. All of these forms have in various ways been associated with freedom of expression, democracy, open access, and so on, although some in the Middle East and North Africa have levied critiques of the forms' culture of origin even while making use of or adapting the forms themselves.

During the 1990s, when *globalization* became a new buzz word, many commentators around the world, particularly in the Global South, noted these intrusions and associated "globalization" with "Americanization," even though the multinational corporations doing business in their midst were not always based in the United States and local businesspeople and innovators had often copied American products and ideas before this point.[32] Those struggling to keep up with the massive changes of the preceding two or three decades—and much of the Global South could not—were especially sensitive to the presence of products and forms that came from afar. Arabs and Iranians often worried publicly about the Americanization of their region in the 1990s.[33] At the extremes, the disenfranchised could turn toward a resurgent fundamentalist version of Islam as an alternative globalism, sometimes with notorious effects.[34] But in the middle, too, the digital revolution made American movies, comics, fiction, music, video games, and websites easily accessible, opening a new way of life that sat uneasily with alleged U.S. imperial designs.

Does the continued circulation of American cultural products and forms prove the prescience of Henry Luce's claim that the twentieth century be understood as "the American century" and demonstrate the persistence of the same conditions in the twenty-first? As I indicated earlier, I believe the answer is no. Even if the contours of the new century seem similar, we have entered a period *after* the American century, with a new set of dynamics that are different from those that Luce outlined. Nevertheless, I invoke Luce's controversial phrase because of the ways he yoked the transnational circulation of American culture and its products to the geopolitical might of the United States as it took on the mantle of global hegemon. However, I want to delimit the logic Luce proposed to a time period that has passed.

The title of this book means to redirect that familiar phrase "the American century"—now understood as a logic of how culture moves through the world—and propose both a replacement that is more truly suited for a period after the American century as well as a method for how to grapple with that movement. I mean to put into service three overlapping resonances of the phrase. First, "the American century" refers to the period of time named in Luce's editorial during which the United States emerges as a political and economic hegemon and a new generation of writers, filmmakers, plastic artists, and innovators take center stage in the cultural theater. Without being overly strict about the periodization, we can define this period as being from 1941 to 1973, which locates the entry of the United States in World War II as a key moment in the move toward political hegemony and follows an economic model noting the collapse of the Bretton Woods system as the advent of financial globalization. Others who attend more narrowly to American cultural and political history have proposed that this periodization extends as late as 1981, before what historian Daniel Rodgers calls the "age of fracture" sets in.[35] Second, the phrase "the American century" names the period during which American studies as an institutional practice is consolidated and flourishes, with the logic of the phrase playing a powerful role in framing the way the new academic field imagines and constructs itself.[36] And third, it refers to the logic that emerges from Luce's essay about the ways in which American cultural products circulate through the world and what the meaning of their transnational circulation portends for U.S. hegemony (both political and cultural).

Luce's logic—what I call a logic of broadcasting because he seems to imagine that by simply receiving or being exposed to American cultural products, those around the world would absorb them—proffered a way to understand the transnational reach of American cultural products before the rigorous analysis of them seemed necessary, precisely at the moment the American century episteme was consolidating. As an Americanist, I am thus attempting to historicize the emergence of the reading formation that I am attempting to discard.[37] I do so not merely because I want to perform an act of deconstruction but because the American century logic of broadcasting remains operative both inside the academy and outside it in the contentious region I engage here—even now, when the importance of the analysis of the transnational reach of U.S. culture seems urgent.

What methods might we summon to move beyond Luce's inhibiting logic, particularly if American studies has an intimate relationship to it?

Thirty years ago in "The World, the Text, and the Critic," Edward Said addressed the debate then prevalent in English departments about whether texts are "self-sufficient"—their meanings immanent—or are what he called "worldly." Though Said's work influenced some scholars in the field of American studies in the 1980s and 1990s, for the most part Americanists ignored his work on colonial discourse and empire, and it was not until after 2001 that they took that work up as crucially important to them. Either way, Said's argument in this now classic essay bears recasting. Said argues that from the start a *text* exists in a time and a place: "[T]exts have ways of existing that even in their most rarefied form are always enmeshed in circumstance, time, place, and society—in short, they are in the world, and hence worldly."[38] Going back to eleventh-century Andalusia, Said summons a debate between Islamic philosophic grammarians over whether meaning in language is internal and concealed within words (and therefore can only be retrieved through "inward-tending exegesis") or whether words have only a "surface meaning, one that was anchored to a particular usage, circumstance, historical and religious situation" (36). The latter position, associated with the Cordoba-based Zahirite school of philosophic grammar, is the one that Said seizes upon. He opposes it both to its original antagonist (the Batinist school) and by extension to those of his own contemporaries who understand the text to be self-sufficient and who are resistant to reading for circumstance. Said writes: "What ought to strike us forcibly about the whole theory is that it represents a considerably articulated thesis for dealing with a text" in which "worldliness, circumstantiality, the text's status as an event have sensuous particularity as well as historical contingency, are considered as being incorporated in the text, an infrangible part of its capacity for conveying and producing meaning" (39).

Said, however, was not content to advance simply a theory of the worldliness of the text without taking on the critic's concomitant responsibility. The final turn of his essay is to show how the critic performs a key role in the text's worldliness. The critic "is responsible for articulating those voices dominated, displaced, or silenced by the textuality of texts. . . . Criticism is worldly and in the world so long as it opposes monocentrism, a concept . . . working in conjunction with ethnocentrism, which licenses a culture to cloak itself in the particular authority of certain values over others" (53). Rather than serving as incidental commentary, the critic's engagement with the text completes it. This final suggestion can be adopted, let us say repeated, for those whom Dilip Gaonkar and I have called "vernacular" Americanists and whom Said might call "monocentrics."[39] We must follow American texts as they circulate into new worlds or be stuck in our own framing orbits. My point is that by not following the circumstance of the text, which I will extend to mean the transnational circulation of it, the Americanist is in peril of being monocentric—the perilous position that worldly criticism seeks to avoid.

Said's insistence that the text's meaning is never divorceable from its circumstance, which for him is what makes it a text in the first place, can be brought together with Michael Warner's work of nearly two decades later. In "Publics and Counterpublics," Warner provides a rich account of the ways in which publics constitute themselves around texts and their circulation, averring that "few things have been more important in the development of modernity." Perhaps most provocative for my purposes is Warner's comment that a public is poetic world making: "There is no speech or performance addressed to a public that does not try to specify in advance, in countless highly condensed ways, the lifeworld of its circulation."[40] Circulation is thus central to his account. Warner's approach helps us to reimagine the stakes of charting and exploring situations where the "lifeworld" of U.S. texts and forms surprisingly takes them to communities in Egypt, Iran, and Morocco (figure 1.4). In different ways across these locations, the creation of a new public extends American texts' lifeworld beyond their imagined address, and thus the realization of that world requires a worldly criticism that accounts for this "circumstance." Yet I want to underline that we should be careful not to collapse Warner's idea of the circulatory fate of a work with a Lucean idea that the reach of American cultural products produces a new American century, a world environment crafted in America's image and in the U.S. understanding of democracy. It is precisely the illegibility and frequent disruption of U.S. texts and cultural forms in these communities—at these new moments of entextualization—that demonstrate otherwise.

I extend Warner and Said to a circumstance that their own considerations of eighteenth- and nineteenth-century texts quite reasonably do not address, the digital age and the digital circulation of texts, which produce a differ-

FIGURE 1.4 The English-language section in a Tehran bookstore. Hemingway, Hawthorne, and Steinbeck share the rack with book versions of *Shrek*, *Jaws*, and *Rain Man*. (Photograph by Brian Edwards)

ent means of summoning a public—a more complex circumstance for the text—than the means used in the analog age. Paul Giles has recently pointed out that the ways in which U.S. culture and globalization interact are a "vast topic interwoven with developments in telecommunications and media as well as the expansion of transnational corporations." For Giles, this interweaving puts in relief how we understand the literature of what he calls the nationalist phase of American literature and culture, which he dates from 1865 to 1981.[41] The turning point for Giles is the election of Ronald Reagan and the advent of a transnational era in which the position of the United States within global networks of exchange became increasingly apparent.[42]

Giles thus associates the arrival of globalization with the waning of the high national moment and urges Americanists to leave behind the older critical mode, including the repetition of the critique of exceptionalism: "Since the 1980s, the rules of engagement have changed so significantly that old area-studies nostrums about exceptionalist forms of national politics and culture, pieties about American diversity or whatever, have become almost irrelevant."[43] Others who would seem to be in the same camp, such as Wai Chee Dimock, have urged Americanists to attend to the transnational routes of American literature and to take a planetary perspective. Dimock perceives that this turn toward the planet requires a different, nonnational conception of temporality and offers a series of math and science metaphors—from fractal geometry and sets and subsets to what she calls "deep time"—to provide models for the ways in which American texts engage other spaces and historical times.[44] I, in turn, emphasize circulation—as opposed to deep time—as a way to address the economic, technological, spatial, and geopolitical dimensions of the digital age, which exist simultaneously with U.S. time, even if at a spatial or social remove.

In so doing, I note the minor strain of the critical term *circulation* in Said's essay: he mobilizes a conception of circulation in his own defense of critical worldliness. Indeed, his essay "The World, the Text, and the Critic"—published in 1983, just after the turn to the postnational or global phase identified by Giles and Rodgers—begins with the discussion of the Canadian pianist Glenn Gould and more particularly an analog, vinyl recording of Gould playing Liszt's transcription of Beethoven's Fifth Symphony. The recording is accompanied by a studio interview with Gould. Said begins with the fact of the mechanical reproduction of Gould's interview; in the interview Gould discusses why he left the concert hall and was only making recordings. Said points out that Gould, despite asserting that he is leaving behind the public audience, is of course addressing a public in this interview, one that he could imagine. To adopt Warner's terms, Gould's discussion of leaving behind the tangible public of the concert hall is addressed to an imagined public of the vinyl recording, and when Said listens to the recording, he helps constitute the lifeworld of that public. That this discussion opens Said's account of textual and critical worldliness is significant, for it allows us to expand his sense of *circumstance* to my own argument about *circulation*. And so I have been increasingly interested in what I am calling the "ends of circulation," where new contexts for American texts (new processes of entextualization) reveal something about the way culture moves through the world in the digital age. It now does so frequently off the expected circuits, out of legibility, but the critic may still chart such movements and thereby unsettle a more bounded or provincial sense of "the text."

Another classic essay by Edward Said deserves a second look with these concerns in mind. "Traveling Theory,"[45] also from 1983, helps us to develop the idea of circulation as ideas travel from one context to another, an idea that is sensitive to the pathways across the alleged East/West boundaries within the digital age. In the essay, Said focuses on the trajectory of Georg Lukács's book *History and Class Consciousness* (1923) as it makes its way into the work of later critics. Lukács's revolutionary theory of totality emerged out of his participation in the struggle against the Hungarian Soviet Republic of 1919. But his student and disciple Lucian Goldman borrowed the idea and employed it in his own study of Racine and Pascal, which Goldman wrote about at the Sorbonne in the mid-1950s. Then in 1970 Goldman gave lectures at Cambridge University, where the great critic Raymond Williams heard him and thus by proxy Lukács. Williams in turn incorporated Lukács into his own new work. In following how the original theory traveled across these new contexts in Paris and Cambridge, which were of course divorced in space and time from the revolutionary Hungary where the theory first emerged, Said tries to account for its renewed uses and for the energies of these later uses. In so doing, he argues against the proposition that such creative readings—those by Goldman and Williams—are in fact misreadings. Though he does not name Harold Bloom in the essay, the latter's book *Map of Misreading*, published in 1975, which had proposed that originality often emerges from misreadings or misprisions of great precursor texts, seems to be on his mind. (Said criticizes the Yale critics in passing earlier in the essay.)

The idea here that I want to bring forward for my own purposes comes from Said's reading of Raymond Williams: "What we also need over and above theory . . . is the critical recognition that there is no theory capable of covering, closing off, predicting all the situations in which it might be useful. This is another way of saying, as Williams does, that no social or intellectual system can be so dominant as to be unlimited in its strength."[46] The last sentence—that "no social or intellectual system can be so dominant as to be unlimited in its strength"—seems to me particularly useful when considering the circulation of American cultural forms across publics. According to Luce's original "American century" logic, those reoccurrences suggest an unlimited power of American culture to circulate and replicate itself. But now in the digital age, we may perceive something else and see that Said offers us a tool by which to pry open the otherwise sealed frames that the "American century" logic had for such situations. Traveling texts in this sense require a kind of cosmopolitan reading, criticism that travels, and critics and researchers who will follow these moving texts where they go and will attend to their uptake. As I delineate further in the next chapter, circulation in the contemporary period takes us from this Saidian understanding of traveling theory and adds an element that seems to be particular to the digital age: the jumping of publics.

* * *

Casablanca, Cairo, and Tehran are the primary sites this book focuses on, and they were not chosen arbitrarily. I have spent the past two decades researching, traveling, lecturing, and teaching in North Africa and the Middle East during a period of major change. Although not always visible to outsiders or to those observers who focused on actors in the upper echelons, the impact of the digital revolution and the changing status of the United States have been clear and apparent to me in the classrooms, cafés, and homes of the hundreds of Arabs and Iranians I have been privileged to know and meet. During that time, I have led research groups, supervised students, and lectured on U.S. literature, culture, and history (with a frequent focus on the role of the United States in the region), and my comments and often my very presence have sparked conversations, both formal and informal, both staged and spontaneous, that have decentered my own approach to American literary studies.

Casablanca, Cairo, and Tehran are three global cities, each the largest in its country, each different from the others even while sharing certain common attributes. Casablanca is the smallest, 3 million people out of Morocco's 31 million; Cairo is the largest, with 20 million of Egypt's 80 million; and Tehran has about 9 million residents (13.5 million in the metro area) in a total Iranian population of about 79 million. These three cities not only bridge a huge region but stand for three different ways of responding to American culture and its forms, as different as these societies and their local histories are from one another. They orient in different directions and have different colonial and postcolonial histories that affect the directions in which cultural products travel in and out of them. Even though American culture is very popular there, Morocco pays attention to France and Spain, former colonizers, and the Netherlands and Belgium, where many Moroccans live in diaspora. Iran looks with an intense focus to the United States and Great Britain, against both of which it has political and economic grudges, while its deep cultural connections to South Asia and Southwest Asia suggest that rival global cultures (Bollywood and Hollywood) are operative there. At the perceived center of the Arab world, Egypt—*umm al-dunya*, mother of the world, as the old moniker described that country—is of yet another order of cosmopolitanism; the popularity of Egyptian films and television shows means that its own cultural products have had an immense regional effect in the Arab world. Despite the particularity and even peculiarity of Egyptian colloquial Arabic, it is the dialect that is best understood across the Arab world—at least until recently, when Lebanese popular music and Gulf-based Arab satellite television put pressure on the positioning of the imagined center of the Arab world.

Although the acts of terrorism that riveted the United States on September 11, 2001, were initiated by a fringe group, the Bush administration's counterresponse simplified the "Muslim world" and painfully reduced its internal differences. Indeed, the State Department had already taken up *New York Times* cultural critic Alan Riding's suggestion that the United States "rerun our cold war cultural diplomacy" four years after the events of September 11.[47] The department's ramping up of cultural diplomacy brought cultural events and music festivals to countries such as Morocco and Egypt and across the airwaves via Radio Sawa (broadcast in local Arabic dialects), Radio Farda (in Persian), and satellite TV stations such as al Hurra (Arabic) and launched a new portfolio of TV and radio programs through the Voice of America. Many of the new events, however, lacked the subtlety of Cold War–era cultural programming. Whereas the famous *Porgy and Bess* tour in Moscow in 1955 brought an acclaimed theatrical production to the Soviets, the Friendship Fest in Marrakech in 2005 brought Christian rock to Muslim audiences in a way that forced local populations to confront the exporting nation's explicit politics.[48]

Such projects surely did more harm than good by their assumption of a unified "Muslim world" that needed to be persuaded of America's good will and tolerance (and news reports through the decade challenged this glossy view). In the cultural realm in the Middle East, what once were innocent cultural products now carried with them the taint of American politics. And this taint extended beyond explicit American cultural exports. In 2002, a large-scale boycott of American products took off in the Arab world. At times, the limits of what counted as an "American" product became vague, an ambiguity that took on comic proportions when a Saudi business owner of a popular donut chain (House of Donuts, with 180 franchises), worrying about the impact of the boycott on his business, publicly offered $300,000 to anyone who could prove that his two-decade-old business had any American ties.[49] American culture and forms associated with it—no less the donut—were increasingly collapsed with U.S. international politics.

Yet some link had already been broken before this point, as Omar Taher and Ahmed Alaidy, two of the more astute observers of the changing scene in Cairo, will help us to see in the next chapter. As I have argued, not only does the digital age give us the metaphors of broken links and noncontinuous sampling, but attention to its logics and to those who have grown up in this age also allows us to glean that by the time the boycott happened, a younger generation had already broken with the older idea that American culture and U.S. politics are necessarily continuous. Some of this rupture was perhaps forced or exacerbated by the renewed propagation of American culture by the U.S. state—that rerunning of a Cold War project was far too blatant—but much of the rupture had already taken place for those who had grown up within digital culture.

Before moving on, I want to say something about the rest of the book— about what this book is and what it isn't, where it places itself in academic disciplines, and why I have made certain narrative choices.

My own presence as critic and researcher is visible across the book. Each chapter begins with an excerpt from my field journals, and each chapter contains passages in which I recount portions of my own research trips and particular research decisions I made along the way. Incorporating these first-person passages is perhaps perilous ground for a literary and cultural critic, but I have made these inclusions consciously for two reasons: first, I am trying to develop a research methodology for thinking about culture in circulation; and second, I am arguing that texts have meaning as they are taken up by new publics where those texts appear.

I might have begun this chapter, for example, by simply discussing the film *Innocence of Muslims* and the controversy surrounding it rather than entrenching it in a discussion set in Morocco a couple of months after the initial protests. But the Moroccan uptake of the film and the controversy that followed it was of interest to me—the controversy over *Innocence of Muslims* was now a part of the rich context within which all films and cultural products from the United States *and* those Moroccan films and cultural products that incorporate, sample, manipulate, or riff on American cultural forms now had to contend. So when Hakim Belabbes began to discuss *Innocence of Muslims* as an American cultural export, he electrified the room. But, as I have argued, the younger members of my audience that day were not otherwise burdened by the idea that listening to Moroccan hiphop that incorporated American forms or that cherishing Nour-Eddine Lakhmari's latest film *Zero* (the one that looks like the American TV drama *CSI*) meant that they were somehow condoning U.S. politics or the offensive YouTube film.

This book is not, to be sure, confined to literary criticism or literary-style analyses of various texts, though such readings are included here, too, because I am convinced that it is worth our time to look carefully at the content of important films and works of fiction. I do not mean to equate a society and its representation in literature and film or to ignore the fact that these works are circumscribed by their relationship to the audiences they address, whom anthropologists would consider an elite audience (because educated and able to afford to consume culture), though not nearly as elite as many social scientists might argue. (In Casablanca, Cairo, and Tehran, the Internet was either very inexpensive or at times freely accessible, and books and pirated DVDs were extremely inexpensive.) Although I am interested in the content of the works I look at and in their local arguments and scenarios, I am also attentive to what they do with the outside, American form or intertext that launches them. What linguistic anthropologists Michael Silverstein and Greg Urban call the entextualizing process—or the "natural history of discourse"—or what Said calls the worldliness of a text enables me to examine the interplay between content and context.[50] The debates over individual films and novels—for instance, the vivid Moroccan discussion of Abdellah Taïa's apparently autobiographical novels or how the Egyptian literary establishment responded to Ahmed Alaidy's 2003 cyberpunk novel *Being Abbas el Abd* or the ways Iranian publics discussed and debated the meaning of filmmaker Abbas Kiarostami's popularity in the West—tell us as much if not more about the contemporary discussions animating Casablanca, Cairo, and Tehran as political scientists' analyses of demographic trends—more, I would contend.[51]

I am just as interested in the debates around such texts, the conversations that happen around the worlds of literature and film, as I am eager to provide a new way to understand literary and film texts from North Africa and the Middle East that are unfamiliar to most of the readers of this book. Throughout the book, I track the presence of American and other foreign objects and cultural forms in the local to open the local up to a better account. I am of course addressing the yet broader audience of those who follow the American project—whether in the academic conversation of American studies or in the public conversation. Ultimately, if what we find is a world "after the American century," we will also see America—its culture, its politics—from outside the prism of American exceptionalism. This is an ambitious project, perhaps even too big for itself, I fear. But if its focus on the movements of refracted objects can help us finally to shed the logics of the American century, it will have been a good first step to inhabiting and understanding a world that has already changed around us.

2

JUMPING PUBLICS

Egyptian Fictions of the Digital Age

Cairo, spring 2005, not far from the Arab league headquarters. We are stuck in traffic, two Egyptian friends and I, and a man pushing a hand-cart walks past our stopped car. On his cart, those little bobble-headed dogs that grace the dashboards of many cars in the United States and elsewhere. He calls out in Egyptian Arabic: "These are a gift from America! America wants you to have them!"

I'm confused. I ask my friends to explain. They instruct me: "America sends us lots of things we don't want. The man is using the joke to sell his objects. You may not want them, but America tells you to want things, so please take a look at these."

"But people know the bobble-head dogs are made in China, right?" I ask.

"Yes, of course. That's not the point."

THE SEQUENCE OF EVENTS that has come to be called the "Arab uprisings" was clearly a turning point in the history of the Arab world. Since the events of January and February 2011, countless articles, books, special issues, and now anniversary accounts have reassessed the meaning of those revolts as they attempted to keep pace with the changing situation in Egypt and other countries whose political systems were transformed that dramatic winter the West calls a "spring." I do not attempt here to offer a comprehensive account of the meanings of those events. Rather, I pick up on the lesson I learned from the man selling bobble-headed dogs in 2005, years before Tahrir, as a means by which to understand something about the changing cultural scene in Cairo, both as it undergirds and reflects the historical transformations of the past years and as a key building block of a reading strategy that puts circulation at the focal center. At the core of that anecdote, which I recorded during my first research trip to Egypt, is the disconnect between the origin of a manufactured object and the meaning it carries. Were the bobble-headed dogs American at all? I asked my Egyptian friends. I was missing the point, they responded. The vendor was using a cheap plastic toy made in China to make a point about the American export of democracy. The vendor was a sophisticated critic of globalization itself: the object itself might be made in China, but to Cairenes it both signified an American thing and neatly symbolized the interplay of American products (useless toys) and American ideologies (democracy for export). "You Egyptians must consume these things, adopt these ideas, because America tells you to!" And the joke was funny to my Egyptian friends, a satire they appreciated. No longer was the bobble-headed dog simply a silly toy intended to sit on a car's dashboard. Now it signified something completely different.

This chapter takes an extended look at a more complex version of this situation, wherein cultural forms associated with the West in general and with the United States in particular—cyberpunk fiction, superhero comics, social networking software, and text-messaging language—make their way into the Egyptian cultural scene and are imbued with rich new sets of meanings. In Cairo, however, in the cases I take up, these forms no longer tell a joke about the West. Rather, they jump publics: they have new sets of meanings that adhere to and build on their authors' use of them and now serve as fodder for a range of local meanings and new forms. There seem to be familiar elements in the new uses of these forms, but the American reader no longer comprehends them, just as I misunderstood the Cairene vendor even while I grasped his words. As a result, the message of these cases reveals the limits of American models of democracy as they are imagined in the West as exportable products. We are witnessing what the end of the American century looks like.

And yet, paradoxically perhaps, the first months of 2011 were a period in which American eyes and pens turned back on Cairo and revisited the narratives by which Orientalist tradition had previously translated a storied city. As Cairo was transformed in the revised American narrative—from ancient city to young metropolis—many American chroniclers found themselves identifying with a young Cairo, even when they least understood it.

* * *

In the wake of the Arab uprisings of 2010–2011, which in Egypt were especially widespread and dramatic, Western observers gave significant attention to the role of youth and their use of digitally enabled forms of social organization. Egyptian literary fiction had already been associated with the big political and historical questions, and many agreed with its major critic, Richard Jacquemond, when he called twentieth-century Egyptian novelists "the conscience of a nation."[1] In the first decade of the current century, a new generation of Cairo-based writers—those publishing their debut novels in the 2000s—frequently employed innovative forms and linguistic experimentation drawn from a global cultural palette while exploring domestic or local social and political themes. Their work, because of how it seems to anticipate aspects of the uprisings, begs the question of whether and how the new Egyptian novel is democratic. It also offers a stark alternative to the patterns by which Western analysts understood and explained what was happening in Tahrir Square and elsewhere in the country. Democracy and narrative, whether Egyptian or Western, are intimately linked, of course, because the series of explanations that Western journalists and other alleged experts gave to translate the unfolding "Arab Spring" were ciphers for Western attitudes toward Egypt; these explanations also changed dramatically when the public they addressed rejected them—the Western narrative—for what was happening.

Discussions of democracy and the twenty-first-century Egyptian novel tend to replicate the categories by which we understand the novel in the nineteenth and twentieth centuries, so such discussions have yet to account for significant changes in the context within which the Egyptian novel operates during the digital age. In her introduction to a special issue of *Journal of Postcolonial Writing* dedicated to Egyptian literary modernity, for example, Caroline Rooney foregrounds the question of democracy. The issue went to press in the wake of the 2011 uprising, and in order to highlight the link Rooney, the issue's editor, quotes the major Egyptian novelist Bahaa Taher (b. 1935), whom she asked in 2010 whether "we might think of literature as a form of democracy." Taher replied emphatically: "Yes, of course. It not only promotes democracy, it *is* democracy."[2] Taher's statement, in the context of his own previous novels, suggests that the dialogic qualities of the novel in general and the ways in which the Egyptian novel in particular weaves debates about the nation into its very fabric constitute the democracy of the genre.[3]

Something different is going on in the twenty-first-century novel. To be sure, younger Egyptian writers have addressed social and political questions in their work and in general are deeply conversant with their literary forerunners (including Taher). But the social and geopolitical context within which they work has altered so dramatically during the digital age that it should come as little surprise that their work has a markedly different relationship to democracy. Taher's statement does not capture it.[4]

Part of the challenge is that we do not yet have a developed methodology for thinking about literary production within the context of globalization or the digital age. In chapter 1, I argued that critics of the contemporary novel must attend to logics and contexts of circulation in order to address the changed episteme that has been ushered in by the massive economic and technological revolutions of the past four decades. Following discussions in sociocultural anthropology of the influential "cultures of circulation" argument by Benjamin Lee and Ed LiPuma, my contention is that the massively changed context within which the novel operates in the twenty-first century requires a different method of critical reading, one always localized to the particular framework of the work in question.[5] What this means in practice is that the global flow of cultural forms across national literatures—fueled by digital technologies that allow easy and rapid transport of literary texts and of visual and aural material—must be attended to without ignoring or occluding more local (i.e., national) contexts, literary traditions, and meanings. Critics should seek to achieve a balance of attention between moments of transnationally inspired cultural encounter and that which remains local and difficult to translate. Perhaps this balance will help us to avoid the pitfall of celebrating the "literature of globalization" in terms of diffusion, hybridity, appropriation, influence, or any other short-hand characterization that tends to be overly triumphant regarding globalization's capacity to collapse local difference for its own economic purposes.[6]

What does attending to the transnational circulation of cultural forms mean for the recent Egyptian novel? And what does it mean for the question of democracy? Let me first back up before I argue for the particularity of the twenty-first-century Egyptian novel.

In the second half of the twentieth century, a distinguished body of Egyptian novels addressed contemporary Egyptians' relationship to their history and the Egyptian nation's failure to live up to its own potential. Naguib Mahfouz, Bahaa Taher, Sonallah Ibrahim, each with a dramatically different style, belong to this rich literature. It is fair to say that Egyptian novelists of this period were both richly aware of their own literary tradition and conversant with other national literary trends and forms. But during the 1990s, a younger generation of novelists turned away from such political concerns and apparently national questions and moved instead toward technical innovation. Samia Mehrez, a leading critic based in Cairo, links this shift to this generation's awareness of "dismal reality, at both a personal and a national level, that prompts them to write what they want."[7]

In the 2000s, as the long state of emergency under President Hosni Mubarak persisted and Egyptian society and politics seemed ever more stagnant, a still newer cohort of young writers and artists looked outward beyond the nation's boundaries. The digital revolution brought a variety of cultural forms—including cyberpunk, graphic novels, and social networking—into the Egyptian cultural milieu and made access to a world outside Egypt immediate and more easily accessible than ever before. This access was evident formally, linguistically, and thematically in the work of several of these writers. In the second part of this chapter, I explore this point with respect to a specific case, but first I want to ask, Is the new Egyptian novel democratic?

In order to answer the question, we must first understand how fraught it is in Egypt even to ask it. "Democracy" and the "democratic" novel are two of the forms in circulation—part of what Arjun Appadurai called the "ideoscape," a landscape marked by a transnational movement of ideas and ideologies, in his now classic account of the cultural aspects of globalization[8]— that were accelerated with the neoliberal aspects of globalization. It is what everyone in the West wants of Egypt—to be democratic—and so we asked the question with the Arab uprisings of 2010 and 2011, and we asked it again in 2013 in the wake of the popular uprisings against President Mohammed Morsi and the military coup that ousted him. In late 2014 and early 2015, we are deeply pessimistic about the question, but we still ask it of the new Egyptian novel. Will you be—can you be—democratic? Foreign aid and military intervention depend on the answer.

In the wake of the so-called Arab Spring—which more accurately in the Egyptian case should be referred to as the #Jan25 movement (the Twitter hashtag antigovernment protesters used to coordinate communication)— many Western commentators attributed the speed and impact of the mobilization of young Egyptians to their use of U.S. technologies such as Twitter and Facebook. This attribution seemed a way of managing a more uncomfortable realization by Americans at the time: that the United States might increasingly be allied with antidemocratic forces in the Middle East, as its long support of Hosni Mubarak and his police state seemed to suggest.

If American innovation offered an antidote to U.S. financial and military support, the argument goes, the circulation of U.S. culture and cultural forms such as social networking media represented a "good" aspect of America in circulation. The putative democracy of Facebook and Twitter, both how they worked as spaces of open deliberation and through their alleged ability to topple a dictator, could stand for a "good" export of American-style democracy to the Middle East to counter the "bad" version exported via the Bush administration's militarism under the guise of spreading democracy. Thus, it seems almost overdetermined that U.S. media venues covering the Egyptian protests of early 2011 paid particular attention to the role of these American technologies and forms. When a small item in *al Ahram* about a young Egyptian man who named his newborn daughter "Facebook" quickly went viral across Western newspapers and websites, taking an unsigned one-inch article from the inside pages of a Cairo daily and broadcasting it to tens of millions of Americans, the celebration of Facebook reached absurd proportions.[9] Such accounts overemphasized the role of digital technologies and social networking in accounting for the Egyptian struggle for democracy.[10] They also borrowed from the now pervasive misreading of the global circulation of American cultural forms wherein social networking media constituted the new space of democratic deliberation.

So, returning to the question asked earlier, we can now identify a question to ask of the new Egyptian literature when it seems to employ or invoke American forms or be in dialogue with American literary genres, software, and popular culture and then apparently leaves behind or transcends its American referents. Without a renewed paradigm for considering such texts' engagement of the outside form as more than derivative, we may miss what they show us: the ways in which creative Egyptian writers and cultural producers play with apparently legible American forms in circulation are in fact more subtle than a mere import and appropriation of outside forms. When young novelist Ahmed Alaidy invokes Chuck Palahniuk's novel *Fight Club* (1996) as a source of inspiration, for example, and Magdy El Shafee names as his inspiration graphic novelist Joe Sacco, whose novel *Palestine* (1996) found a unique way to represent the noisy and crowded Cairo street, much more is going on than simple "diffusion" of two American authors' creative work about democratic counterpublics. Circulation, contrary to one of its operative fictions, is not a two-way street, *aller-retour*, it turns out. There are many endpoints from which cultural forms do not return.

In the third section of this chapter, I focus on the comics of Magdy El Shafee (b. 1961), whose book *Metro* (2008) is generally considered the first Egyptian graphic novel, to push the "ends of circulation" idea further with a reading of a particularly intriguing author. I extend the discussion in the fourth section to include remarks on the prose novelist and poet Ahmed Alaidy (b. 1974) and the creative nonfiction writer and dialect poet Omar Taher (b. 1974), and give an extended reading of Alaidy's major novel in the fifth section. But several other writers from this generation can also be discussed in these terms, including Mansoura Ez Eldin (b. 1976), Ahmed Nagy (b. 1985), Muhammad Aladdin (b. 1979), Khalid Kassab (b. 1974), and Ghadah ʿAbdel ʿAl (b. 1978), author of the hugely popular blog *I Want to Get Married!*[11] What these writers' work helps us to understand in various ways is how circulation is both a useful rubric for thinking about democracy in the twenty-first-century Egyptian novel and a problem. First, however, I want to take a more careful look at the American narrative of the Arab uprisings as it developed in real time.

NARRATING TAHRIR

By telling the story of the uprisings as a revolution produced by social media, American commentators were taking a stand in a debate that has been waged among scholars of global culture and that may help us to see the interplay of the global and the local with more nuance. Should cultural critics who are attentive to the rapid and transnational circulation of images, ideas, and public forms focus on the circulation itself—how it happens, what circulates, and so forth—or on the more local meanings that adhere to or emerge from or are hidden by these forms in motion?[12] By attending somehow to both, we can move beyond the limits of a strict postcolonial critique, which might focus on the ways in which Egyptian creativity appropriates that which comes from the imperial center as a form of resistance to neoliberalism, and beyond an approach focusing only on movement, which eliminates from cultural production its rich sets of meanings. Mainstream media accounts of the uprisings, for their part, focused more on the movement than on the local meaning. What was common in many such American accounts was that youth—a new generation—were enabled by the new media technologies to do something unexpected in the Middle East.[13] Looking for heroes in a revolution without them, these accounts zeroed in on Wael Ghonim, Google's head of marketing for the Middle East and North Africa. In July 2010, Ghonim had created the important Facebook page "We Are All Khaled Said" to bring attention to the Egyptian police's torture and killing of a young man from Alexandria; the page was seen as a key method of organizing the January 25 protests. (Months later, in the fall of 2011, American media would speculate that Ghonim was a likely choice for the Nobel Peace Prize.)

In detecting a pattern among many American accounts of the Egyptian protests and uprisings of late January and February 2011, I do not mean to suggest there was some collective decision by media moguls on how to tell the story. Rather, we can note how the narrative employed to explain a complex situation distant from American audiences *shifted*. There are two aspects to this claim: first, that there was a prevailing narrative and, second, that it shifted. Like any narrative, this one had to organize disparate information in the effort to explain a complex situation with many unfamiliar characters, histories, and settings to a distant audience not yet initiated into the plot or its details. Subtlety had to be left behind or out. As an explanatory device, though, a narrative may also be blind to information and interpretations that do not fit, or it might absorb them to better hide their challenge. And like other American narratives about foreign settings (especially about the Middle East), this one would reflect as much about American self-understanding as about Egypt. After all, the story must captivate its audience, and to maximize its reach it must orient itself around its audience's interests, preconceptions, and desires. When there is a mismatch—when the narrative does not reach or captivate its public—it must change or shift.

As the narrative of the uprisings in Egypt shifted, it replaced a residual account of the contemporary Middle East that was notably different. During the previous decade, scholars such as Bernard Lewis and Fouad Ajami had professed an account of the Arab world that had become influential far beyond the academy and extended into the White House itself. With titles such as *What Went Wrong?* (2003, Lewis) and *The Foreigner's Gift* (2006, Ajami), the new Orientalism of the 2000s looked much like the Orientalism of the twentieth century. Arabs were caught up in old grudges, mired in the past, unable to forget defeats either decades or centuries old. A new crop of native intellectuals and writers from Iran and the Arab world had emerged to craft what Ali Behdad and Juliet Williams call "neo-Orientalism": "a mode of representation which, while indebted to classical Orientalism, engenders new tropes of othering."[14]

The coverage of the first days of the protests in Egypt demonstrate how older "truths" from the Orientalist storyline about Egypt were repeated. As the Tunisian uprisings of December 2010 and January 2011 seemed to pass the baton to Egypt, where momentum grew quickly, U.S. media turned to journalistic "experts" for explanation. For example, on January 30, 2011, *Meet the Press* featured a six-minute interview with Thomas Friedman, the *New York Times* columnist and author whose book *From Beirut to Jerusalem* (1989), winner of the National Book Award, established him as a Middle East expert in the eyes of many in the media. On the sixth day of massive protests in Cairo, *Meet the Press* host David Gregory asked Friedman a simple question: "Is there any way that Mubarak can stay?" The way Friedman formulated his reply is revealing: "You know, I don't want to make any predictions. That's going to be determined by the Egyptian people. To me, what I think the United States should be focusing on are three things. One, emphasizing that we hope that whatever transition there is peaceful. Two, that we hope it will be built around consensual politics, not another dictatorship. Three, that whatever regime, whatever government emerges, whether it has the Muslim Brotherhood or not, it's a government that is *dedicated to ushering Egypt into the twenty-first century*" (emphasis added).[15]

Friedman would repeat this last phrase, "ushering Egypt into the twenty-first century," later in the interview. But first he would give a more resonant image of Egyptian backwardness: "Egypt, and really most of the Arab world, *has been on vacation from history for the last 50 years, thanks largely to oil.* Egypt didn't have oil. It had the peace treaty with Israel. What peace with Israel was to Egypt, oil is to Saudi Arabia. It got Egypt all of this aid, it allowed the regime to move very slowly on democratization. And now it's got to play rapid catch up" (emphasis added). Friedman here provided a startling image of Egypt on vacation from history and then attributed that absence, bizarrely enough, to oil. As if hearing himself, he noted that Egypt doesn't have oil and then substituted a contradictory and completely enigmatic explanation for why Egypt is "on vacation from history," one that turns out to be very historical: its 1979 peace treaty with Israel. Gregory never questioned him on this confusing explanation, so it stood as given. The Orientalist logic here is multiplied: out of history, in history, oil, Israel—it all blends together in Friedman's statement.

I am using Friedman as shorthand for the narrative that would be supplanted. But because Friedman is already notorious (in many circles) for his sloppy forms of argumentation and is in any case a celebrity columnist with a sometimes idiosyncratic perspective, let me give an example from another media outlet: *ABC World News* with Diane Sawyer. On January 25, 2011, the first day of the protests in Cairo, Sawyer turned to young correspondent Alex Marquardt, who was reporting on the "the latest violence to spread across the Arab world in the wake of the stunning overthrow of Tunisia's president." The key word here is *violence*, and the idea that it was spreading across the Arab world is the main point. Marquardt continued: "Diane, today has been called a day of rage in Egypt, and it's living up to the name." The date January 25 was indeed called a day of rage for Egyptians, and yet the focus on emotions commanded the story. Because this is broadcast news, very few words were allowed to relate the account (about four hundred words, by my count), and so the emphasis on rage, violence, "chants," "anger," and so on undergirded previously given impressions of a chaotic Middle East. Now there are certainly sophisticated things one might say about the role of emotions or affects on politics.[16] But here they perpetuated older stereotypes of "the Orient" as a place of massive emotions, violence, and danger. The following day, again on *ABC World News*, Sawyer focused her opening on what she called "a kind of chain reaction across the Middle East," emphasizing that "the chaos could have serious repercussions right here in the United States." In a clear attempt to make the distant story relevant to her domestic viewership, she asked correspondent Martha Raddatz "to tell us what those repercussions could be."

A graphic filled the screen, asking in all caps: "WHY IS EGYPT IMPORTANT?" Instead of providing her own analysis, Raddatz instead channeled the official U.S. position: "Listen to the president today." The screen cut to President Barack Obama saying, "You know, Egypt's been an ally of ours on a lot of critical issues." Back to Raddatz, who provided a shorthand elaboration of his statement: "Issues like the Mideast peace process and fighting terrorism." There, in almost telegraphic phrases, were the key repercussions that apparently mattered to the American audience. Then, for further backup, Raddatz offered a quote from an expert: the camera cut to a white American man wearing business attire, sitting at a desk. The caption provided his name, David Bender, and position, the vague but professional-sounding "Analyst, Eurasia Group" (the Eurasia Group is a global political risk consulting firm, founded in 1998, whose motto is "Defining the Business of Politics").[17] Bender then stated on camera: "If the Egyptian government falls, then, sort of, all bets are off throughout the region." Anxiety, rage, instability. Then, by the logic of chain reaction that Sawyer led the news with, the 2:15 segment turned to Yemen. Raddatz's voice grew increasingly worried: "The protests have even spread across the water, through the deserts, to Yemen." And another graphic on the screen asked: "WHY IS YEMEN IMPORTANT?" Raddatz provided more fear: "The list is long and frightening. A training ground for al-Qaeda. The home of Anwar Al-Awlaki, a terror leader more dangerous than Osama Bin Laden. . . . If the Yemeni government falls, no one will be there to challenge the terrorists." ABC's quick tour around the Middle East showed that the chain of protests against authoritarianism was ultimately to be seen as frightening. Raddatz, ABC's senior foreign affairs correspondent, cast the revolution not as something in the American tradition of liberty from tyranny but rather as something with a likely negative impact for Americans: "So while protests may be cause for cheering in some places, in others these scenes should make Americans *very* nervous."[18]

These accounts stand for scores of similar accounts from those early days in late January, with American journalists repeating the "truths" perpetuated by the Washington political establishment: Mubarak was corrupt, perhaps, but the alternatives in Egypt (chaos, *fitna*, Islam) were worse. Reporters showed themselves in harm's way. ABC's Alex Marquardt, for example, showed himself after having been tear-gassed, his eyes watering while a bumpy camera ran down the street with him. They created fear on the American viewer's TV or at least told the viewer to be fearful. Sensationalism ruled, and the official U.S. line—which Egyptians themselves were highly critical of—was literally parroted to American audiences via the media.

But then somewhat abruptly the story line changed. Within a week, the "chain reaction" of rage and chaos could be characterized in a new way: as youth driven, digital, and fun. A utopia in Tahrir Square. What changed, and why? In some ways, the collective shift in narrative about the Egyptian protests was market driven.[19] As Mubarak stayed on the stage in the largest city and largest country in the Middle East, the reporting by U.S. media thus far wasn't sufficient for American audiences either in quantity or quality. Because of the way the Internet had affected how readers got their news, Americans had numerous options. Hungry for more news, they had encountered other interpretations of what was happening on Arab media.

Al Jazeera English (AJE)—a twenty-four-hour news broadcast channel that was long suppressed from U.S. cable and satellite platforms—offered streaming video of its coverage of Cairo. And it was good. (In August 2013, Al Jazeera Media launched Al Jazeera America, a separate channel with American programming that has since made inroads into U.S. markets, but in 2011 AJE was available almost exclusively via the Internet.) Although AJE has its own tendencies toward sensationalism, to be sure, its prevailing story line in this case was not fear that a flood of al-Qaʾida terrorists would be unleashed upon the United States should Mubarak fall but rather a historic struggle for freedom from the tyranny of regional dictators. U.S. viewership of AJE surged in a few days. (Reflecting back on their own coverage of the Arab Spring, American media outlets took a variety of positions on AJE's coverage, but none ignored its major role.)[20] Eager to compete, U.S. media corporations sent their own reporters to Cairo. American audiences were evidently seeking a different account or were at least able to see that the prevailing one in the United States might have some holes in it. The new account embraced a logic of the digital revolution suited to the medium—which required it because AJE was viewable for most only via streaming video.

If the new message about Tahrir fit well with the medium, a story about Tahrir as a digital revolution was ready made for the Internet consumers of news. And the message did change starkly as CNN's Anderson Cooper and a slew of other celebrity journalists, including Christiane Amanpour for ABC and Katie Couric for CBS, arrived in Cairo in their khaki foreign-correspondent shirts.[21] I point out these journalists' attire because of the way it plays into the performance of foreign correspondence, itself a part of the entertainment factor of the news. Amanpour favors the khaki, which recalls old-time war correspondents from the Vietnam era. Cooper quickly gave up his vest for a more contemporary dark-hooded sweatshirt. Couric was seen wearing both khaki and the hooded sweatshirt.

On the print side, a second bureau of the *New York Times* now competed with the first. Michael Slackman, veteran correspondent aided by young Lebanese assistant Nadim Audi, worked across town from newly arrived correspondent David Kirkpatrick, a generation younger than Slackman. The *Times* had also hired Liam Stack, a Columbia graduate student who had taken a hiatus from graduate school to write for the *Christian Science Monitor*, and he, like Audi, sometimes shared bylines with Slackman. Kirkpatrick, with no Middle East experience and little foreign reporting, challenged the veteran Slackman, who had years of experience in the region (and would eventually be sent home to become deputy foreign editor). The personalities were important to the coverage. Rivalry was barely hidden. Gender and sexuality were key. When CBS's Lara Logan was sexually assaulted by a crowd on the very night that Hosni Mubarak stepped down, the vicious and deeply disturbing attack became a referendum on "true" Middle Eastern attitudes in the wake of the apparent democratic revolution (the story itself wasn't reported for four days).[22] Scholars of the Middle East created their own websites to challenge the superficiality of mainstream media coverage, and the excellent website Jadaliyya emerged as a go-to source for those interested in more depth and has since become a staple of analysis of events in the Middle East.

Edward Said notes in *Culture and Imperialism* that American attention to other parts of the world works in "spurts": "The foreign policy elite has no long-standing tradition of direct rule overseas, so American attention works in spurts; great masses of rhetoric and huge resources are lavished somewhere (Vietnam, Libya, Iraq, Panama), followed by virtual silence."[23] There is nothing, and then there is a barrage of information, almost overwhelming in its scope and intensity. Here was one of those spurts. Much good reporting was done, of course, particularly by those working for the

New York Times, the *Los Angeles Times*, and sometimes the *New Yorker*, where the long form allowed for more nuance, and the ease of access to publics meant that citizen journalists and anyone with a smart phone could upload their videos or break some news. To be sure, I have relied on the work of many of these journalists to understand what was happening. Ironically, the massiveness of the attention to the events in Tahrir allows us to discern a pattern, a narrative, more easily. No doubt there are exceptions, and some analysts did not fall into the new narrative trap. In general, however, the narrative told by Lewis and Ajami and repeated by Friedman in the coverage at the beginning of the uprisings—of a Middle East stuck in its own past—gave way now to a narrative about a Middle East in its "spring," driven by a new generation of tech-savvy, Blackberry-carrying Tweeters. This was not your grandfather's Middle Eastern revolution.

Can we step back to compare the old and the new narratives and ask what the blindnesses of the new narrative were? I cannot hope to be comprehensive, of course, and this is not a chapter about what happened during the Arab uprisings or about the series of disappointments that would follow in Egypt, leading to a return of the police state under General Abdel Fatah el-Sisi, who assumed the presidency of Egypt in June 2014. The role of religion was important but poorly understood, as would become clear in the next wave of media attention when Muslim Brotherhood leader Mohammed Morsi was elected to the presidency. There were excellent guides to the complex negotiation of religion within contemporary Cairo punctuated by new technologies and forces of globalization.[24] These types of insights and their subtlety were lost from the mainstream coverage, but for those readers interested in pursuing questions further, Jadaliyya offered extensive resources.

Thus far I have addressed the changing narrative about Egypt and the way American journalists and writers translated the foreign through the lens of the domestic. But rather than dedicate the remainder of this chapter to a deconstruction of Western discourse on the Arab Spring, I want to turn to contemporary Egyptian narratives, especially those from the decade leading up to that spring. Whether these narratives "predicted" the Arab uprisings—as some later claimed—or not, they help us to understand the tension between the local and the global that was elided or misunderstood in American accounts. Despite the focus on a youth revolution engaged with new technologies, a cohort of Egyptian writers whose work embraced precisely this juncture and were instrumental in creating a key Cairo counterpublic prior to the revolution has not been given due attention. A handful of academic readers of Middle Eastern literature and their students noted these writers, and a few of the writers were published in American periodicals and daily papers during the January–February 2011 spurt of attention, with at least one of them (Magdy El Shafee) securing a translation contract with a New York trade press (Metropolitan/Henry Holt) in the wake of that attention. But their work needs more extended attention for two reasons. First, appreciation of it helps us get beyond the easy formulation about circulation, technology, and Arab revolution that dominated the mainstream account. Second, their work shows how new American forms could enter Cairo's cultural scene *without* any sense that those who took them up were beholden to U.S. politics or "American values." In other words, innovative works that might at first come into being via the presence of or engagement with American forms could lead eventually to texts in which American meanings are absent. They thus provide a vivid case of the process by which texts or forms in circulation jump publics—one of the many places where circulation ends.

CREATING CAIRENE COUNTERPUBLICS

In the Egypt of the past decade, if not longer, American forms in circulation became increasingly visible in the Cairene social and cultural landscape. Two apparently different American exports were especially prominent. First were the cultural products such as Hollywood and hip-hop, of course—which was nothing new, though now ever more ubiquitous—but also, increasingly, software, digital video games, and social networking sites. Second, there was an increasingly loud American discourse about democracy in the Middle East, whether the propaganda during the initial

years of the U.S. occupation of Iraq (2003–2011), media and political commentary about the victories of the Hamas Party in the 2006 Palestinian parliamentary elections, or, closer to home, President Barack Obama's speech
in Cairo on June 4, 2009. Obama's speech, titled "A New Beginning," met
with a mixed reception locally because of its apparent hypocrisy in the wake
of the continued U.S. occupation of Iraq, firm support of Israel, and ongoing support for the Mubarak administration.[25] The increase in visibility
and volume of these competing if complementary U.S. exports was due in
part to the belated arrival of the digital age in the Egyptian capital and in
the universities and urban centers of the rest of the country, which brought
with it a flood of easily accessible Western cultural forms and discourse.
But it was also due in part to the new pressures on Egypt in the wake of
the events of 2001 and the so-called war on terror.

As the writer and dialect poet Omar Taher put it in *Shaklaha bazet*
(Looks like it's falling apart, 2006), which established him as one of the
leading voices of the new cohort of Egyptian writers and artists, a generation was born of this collision. In 2009, I was gathering literary texts by
young Cairene authors to translate for a special portfolio to appear in a New
York literary journal. As part of my research—inspired by the idea of a literary field, interested in the social and professional links between writers, and
playing on the sociologist's technique of snowballing—I asked prominent
writers of the 2000s generation for recommendations on whom to include
in the portfolio. I had started with Ahmed Alaidy, then thirty-five years
old, whose novel *An Takun ʿAbbas al-ʿAbd* (2003; *Being Abbas el Abd* [2006])
had first caught my attention. The name "Omar Taher" kept coming up (no
relation to Bahaa Taher), especially his manifesto-like introduction to
Looks Like It's Falling Apart: "I am the son of the generation who got the
shock of multimedia in my face after university. Attention was dispersed,
all the world pressing upon me without mercy after years of deprivation,
through the internet and satellite channels, and lay down on the floor in
front of the power of the communication revolution, whose slogan was 'the
world is a village.'"[26]

Taher's book of literary nonfiction named a condition—a new generation's encounter with both national and global crises and their interplay—

that suggested, or required, an appropriate literary style. Taher's particular and noteworthy fusion of Egyptian dialect (*'ammiyya*) and standard Arabic (*fusha*) and his invocation of comics as genre and cultural logic (as in his book *Kabitan Masr* [Captain Egypt])[27] were born, according to the manifesto, from a generation's experience of both geopolitics and digital technology. Taher collapses this experience nicely in the phrase "the world is a village," with its layered suggestions of technological innovation and neoliberal political imperative (and echoing Hillary Clinton's best-selling book *It Takes a Village*, published in 1996 when she was First Lady). And he thereby shows the link in the dual logics of *circulation*—which here means both the technologies of the digital age and the transnational ideoscape in which an empty slogan, "democracy for all," becomes an American export.

I came to agree with his peers that Taher had named or depicted something crucial about his generation. In turn, his description of the way his generation grew up shows the link between a highly mediated youth and the literary evocation of a Cairene counterpublic no longer bound by national concerns—but not able to escape them fully either. First, his manifesto efficiently and accurately shows how global culture, including global politics, and local (Egyptian) culture and politics exist simultaneously in a layered palimpsest. Second, in the manifesto Taher summons up his own *public* both by invoking it (or calling it into being) and by grouping shared media experiences (and shared experiences of media) as productive of that public. In other words, the public that Taher names, invokes, and creates is a public in large part because its members have had similar experiences of the global mediascape.

In his manifesto, Taher repeats through anaphora a series of experiences shared by what he calls his generation (*al-jil* or *al-gil* in Egyptian pronunciation). "I am the son of the generation whose consciousness was opened by Mama Nagwa and Bo'louz, and with 'Al-Sindbad' Baba Magid Abdelrazaq and *Children's Cinema* with Mama Afaf Al-Halawi" (135). The manifesto begins with the shared television viewing of children of his generation, a series of programs so local, both generationally and nationally, as to defy translation. He moves through sequences of television programs, music, commercials, public-service announcements, and finally a barrage of global and local media events that converged in the young Egyptian consciousness: "I am the son of the generation that witnessed Egypt make it to the finals of the World Cup. . . . And we witnessed the rise and fall of stars beginning with Maradona going to Ali Hamida, and ending with Princess Diana" (135). Taher is doing more than rhapsodizing or waxing nostalgic for the cultural products of his youth. "Dear Reader," he begins, "it's possible that this book will not represent anything of importance to you, but it will mean a lot to you if you are one of the children of the generation" (135). This opening is the constitution of a public, which, as Michael Warner has argued, "requires preexisting forms and channels of circulation. It appears to be open to indefinite strangers, but in fact selects participants by criteria of shared social space (though not necessarily territorial space), habitus, topical concerns, intergeneric references, and circulating intelligible forms (including idiolects or speech genres)."[28] If Taher speaks to you, the opening declares, you are one of the generation; that is, you are a member of his public. If not, his words will not seem important. They will not address you; you are not part of his public.

Taher's sequence of media events—and the pleasure of their juxtaposition in a catalog that feels Whitmanian via Allen Ginsberg—demonstrates something very much like an awareness that the public of his text is not endless and infinite but requires shared social spaces. But note that the public here does not require shared "territorial space," as Warner notes, though it does rely on a common orientation toward the media-saturated spaces of Cairo. Thus, Taher gives us the precise time that certain programs of his youth aired ("And in the evening, *The World Is Singing* and every night at exactly nine-thirty *Window to the World*" [135]). Warner points out that publics are forms of poetic world making: "There is no speech or performance addressed to a public that does not try to specify in advance, in countless highly condensed ways, the lifeworld of its circulation."[29] With great efficiency and with a literary voice that fuses the Egyptian dialect of Taher's own ʿammiyya poetry and a higher literary style, his manifesto specifies its own lifeworld.

It is appropriate, then, that although several of the events listed in Taher's catalog are familiar to non-Egyptian audiences (or even to Egyptian audiences of different generations), most are highly local, which in turn allows us loosely to identify Taher's public. Despite the sequence of global media events and outside cultural products that converge here, those same transnational flows of global culture *end* here in Cairo. Yet that does not mean they are legible in full to an outsider. Indeed, when I finally met Taher and told him that I wanted to translate and publish his manifesto for the portfolio I was editing, he consented but told me it would be impossible to translate: no one outside Cairo would understand its references. I translated the essay nonetheless, annotated it heavily, and in the process killed the pleasure Taher's designated public might take in it. My initial understanding of Taher's "untranslatable" creative work was that he was addressing a counterpublic.[30] Now I think that the central point of Taher's manifesto is that the dead end his generation had reached might in turn constitute a new Egyptian public if only it could recognize itself as such. The events of #Jan25 in Tahrir Square suggest what such a productive dead end might look like.

Understanding Taher's work in this way has implications for the larger project of reading new Egyptian fiction as global and as engaging outside forms creatively. Older models of comparative literature that imagine Egyptian fiction and other national literatures as cut off from the world—or on the receiving end of literary influence—cannot hold sway from the perspective of the give and take of the digital age. When young Egyptian novelists take on Western cultural forms for local projects, as El Shafee does, it seems to me that the proper questions to ask are not about influence, cultural hybridity, or diffusion. Questions about the Egyptian novel can no longer be innocent of the interplay of the transnational circulation of abstract political ideas and ideologies (e.g., "democracy," the "global village") and global flows of literary and cultural production.

MAGDY EL SHAFEE'S CAIRENE COMICS

Indeed, such questions are not innocent, as the obsessions of mainstream American media indicate. When the journalist Robin Wright wrote a chapter on Egypt for her best-selling book *Rock the Casbah* (2012), she decided to feature a profile of a young Egyptian woman many of us had not heard of before: Dalia Ziada.[31] Though Ziada's name was not familiar, her story was. During the Arab uprisings, as U.S. journalists looked for ways to account for the massive organization of young Arabs and, most of all, for their effectiveness in ousting a president whom the same media had previously been telling its readers was permanent—the best option in a world marked by "extremism" and "corruption"—they grasped continually at examples of these American forms in circulation for evidence of what had changed. Most notable was the obsession with social networking sites such as Facebook and Twitter, as I have suggested. But Ziada was a particularly enticing case, for she had engaged in a surprising cultural act. As reported in the *Washington Post*, in 2008 she translated into Arabic a fifty-year-old nonfiction comic book called *Martin Luther King and the Montgomery Story*. The original was published, with King's agreement, in 1956 by the Fellowship of Reconciliation in the wake of the Montgomery bus boycott. According to an article on Ziada by Barbara Becker in the *Huffington Post*, apparently channeling statements by the American Islamic Congress (the congress had funded the translation project), "With the aim of disseminating information about nonviolent protest to the semi-literate, the group [Fellowship of Reconciliation] decided upon the quick-to-grasp comic book format."[32] Ziada translated the work, had it published, and with the help of the American Islamic Congress, according to Michael Cavna, "distributed thousands of Arabic-language issues . . . in the Middle East, including in Tahrir Square at the height of January's revolution." Cavna, the author of the *Washington Post* article on Ziada and the comic book, was entranced by the link between the King comic as American document and its potential to influence the "hearts and minds" of young Arabs: "The book is testament not only to the power of King's message . . . but also to the popularity of cartooning in the Arab world, especially among the younger generation. And [Ziada] is just one of many Arab comic publishers and cartoonists who believe passionately that their work can help inform, inflame and open the hearts and minds of their Mideast readers in the throes of revolution."[33]

Wright accepted this version of Ziada's story with little apparent additional research. As a result, the interpretive error Wright made was the assumption that Martin Luther King Jr. was an important inspiration for the Arab uprising and thus that the Arab uprising might be expected to follow a model with which Americans were familiar. At first blush, this assumption seems to extend an older tradition of American Orientalism in which Arabs' struggle for independence and full citizenship was understood in terms of African Americans' demands for equality in the United States. The African American press explored this possibility during the North African campaign (1942–1943) in World War II, and what I have called the ur-text of American Orientalism, the film *Casablanca* (Michael Curtiz, 1942), hinted at it by allying the African American piano player Sam's subjugated role with that of the Moroccan characters in the background.[34] Here, the role of the graphic adaptation suggests that the form itself—a comic book version of the Montgomery story—is particularly suited to an Egyptian audience. The link between what Becker referred to as the "semi-literate" audience of the 1956 original and the young generation of Egyptians was implied with a heavy hand. As such, Ziada's is one of many such stories that Wright tells—about Arab hip-hop, Arab and Arab American stand-up comedy, Arab versions of *American Idol*, and so on—in which U.S. cultural forms contribute to making a new Egypt, a new Arab world, crafted in an image with which the West can (and should, in her account) feel comfortable.

The story of the role of *The Montgomery Story* in the uprisings in Cairo, however, so far as I can tell, was greatly exaggerated. I do not question that Ziada translated the work or that the American Islamic Conference distributed it, but I do dispute that it had any substantial audience in Tahrir Square in 2011. Wright failed to inquire about the public of the *Montgomery Story* translation. Who comprised it? How many copies were out there? (Becker said that 2,500 copies were distributed from 2008 to 2011 throughout the Arab world, which is a mere trickle.) Given the somewhat straightforward images in the graphic adaptation of the story of the Montgomery bus boycott—it is notably *not* a robust version of the graphic novel, with straightforward panels heavy on prose—these seem fair questions, even crucial ones.

A hugely important graphic novel also published in Cairo in early 2008 was available to Wright but did not make it into *Rock the Casbah*, nor did it register in mainstream media discussions prior to 2010.[35] Magdy El Shafee's graphic novel *Metro* would seem, on first look, to be a more sophisticated version of Ziada's *Montgomery Story* translation, one that might have been championed in some of the same Western media venues had it been read. But on closer inspection, it turns out to alter the very story Wright and others in the mainstream media were trying to tell: that the Arab uprising was in fact parallel to American models of democratic discourse. By extension, *Metro* reframes our understanding of the relationship of democracy and the Arab uprising to the new Egyptian novel.

El Shafee's work is important because in creating Egypt's first graphic novel and emerging as the godfather of comics in Egypt, he seems to work in a familiar idiom. And yet to read his work closely, we must recognize that it and its engagement with the graphic novel jump publics, leaving behind the register familiar to Western readers. It is an example of the end of circulation from which an outside form cannot return to legibility. *Metro* cherishes its very locality.

First, where did El Shafee's riveting work come from? He is the author of Egypt's first graphic novel, so the genesis of his engagement with the form seems relevant. El Shafee has told me that his first influences as a comics artist were pharaonic drawings from ancient Egyptian tombs. But he has also spoken of his enjoyment of European comics such as *Tintin*, *Asterix*, and the work of Golo (Guy Nadeau [b. 1948], the French comic artist who illustrated for Egyptian newspapers in the mid-1970s). In an interview in March 2011, El Shafee remarked: "[Golo] is my *patron*, as they say in French."[36] Having encountered the work of the American comics guru Robert Crumb in the 1980s when he lived briefly in Paris while in his twenties, El Shafee returned to Cairo; through the 1990s, he worked in the pharmaceutical industry. In the "About Me" section of his personal website, he refers to his role at this time as "an evil Hippocrate [*sic*] [who] rushes to tell the secret of his intimate colleagues [to] his dummy non-cultured BOSS in order to survive and gain more money. His job description: how clever he is in arousing a charming illusion to the public that drags more and more money from their pockets forgetting all about the right of every individual to get the RIGHT treatment." Referring to this job and the hypocrisy it required, he writes: "I COULDN'T BEAR [IT]" (capitals in original).[37]

But then in 2001, in what El Shafee calls "the change" in his life, he participated in a comics workshop held in Cairo, the product of which was a collective volume. In 2003, he created the comic strip *Yasmin & Amina*, written with Wa'el Saad and published in the Egyptian weekly *Alaa Eddin*. That strip, which revolved around two girls who join their father secretly on board a commercial ship and so are plunged into global adventures, gained a local following. But the publication of *Metro*, a full-scale graphic novel, in 2008 was not only a personal accomplishment but also a signal event in literary Egypt. *Metro* was quickly banned, but El Shafee's influence on a new generation of Egyptian graphic novelists and comic writers was substantial. (It has since appeared in translation in Italian and American editions.)

There are different ways to approach the question of circulation with respect to El Shafee's work. The first seems initially something like literary influence. El Shafee rhapsodizes about the first page or two of Joe Sacco's graphic novel *Palestine* (1996), which begins with a frenetic page set in downtown Cairo.[38] Perhaps it took a foreigner to achieve this image, El Shafee says. "It was the first time I saw someone representing the *zahma* of Cairo," he told me shortly after the fall of Mubarak. *Zahma* here means something more than traffic—a full blockage of not only the Cairene street but the entire social and political situation of Cairo.[39] So we have here the circulation of a formal element from Western comics: the crowded page, images spilling over the frame, with dialogue bubbles mixed and hard to sequence. Is this approach a way to connect what Robin Wright thought was happening in Ziada's translation of *The Montgomery Story* with El Shafee's *Metro*? If so, we would have to argue that Joe Sacco's great Cairo page in *Palestine*—a work written to contest the mainstream American media narrative about Palestinians (as Edward Said underlines in his introduction to Sacco's novel)[40]—offers a new way to represent the *hisa* of Cairo (figure 2.1). (*Hisa* is a word that means more than noise; its closest translation into English denotes chaos, the frenetic, and noise all wrapped into one.) For El

FIGURE 2.1 Joe Sacco's graphic novel *Palestine*. (Image © Joe Sacco. Courtesy Fantagraphics Books)

Shafee, such a formal element was not present in comics previously, whether in the work of Golo or in earlier European comics; he suggests it was a visual innovation within graphic fiction representing Egypt specifically. And as such, Sacco's page allowed him to imagine a graphic form that might explode Cairo from the inside.

Sacco was not the only influence on El Shafee, or, rather, Sacco's work was not the only outside cultural form that found its way into El Shafee's representational repertoire. Sacco's crowded page also allowed El Shafee to imagine graphic possibilities for representing the Cairene underworld as noir and linked with other works of both prose and graphic fiction that he was reading. Among the many interesting aspects of *Metro* are the formal borrowings from Sacco, the way in which El Shafee engages and extends the American superhero comic, and a strain of the dark neorealism of Alan Moore and Dave Gibbons's *Watchmen* series. There are hints, too, of Chuck Palahniuk's punk novel *Fight Club* (1996), possibly filtered through Ahmed Alaidy's deep engagement with Palahniuk in the novel *Being Abbas el Abd*. In *Fight Club* and in Alaidy's novel, a doubling of protagonists is key to the narrative, where both reader and protagonist become confused as to who is directing the action. In *Metro*, characters are doubled, and there is some confusion of identities, but the Palahniuk strain is yet more viral via El Shafee's representation of an underworld where street battles (between neighborhood criminals, corrupt politicians, and businesspeople) operate below the registers of the visible. Before I move to an alternate reading of *Metro*, one that counters an approach I associate with models of diffusion and influence, let me back up to describe the work.

Metro tells the story of Shehab, a software designer and expert in the digital realm who is trapped within Cairo networks that will allow him neither to thrive nor even to live in safety (figure 2.2). A way out presents itself via a wealthy neighbor who offers to finance Shehab's idea for a software project, but the neighbor is murdered because of his involvement with a group of corrupt professionals. Shehab witnesses the murder and is at the dying man's side when the man passes on a confusing message that seems to be the clue to the network's treachery. With his friend Dina, an investigative journalist, Shehab aspires to expose the crime, which is being pinned

FIGURE 2.2 Shehab in Magdy El Shafee's graphic novel *Metro*. (© Malamih Books. Courtesy Magdy El Shafee)

on the wrong person to cover up the dangerous knowledge that the murdered man held. Following his best instincts, Shehab seeks to find a way to deliver "the truth" to some authority above or outside the corruption who might help to expose it. But he knows, too, that there is nothing outside the criminal circles of contemporary Cairo, which go all the way to the top, and so he looks for another way out of the cage. Here, his knowledge of the digital is of some help: he knows how to hack the system as he runs afoul of corrupt Cairo. He can make public phones in the Metro ring to communicate with his friend Mustafa; he can hack into the dead man's cell phone to find clues to his mysterious dying words; and he can transfer funds to his own account by hacking into a bank's secure network. This is not Bahaa Taher's Cairo.

But what I have recounted is merely the plot of *Metro*, not what it is *about*. Alan Moore's great guide *Writing for Comics* (an inspiration to Alaidy and apparently to El Shafee), distinguishes between a comic book's plot and what it is *about*: "The idea is what the story is about; not the plot of the story, or the unfolding of events within that story, but what that story is essentially *about*."[41] For Moore, the distinction is particularly important for comics art because of the particular fusion of frame transitions, image, and text. In this sense, *Metro* is about the cage of Cairo and the impossibility of escaping it, whether it is composed of corrupt businessmen or the thugs who beat street protestors chanting for their rights. Foreshadowing the #Jan25 movement of 2011, El Shafee represents the Kefaya movement of 2004–2005, an important protest movement (the word *kefaya* means "enough!" in Egyptian Arabic) that was often overlooked in many mainstream accounts of the Arab Spring.[42]

Metro is, of course, an underground story, and, like the underground train system for which it is named, the novel is concerned with networks of communication, transportation, and circulation, all of which lead nowhere except to political and social stasis. Maps of the Cairo metro permeate the narrative, and like most urban metros, the lines eventually come to an end (figure 2.3). Shehab tells Dina: "We're all in a cage. The way is wide open, but we're stuck inside because no one ever tries walking out of it."[43] Reflecting the *zahma*, or blockages, of Cairo, *Metro*'s pages are punctuated

FIGURE 2.3 Shehab and Dina in Magdy El Shafee's *Metro*.
(© Malamih Books. Courtesy Magdy El Shafee)

by propagandistic signs and sayings by Hosni Mubarak—a banner inscribed "For a better tomorrow: Mubarak" hangs over a street (42); pro-government thugs chant, "Long live our leaders! Long live our democracy! Enemies of the state go home" (66)—and represent protesters from the Kefaya movement and their chants: "No justice on the street! Nothing for the poor to eat!" and "Why turn on the victim? Why not the oppressor?" (67). In this sense of what *Metro* is about, the graphics advance its meaning more surely than do plot or text. Its noir look and multiple graphic styles (including El Shafee's incorporation of two pages by a comics colleague from Cairo, Muhammad Sayyid Tawfiq) are animated by fight sequences that combine superhero comics, the *Watchmen*, kung fu, and *parkour*.

In *Understanding Comics*, his now classic guide to reading graphic fiction, Scott McCloud catalogs the different kinds of movement between frames that are available to the comics author. It is in "the gutter," or the space between frames, McCloud writes, that the comic book distinguishes itself as a particular art form: "Despite its unceremonious title, the gutter plays host to much of the magic and mystery that are at the very heart of comics."[44] McCloud differentiates Western from Eastern techniques for comics transitions and argues that Western comics tend toward forward narrative progress in such transitions, whereas *manga* and other Asian comics have a notably higher percentage of atmospheric frames in which multiple aspects of a scene, landscape, or character are shown. Forward progress is in such frames stalled; pacing is slower. McCloud offers statistical evidence for this assertion, but my critical impulse is to resist this binarism, which is redolent of Orientalist tropes about Eastern stasis and Western "progress." In any case, given the global popularity of both *manga* and American superhero comics, McCloud's strict division of East and West may not hold true anymore (if his original analysis was correct in the first place) for the *readers* of comics. The atmospheric frame transition may be characteristic of *manga*, but it is hardly unfamiliar to the Western reader. Nonetheless, McCloud's larger point about the effects of these different transition styles is useful.

In *Metro*, whether El Shafee attributes the two types of frame transition to "Eastern" and "Western" styles or not, he clearly plays on both techniques. The novel reads at first as noir and quickly builds plot and narrative momentum. But then it slows down its narrative drive and lingers in the Metro itself, building atmosphere, depicting street fights that spill over the pages' frames, and employing a consistently changing graphic style. None of this is impossible within what McCloud attributes to comics from the West, of

course, and film noir in American cinema is well known for its atmospheric shots. Nonetheless, it is in these atmospheric, static frames, gut-
ters, and transitions that El Shafee tends to leave his American reader
behind—or, rather, where he seems to be less concerned with his international, non-Egyptian public. It is in these frames that he addresses his Cairene public in particular: that public knows the local referents of particular
places and situations, and these localized frames do not resonate for the outsider. In other words, the crowded page of Joe Sacco's Cairo cedes to a
Cairene cage that is poetic world making for a different public.

El Shafee's work jumps publics, and rather than stand as an example of
the diffusion of the Western form, it takes aspects of that form, combines
them with Egyptian literary traditions (the social protest novel, the nationalist novel, and so on), and summons up its own local public. In this way,
it is similar to Omar Taher's manifesto and to Alaidy's fiction. It is new in
Egyptian fiction, but it is not derivative or the simple diffusion of a
Western form. The disjuncture in it pushes us to ask questions about the
democratic aspects of the new Egyptian novel but also more generally to
argue that critics of Egyptian fiction, among others, need to take seriously
younger Egyptian writers' engagement with both their own literary traditions and Western literary and cultural forms.

Because I have placed a heavy burden on the idea of jumping publics, let
me offer a brief discussion of a short work in which El Shafee, here collabo-
rating with Alaidy, plays with the very idea of "jumping." In 2009, as I edited the Cairo portfolio, I wanted to include an excerpt from *Metro*, and I
approached El Shafee for his permission. My editor in New York was resistant to novel excerpts in general, which are harder for the reader with no access to the complete work to comprehend. El Shafee had a solution. He had,
he told me, already plotted a short work of graphic fiction with Ahmed Alaidy,
estimated at six pages, and accepted my offer to translate and publish the
shorter work. Titled "The Parkour War," the six-page comic extends some
of *Metro*'s concerns in brief and with new characters. Again, it is *about* a
Cairo in which state corruption is generalized to the local, daily level. The opening page sets the scene with an atmospheric drawing of an
apartment building in a nondescript, lower-middle-class Cairo neighbor-

hood. On the second page, a fat man is depicted coming to collect bribes from local shopkeepers—for their protection, one assumes. The text reads: "Like any filthy morning, people feeding off of other people. . . . Pulling the life right out of you. . . . They smell . . . like ashes." But the corrupt man encounters a slim man, standing in a doorway, who decides to fight back. "They wouldn't know . . . that some folks have . . . tough meat" (ellipses in original).[45] Over three pages, drawn with superhero-like colors and swooshes of combat and with sound effects such as "SCRAAAATCH" and "SPLAAAAASH," the slim man fights the fat man and brutally beats him (figure 2.4). In the final frame of the penultimate page, the slim man wins the fight by decapitating the fat man, whose head rolls to the ground.

Commencing in the last frame of the penultimate page, however, a dialogue bubble interrupts the action. The line in the bubble wraps from the penultimate page to the first frame of the last page; in other words, it starts on the fifth page of the comic and concludes on the sixth page. In the original Egyptian Arabic, the line derives from a then recent Egyptian film called *El Gezira* (The island, Sherif ʿArafa, 2007), about a community of Upper Egyptians living with their own rules; the line would be familiar to many Egyptians at the time. I come back to it in a moment, but first let me remark that the final page has a surprise in it. The battle that we have been witnessing between the fat man and the slim man, it now becomes clear, was not a street battle at all, but rather a battle in a video game (figure 2.5). And the elusive title of the short comic, "The Parkour War," seems in retrospect to be the name of a video game that two young men in their teens, one fat and one slim, are playing on a PlayStation in a small apartment. Next to them, a child perhaps ten years old is watching a movie on a second TV set, dangling a remote, weary from watching too much television. The slim man, who has lost the game, throws the television being watched by the child out the window. "Didn't we say no TV till the weekend?" he shouts. Perhaps he is the older brother of the child. He addresses his friend again: "Dude, let's play again. Where's my Pepsi?"

There is a lot going on in a short amount of space. On the first level, the heroic story of battling and defeating corruption cedes to a critique of young Egyptians stuck in their apartments, consuming media from televisions and

FIGURE 2.4 Scene from Magdy El Shafee and Ahmed Alaidy's graphic story "The Parkour War." (Courtesy Magdy El Shafee and *A Public Space*)

video game consoles. On the one hand, El Shafee seems to suggest that these technologies are social soporifics, stamping out the political potential of Cairene youth. The boys stay in their apartment, playing video games as they suck down Pepsis. What the French ruefully called America's "Coca-Colonization" in the 1950s is here present in its digital form: the Play-

TRANSLATED BY BRIAN T. EDWARDS

FIGURE 2.5 The final frame in Magdy El Shafee and Ahmed Alaidy's graphic story "The Parkour War." (Courtesy Magdy El Shafee and *A Public Space*)

Station games of the 2000s are like the Coca-Colas and Pepsis of another era (and Pepsi is still present as an addictive, foreign commodity). But *parkour* — that urban sport wherein athletic young people learn to scale walls, jump fences, and leap from rooftops—offers another possibility, one that competes against the easier and we might say older generational lament over cultural imperialism and political apathy. The flight of *parkour*, which here is structured into a video game that we (as readers) do not realize the boys are playing, with Cairene referents difficult to translate, reveals a break. (El Shafee told me that he had joined *parkour* clubs in Cairo, and here he brings it into his fiction.) That dual strand of circulation—the one easy to read, the other more elusive— suggests the double valence of an Egyptian fiction of the digital age.

In my attempt to translate El Shafee and Alaidy's comic into English without reducing it to a translatable value or a bit of exotica from Egypt, I encountered many challenges.[46] The Egyptian Arabic used is especially colloquial and employs phrases that barely translate when rendered into English except as phrases indicating violence and resistance (for example, "They'd have you for lunch. They wouldn't know . . . that some folks have . . . tough meat" works well enough in English but loses the immediacy of the original). Egyptian argot was one thing, but the line of dialogue from the Egyptian film *El Gezira* posed yet another problem. This short comic was clearly invested in exploring various forms of media in circulation in Cairo, so it is worth some further consideration of the problem posed by the line that wraps from the penultimate page to the final page. Here, the line from the Egyptian film being rebroadcast on TV references national culture, even if Egyptian cinema had and continues to have a transnational reach, at least in the greater Arab world. The line itself signifies a breakdown of the system: "From today there is no government. / I am the government" is a literal translation of the line as El Shafee has it in his original. But the TV set that the younger sibling watches competes against the TV on which the older boys play their video game (note the different styles of console and the multiple digital inputs on the older boys' set). How to translate the line from the film? When we discussed it, El Shafee argued that comics should be clear and apparent on the first reading, and thus the Egyptian dialogue must be changed for an American audience. After offering a number of alternatives and some deliberation, I proposed a line from *The Godfather Part II*: "I don't feel I have to wipe everybody out, Tom. . . . Just my enemies." El Shafee was enthusiastic and gave his full consent.

In using this line as a translation, had we made "The Parkour War" a translatable value to be carried along with the global flow of discourse from

Egypt back to the United States? Or had we done some disservice to the very idea of jumping publics that I have argued is central to the theme of "The Parkour War" and at the heart of the genius of *Metro*? Although I cannot claim that this substitution of a line from *The Godfather Part II* was the best solution to the translation problem posed by the text, I want to end my discussion of "The Parkour War" by suggesting that the work still resists translation and has not become fungible and that it has not even really jumped publics back to the United States via this new line of dialogue. Like Omar Taher's manifesto in *Looks Like It's Falling Apart*, El Shafee and Alaidy's comic is ultimately impossible to translate in the sense that the public it addresses is one that uniquely comprehends both the national or local Egyptian *and* the transnational references and referents. That comprehension is so deeply inscribed in the text that it cannot be loosened even with a line of dialogue from Francis Ford Coppola. Indeed, one can imagine a line from *The Godfather* in the Egyptian novel or comic quite naturally as an element of global culture, but it is much harder, if not impossible, to imagine a line from Egyptian cinema or an Egyptian comic moving as naturally in the other direction.

PUBLICS AND COUNTERPUBLICS: ALAA AL ASWANY AND AHMED ALAIDY

If the Internet, digital downloading, and satellite technologies made access to a world outside of Egypt immediate and more easily accessible to Egyptians than ever before, the effects of this access are seen formally, linguistically, and thematically in the work of several of the writers of the 2000s generation. And yet, as I argue, these effects were the endpoints of global circulation: these writers' engagement with the foreign—the global—was visible to Egyptian audiences and indeed figured in some of the most ambitious works, but it was difficult to circulate back to the West. When those works did circulate back to the West—say, in a classroom or through an individual American reader's interest—the disconnect was such that the works did not register as interesting or innovative or even "Egyptian" enough. They seemed merely derivative, or they confirmed the erroneous position that democracy and technological innovation begin in the West and find their acolytes and imitators in an otherwise chaotic East.

The staggering popularity of Alaa Al Aswany (b. 1957), a writer first published by the intrepid Cairo publishing house Dar Merit, in the United States would be the exception that proves the rule. Dar Merit was run by Mohamed Hashem, who had been a key member of the Kefaya movement earlier in the 2000s (in particular its Writers and Artists for Change group) and through that decade had published daring fiction—and to a lesser extent poetry and nonfiction—out of a small office near Tahrir Square.[47] In the back room, evening gatherings brought together intellectuals, writers, and filmmakers. For Al Aswany, launched by Dar Merit, Hashem's operation was apparently not going to reach a broad enough public; circulation mattered to Al Aswany. His novel *The Yacoubian Building*, first published by Merit as *'Imarat Ya'qubian* in 2002 but then reprinted by bigger Cairo publishers Maktabat Madbuli and later Dar al-Shuruq, quickly became the best-selling Arabic-language novel in the world.[48] With a film, a TV mini-series, and then a major U.S. launch for the translation of his novel in 2007, Al Aswany became the Arab author, aside from the late Nobelist Naguib Mahfouz, whom Americans had heard of if they had heard of any Arab novelists. The 2008 edition of Al Aswany's second novel *Chicago*, published in the United States by Harper Perennial, garnered a full publicity campaign; the *New York Times Magazine* had Indian novelist Pankaj Mishra write a full profile of Al Aswany.[49] (I am not aware of another translation from Arabic to garner such resources.) Despite the greater publicity and as entertaining as it is, Al Aswany's first novel does not capture the fusion of national critique and global cosmopolitanism that characterizes El Shafee's or Omar Taher's work in terms of either content (there are no digital hackers here) or especially literary form.

Scholars of Arabic-language literature debate whether *The Yacoubian Building* is innovative, "serious," and interesting from the standpoint of its language and technical craft or merely commercial, but most take the latter position. A literary soap opera with multiple intersecting story lines focusing on a corrupt business magnate, the gay neighbor, and a terrorist, it certainly has aspects of the melodramatic television serials that are popular in Egypt. But serious scholars of the Arab novel—such as Marilyn Booth, Richard Jacquemond, and Samia Mehrez—have encouraged readers, implicitly or explicitly even if sometimes a bit reluctantly, to take *The Yacoubian Building* seriously as a document of the changing market for popular fiction.[50] Mehrez calls Al Aswany's success "mind-boggling and overwhelming" and points to the Egyptian literary establishment's contrasting perception that he is the author of "scandal literature."[51]

For my purposes, though, what is important is how this novel's depiction of the grand sweep of contemporary Cairo, realist and melodramatic, assured its circulation in U.S. markets. American publishing circles treated Al Aswany like a new Mahfouz. The front cover of the paperback edition features a quote from the highbrow *New York Review of Books*: "Captivating and controversial—an amazing glimpse of modern Egyptian society and culture." The *New Yorker* ran a five-thousand-word profile on Al Aswany, calling him "Egypt's leading novelist" in the subtitle, with no mention that Egyptians would have to qualify such a statement to be able to accept it. Bahaa Taher and Sonallah Ibrahim, among the more obvious candidates, would need to be mentioned, unless sales figures alone undergirded the statement by the *New Yorker*. Mehrez puts the disconnect between the judgments of American and Egyptian literary establishments well: "Much to the veteran scribes' dismay, Al Aswany's spectacular success came to confirm that the way into the international republic of letters may depend not on the scribes' local status in the alley but rather on the global village and what *it* deems to be a 'classic.'" She compares *The Yacoubian Building* to Ibrahim's major novel *Dhat/Zaat* (Self, 1992), both of them exposés of contemporary Egypt, and asks why Al Aswany's sales dwarf Ibrahim's. The answer is clear enough: Ibrahim's style is experimental, avant-garde, whereas *Yacoubian Building*'s trade in classical realism allows it to appeal to "a much wider spectrum of uninitiated readers in the global village."[52] But we should also note that technology and global culture do not figure largely in Al Aswany's work; his is a Cairo that translates easily to the West. His much promoted second novel, *Chicago*, for example, about Arab residents in the American city, is set in the United States well before September 11, 2001, an era without social networking, mobile phones, or Skype, all of which in the intervening years would come to punctuate daily existence. Questions of literary sophistication aside, it is precisely this nostalgic sensibility regarding an Egypt that remains distant that allowed Al Aswany to circulate within the global marketplace—what Pascale Casanova has called "the world republic of letters."[53] In other words, the exotic difference of the Egypt Al Aswany portrays in *The Yacoubian Building* perhaps paradoxically allows that novel to circulate more easily than El Shafee's *Metro*, even if the latter portrays a Cairo that should be more familiar to readers because it is full of digital phones, hackers, and other contemporary motifs.

Al Aswany's popularity masked the ways in which his contemporaries a few years younger were doing more radical things with the global and interrogating the local more intimately, without the familiar formulas of Egyptian cinema or serial drama. His success should have opened up a space for other writers from Egypt (and profiles such as Pankaj Mishra's and Wendell Steavenson's point out that his weekly salons introduced other writers to that immediate crowd) and encouraged American critics and journalists to look further at the contemporary Egyptian literary scene, but it did not.[54] Cairo, in all its complexity, with all its millions of unheard people— at once bleak, saturated from a thousand directions, and disruptive—is opened up by the authors who published in the years leading up to #Jan25. In ways that Al Aswany does not, writers such as El Shafee, Omar Taher, Alaidy, Nagy, Ez Eldin, Aladdin, and Mohamed Al-Fakhrany (b. 1975) featured a Cairo that spoke to a young and large public in Cairo but barely circulated outside it. Whether in Aladdin's taboo-breaking tale of desire and sexuality in urban Cairo—which, contra Al Aswany, challenges the reader with a complex literary structure and challenging use of Arabic—or in Al-Fakhrany's postmodern novel of street children fighting to survive outside the five-star hotels and luxury night-club boats anchored on the Nile or in Nagy's novel *Rogers* (2007), in which a young Cairene's angst is punctuated by a Pink Floyd soundtrack, the generation of the 2000s was especially agile in shifting registers, of seeing in the close-up detail a more shattering meaning that reverberated through that densely packed city. That their work did not resonate beyond Cairo, despite its vibrancy and its embrace of outside and contemporary forms suggests another endpoint of the circulatory process. Indeed, Al Aswany quickly left the publisher Dar Merit behind for Madbuli precisely because of the former's inability to and lack of interest in circulating his work broadly.

BEING ABBAS EL ABD AND FIGHT CLUB

Ahmed Alaidy's novel *An Takun ʿAbbas al-ʿAbd* (2003) was the work that led me to the cohort of Egyptian writers discussed in this chapter. When I first read it, it seemed to me a novel that demonstrated what the encounter of literature and the technologies of the digital age might look like and offered a less obvious example of "literature and globalization" than the first round of critics working to establish that category had identified. Alaidy's short novel has drawn attention from specialists of contemporary literature from the Middle East, and it is finding its way into American university classrooms via the English-language translation by Humphrey Davies, *Being Abbas el Abd* (2006). The rich novel is beginning to generate critical discussions as well, so I limit my comments here to the way in which it helps craft a different narrative about Cairo on the verge of the Arab uprisings via the engagement of or with an outside form, here the American punk novel *Fight Club* (1996) by Chuck Palahniuk. *Being Abbas el Abd* both portrays the end of circulation and shows us what it looks like.

Being Abbas el Abd, then, helps to advance the larger argument of this book and to demonstrate the reading strategy based around circulation. The novel teaches us how to read literature in the context of globalization, where globalization is understood as an episteme, a context within which we all operate. I have been attempting to show how the acceleration of transnational cultural flows—how cultural products and forms make their way from one place or context to another with fewer restrictions or time lag then ever before—requires a particular reading technique or approach. As I contended in chapter 1, circulation and literary influence are quite different from each other. We already have a long tradition in literary criticism of reading influence, but circulation is something else.

Like El Shafee's *Metro* and Omar Taher's *Looks Like It's Falling Apart*, but unlike Al Aswany's *Yacoubian Building*, Alaidy's *Being Abbas el Abd* represents a Cairo permeated by global culture and the digital: cell phones, computer keyboards, international media, American movies, shopping malls, international pharmaceuticals, and so forth. That is its *content*, what it is "about": a changing city for a new generation. The generation here is the one that follows the Generation of Defeat and that Alaidy's narrator calls "the 'I've-got-nothing-to-lose-generation'" and "the autistic generation."[55] The novel's form has a sophisticated linguistic and formal relationship to the global. The form and the content complement each other, of course. In this challenging and often confusing novel, Alaidy is occasionally direct, even pithy: "You need to UPGRADE your wisdom and UPDATE your experience: *The worst thing that can happen is to have nothing worse to fear*" (36, emphasis in original). Despite the frequent references to the global, it is precisely the ways in which the form and content overlap, particularly in the Arabic original, that help us to understand why certain works (such as *Being Abbas el Abd*, *Metro*, and others) do not quite circulate back to the West. Circulating back ultimately is not their concern, nor is not doing it something their authors would see as a shortcoming. Indeed, that these works do not circulate back offers a rejoinder to the easy or celebratory account of American culture's circulation in Egypt as intrinsically liberatory. The cyberutopian and the neoliberal positions expect a two-way flow of culture and capital. Alaidy refuses to deliver it.

First, the briefest of recaps to orient the reader who hasn't encountered the novel, even though *Being Abbas el Abd* is hardly the kind of book for which a recap makes sense, both because its forward momentum is not always clear or important and because it plays on the very collapsing of identities and doubling of situations that make plot summary frustrating. The book's narrator, who takes on multiple names throughout, navigates contemporary Cairo, possessed by the voice of a double named Abbas el Abd. The narrator himself is fascinated, haunted, and perhaps possessed by doubles, and the novel itself repeatedly offers doubles, beginning with the doubling of the narrator and Abbas and then later including the doubling of the narrator and his psychologically abusive uncle Awni, an experimental psychotherapist, based in Cairo but then trained in the United States, who has conducted various forms of something the novel calls "Dissociative Emotional Regression technique" (118), a risky technique because if "the doctor fails to cure himself, he remains a prisoner of his condition for the rest of his life" (118). The two primary female characters of the novel, both named Hind, also double each other. In one of the more memorable scenes of the novel, Abbas invites the two Hinds to the same café (the Mohandisseen Bakery [23]) at the same time and sends the narrator there to decide which woman he (Abbas) wants to pursue. The narrator goes to the café and gets caught in a complex cycling back and forth between the two Hinds. Permeated by cell phone calls, graffiti, lists of phobias and conditions provoked by contemporary Cairo and haunted by his mysterious double, the narrator's voice jumps off the page, analyzing but also exemplifying the symptoms of a Cairo overrun by the complexities of globalization, where it is no savior: "Anyone who reads the history of most Third World countries will discover a painful tragedy. Many have been liberated by the Revolution from 'the foreign occupier' only to fall into the clutches of 'the national occupier.' In a third of the countries of the Third World—approximately— you need to have an American passport if you want to be treated like a respectable citizen" (36–37).

In a group dedication that is reminiscent of Ginsberg's dedication to *Howl*, Alaidy names several "partners in crime," whom he lists "in order of involvement." After his parents, he records several "mentors." The first three are Chuck Palahniuk, Mohamed Hashem, and Sonallah Ibrahim. Hashem published *An Takun ʿAbbas al-ʿAbd* at Dar Merit, dramatically different in form and content from Al Aswany's novel *The Yacoubian Building*. Palahniuk and Ibrahim, though, garner my attention now. As the narrator of *Being Abbas el Abd* catalogs and spoofs the symptoms of contemporary Cairo, Alaidy's engagement with the work of Sonallah Ibrahim is apparent to readers versed in Egyptian literature, even if the style is quite different. I mean Ibrahim's great first work of fiction, the short novel *Tilk al-Raʾiha* (1966;

The Smell of It [1971] or *That Smell* [2013], as Robyn Creswell has recently retranslated it), and perhaps especially his novel *Al-Lajnah* (1981; *The Committee* [2001]).[56] As the critic Muhsin al-Musawi has shown us in his extended discussion of the latter novel, *Al-Lajnah* is a key text from an earlier moment in the advent of globalization and a landmark in rethinking the relationship of neoliberalism to the state of Egypt.[57] If *That Smell* depicts a decadent Cairo that the narrator, newly released from prison, can see in its squalor, *The Committee* demonstrates how global products and forms are as much a part of the changing landscape as traditional Egyptian ones. Perhaps the key moment comes when the committee members ask the first-person narrator, who is in front of them to be judged for unspoken crimes, by which single "momentous event" we will remember "our century" in the future.[58] The narrator mentions Marilyn Monroe and several global products and brands and eventually lands on "one word, although some would consider it two: Coca-Cola" (18). His long discussion of why he has landed on this single product/word associates the reach of the commodity with the language used to name it or describe it: "While the words used for God and love and happiness vary from one country to another and from one language to another, 'Coca-Cola' means the same thing in all places and all tongues" (19). For Musawi, this focus on language and rhetoric is a trademark of Ibrahim's work: "The hearings in *The Committee* seek to legitimize the national through the global rhetoric, a language that is menacingly repetitive, overladen with emphasis on democracy and freedom, to the extent that their human connotations and implications are negated."[59] Sonallah Ibrahim's cultural heroism was, of course, in ascendance at the time Alaidy was writing. On October 22, 2003, from the stage of the Egyptian Opera House in front of the Minister of Culture, Ibrahim publicly refused the award granted him by a system whose corruption he proclaimed from the very stage that would honor him, a refusal that again elevated him in the eyes of Egyptians, including the younger generation of writers.[60]

Although Alaidy's engagement with and debt to Ibrahim are obvious and link Alaidy to the Egyptian literary tradition, what he does with Palahniuk takes us further with respect to the way a "global rhetoric" may be employed in the new Egyptian novel. Here the rhetoric and form of the novel show us something new. If the narrator is obsessed with doubles, re-creates them, and is ultimately killed by them, the relationship of *Being Abbas el Abd* to *Fight Club* is another double, which both exists and then is masked in the work to the point where the reader forgets or is unable to answer the question whether *Fight Club* exists as the other of *Being Abbas el Abd* at all. The narrator himself is a massive consumer of American culture. He works at the Amerco Video store and offers cures for customers via Hollywood prescriptions: "WATCH Robert De Niro in *Cape Fear* and you'll thank me later"; "WATCH Richard Gere in *Final Analysis* and you'll thank your Uncle Awni later"; WATCH Meg Ryan in *When Harry Met Sally* and, uh . . . Are you seeing anyone?" (17–19). American culture may offer a cure, but America is also a negative force: "Lords of the world, inventors of AIDS and CNN, / Lords of the world, who discovered the ozone layer and then put a hole in it" (12). But the arrival of "the West" via digital culture also gives it a unique voice and form.

The first thing those who read the novel in its Arabic original notice is the explosive way it disrupts the language itself. Humphrey Davies describes this effect best in his translator's note, where he points out that contemporary Cairo for Alaidy's generation is marked by "the culture of the shopping mall, the cell phone, the SMS [Short Message Service], the computer," all of which find "a wide-open area for havoc in language" (128). The latter comment requires a bit of an explanation for those readers who are not familiar with the relationship of the various colloquial variants of Arabic (*ʿammiyya*) to what in the West is called Modern Standard Arabic (*fusha*), which I mentioned earlier in the description of Omar Taher. Of course, all languages have more traditional or formal variants that are affected by new colloquialisms. But Arabic has a more complicated relationship to the colloquial because of its relationship to the sacred (classical Arabic language finds its most perfect form with the revelation of the verses of the Qurʾan, recited by the formerly illiterate prophet Muhammad), its formality, the fact that it is used in published writings but not in everyday speech, and the fact that colloquial Arabic (of Egypt, Morocco, or wherever) is considered an informal language, generally not used in print (with the exception of, say, dialogue in novels, dialect poetry, and a newer generation of hip publications).

Despite the fact that Egyptian writers in Alaidy's cohort, including Omar Taher, had begun to play with the colloquial in more interesting ways in their creative nonfiction and prose fiction, Alaidy's linguistic innovations are notable. Davies, the eminent translator, explains that the author "revel[s] in the deployment of modern Egyptian Arabic in all its newfound and multi-layered diversity, mixing and matching idioms as the creative urge demands, often using the contrast for comic effect. An impeccably classical sentence may, for instance, have at its syntactical center an undeniably colloquial verb, resulting in what, from a traditional perspective, is a disorienting sense of a breakdown of borders" (128–129). If Alaidy does this differently from Taher, he is surely in dialogue with him. The strand is present, too, in Hamdi Abu Golayyel's novel *Lusus mutaqaʿidun* (2002; *Thieves in Retirement* [2006]), another of the new Egyptian novels emerging from this cohort (Abu Golayyel [b. 1967 or 1968] is named in Alaidy's group dedication as another of his mentors). Marilyn Booth, the translator of Abu Golayyel's novel, perceives that the signs of globalization that mark the landscape of Cairo are also present there on the level of language, the alternating registers of Arabic—a higher *fusha* and a vernacular *ʿammiyya*—and the play on Nasserite language, hopes, and dreams (as well as on the literary vestiges of that generation).[61] With Alaidy, however, you can see this complex fusion on the page itself.

If *Being Abbas el Abd* commands attention because of its play with language, the way it imagines a new relationship to history itself is yet more notable. Of the several critical readings Alaidy's novel has garnered thus far, Tarek El-Ariss's recent discussion is for me the strongest. El-Ariss calls *Being Abbas el Abd* a novel of hacking, by which characterization he offers a more sophisticated reading of the work's relationship to globalization than those whom he critiques for misreading Alaidy as merely a reflection of globalization and the market. For El-Ariss, the novel is a "postmodern manifesto for a new writing characterized by textual disruption, sabotage and mimicry." He describes the dynamic aspects of Alaidy's Arabic in ways that go beyond Davies's explanation. For El-Ariss, Alaidy "infiltrates the publishing establishment from which he was excluded and disrupts the codes of Arabic literary production." Hacking is a form of code disruption with its own aesthetic, what El-Ariss calls an "aesthetic of subversion and a call to action, staged as an active participation in cultural production." Thus, Alaidy employs hacking as an act of cultural violence, but one that allows him and his generation to take control of cultural production "through acts of violence, dissimulation, negotiation, and play."[62]

El-Ariss's reading of hacking in the novel helps us connect Alaidy's social critique with those made by Omar Taher and El Shafee, wherein Alaidy suggests an "upgrade" to the young Egyptian's "software" as a philosophy of historical change. But it also allows us a means by which to understand the silent way Alaidy plays with Palahniuk—the way *Fight Club* makes its way into his novel, a process that is both cosmopolitan and untranslatable. In other words, what we see is that *Being Abbas el Abd* explores what I am tempted to call a "cosmopolitan sensibility"—by which I mean bringing two opposed, competing worldviews simultaneously into being— but one that the West cannot quite grasp. *Being Abbas el Abd* is the most readily available bridge to the cohort of young Egyptian writers, but it, too, is an endpoint of circulation.

The relationship of *Fight Club* to *Being Abbas el Abd* matters, although it is not perhaps the first thing you care about after reading the novel. El-Ariss's hacking metaphor and his underlining of Alaidy's own metaphor of upgrading the software are perfect. He, too, remarks in passing that the book is influenced by *Fight Club*. What would influence mean in this context? Is doubling a better metaphor? What is it that is in circulation here?

Palahniuk himself ironically gives us a way of understanding the circulation of his own work beyond the public addressed by the work itself, in which something about the work leaves the text itself and certainly its author behind. In a recent reissue of *Fight Club*, Palahniuk recounts a story of the book's reach, which he claims surprised him. He tells of encountering a tour guide dressed as a cowboy on a "Haunted Tunnel Tour" somewhere in the United States, who as part of his schtick says, "The first rule of the Haunted Tunnel Tour is you don't talk about the Haunted Tunnel Tour."[63] This statement of course is an adaptation of the line from *Fight Club*, "The first rule of Fight Club is you don't talk about fight club." Palahniuk confronts the tour guide:

I say, I wrote that book.

The rope between us going tighter, tighter, tight.

And the rope stops the cowboy. From the dark, he says, "Wrote what?"

Fight Club, I tell him.

And there, the cowboy takes a step back up. The knock of his boot on a step, closer. He tilts his hat back for a better look and pushes his eyes at me, blinking fast, his breath boilermaker strong, breathalyzer strong, he says:

"There was *a book?*" (210)

Instead of stopping with the recognition that a Hollywood film will trump the book that inspired it or that it was based on, Palahniuk instead catalogs the way the work circulates beyond itself:

Before there was the movie. . . .

Before 4-H clubs in Virginia were busted for running fight clubs. . . .

Before Donatella Versace sewed razor blades into men's clothing and called it the "fight club look." Before Gucci fashion models walked the runway, shirtless with black eyes, bruised and bloodied and bandaged. [. . .]

Before young men started scarring kisses into their hands with lye or Superglue. [. . .]

Before you could walk into Office Depot, shopping for plain, matte white labels, and there on the Avery Dennison package (product item 8293) was a sample label, printed: "Tyler Durden 420 Paper St. Wilmington, DE 19886[.]" (210–211)

So Palahniuk has already a sense that his book has reached an extended counterpublic, circulating on the Avery envelopes for sale at a chain stationery store. It has been mailed to places imagined on the Avery packaging, labels for unnamed packages with undefined contents.

Why this matters is that what is imagined in *Fight Club* is nothing less than a disruption of the status quo itself. Palahniuk's novel, his first, grabs you by the throat. The doubling of the narrator and the character called Tyler Durden is explicit in the novel. At first, via an underground network of illegal fight clubs, men find their wounded masculinity in the age of late capitalism. But then the network expands, explodes, and threatens to take over the world. In the haunted narrator's imagination,

> Human beings had screwed up and trashed and capped on this planet, and now history expected me to clean up after everyone. [. . .]
> This is my world, my world, and those ancient people are dead.
> It was at breakfast that morning that Tyler invented Project Mayhem.
> We wanted to blast the world free of history. (124)

The anarchy unleashed by the characters in *Fight Club* emerges from a sense not just of violence against the planet that must be righted but from a project of world remaking. Of course, *Fight Club* ultimately is limited in its own imagination—its global community of anarchists is made entirely of men wearing black shirts, pants, and socks and living in an underground warehouse. But I am not interested in critiquing Palahniuk here for the limitations of his conception of gender or rebellion. Rather, I am interested in the fact that despite the very circumscribed vision of a counterpublic in Palahniuk's novel, it jumps publics into *Being Abbas el Abd* and *Metro*. Alaidy and El Shafee do not feel themselves outside this public, even if Palahniuk does not invoke them or address them in 1996 or imagine a public that might include a young Egyptian hacking his own system. For Palahniuk's narrator, ancient civilizations are dead. The anarchy will begin in the Pacific Northwest.

Fight Club is something of a dangerous book, and it imagines a form of resistance to power that leaks outside of its covers. That is precisely what happens when the tour guide replicates its key line, the code by which members of the fictional Fight Club operate. But in *Being Abbas el Abd* Palahniuk's book has circulated beyond its public. At present, that point seems harder to make, for the Occupy movement could in the fall of 2011 look back at Tahrir and claim inspiration. But before Tahrir, before Hardt and Negri's *Empire*, could *Fight Club* imagine an Egyptian public? I think not.

Alaidy is not *influenced* by Palahniuk, then, so much as something has made its way from Palahniuk's work into Alaidy's work. As the late Miriam

Hansen showed us in her work on classical Hollywood cinema as a global vernacular, it was the sensorium that moved from Hollywood cinema into other global cinemas.[64] Similarly, what moves from *Fight Club* into *Being Abbas el Abd* is not to be found within the lines of the latter's pages. What Chuck Palahniuk does in *Fight Club* is to reanimate the question of a public making itself as a literary project. *Fight Club* summons its public, and through the depiction of the search for membership in the fight club it mirrors its own summoning of a public. And as Alaidy in *Being Abbas el Abd*, Taher in *Looks Like It's Falling Apart*, and El Shafee in *Metro* created bold works within another context, they addressed and thereby summoned up their own publics. In the process, *Fight Club* could be left behind except as a trace, just as El Shafee could leave behind *The Watchmen* and *Palestine*. The notable appearance of the Guy Fawkes mask in Tahrir Square, which of course has a long history but which was revived in Alan Moore's graphic novel *V Is for Vendetta* (1982; adapted as a film in 2006) is not, then, a mark of Western authorship of the Arab uprisings, as is by now clear. (Note that both Bahrain and the United Arab Emirates banned the wearing of the mask in 2013.) Just as Alaidy moves beyond Palahniuk, these traces, strains of code perhaps, are the residue of what has departed from the original through the circulatory process.

JUMPING PUBLICS

So we arrive back at my original question: Is the Egyptian novel democratic? What would it mean to ask this question with a rigorous definition of circulation in play? In the Cairo joke about the bobble-head dogs with which I began this chapter, there is a wonderful irony at play. The man selling the bobble-head dogs was playing on American rhetoric about democracy, particularly in the wake of the 2003 invasion of Iraq, which, as widely reported (and derided in Arab media), accompanied a logic that Arabs were eager for American-style products and ideas, especially democracy. America tells you that you want this thing, so you *must* want it! Buy my products!

Fictions *about* Egypt in the digital age—such as the fiction that Egypt takes up putatively liberating Western forms uncritically and ultimately derivatively—must be given up if we are to understand the rich contemporary cultural scene in Egypt. In their place, let us attend to these Egyptian fictions *of* the digital age, including the works by El Shafee, Alaidy, Omar Taher, and others, that produced an Egyptian public in the wake of the "shock" of multimedia and the digital revolution. It was these fictions that were taken up by the impulse to rise up in 2011, which in turn extended and expanded their lifeworlds in ways that defy translation. These fictions jump publics, leaving behind the strands of the outside form that often provoked them into being, just as the global flow of culture finds an end to the circulatory path. And though in 2015, those energies seem frustrated, in stasis, theirs is not a dead end, but a vibrant one, whose energies have not been depleted. These works are powerful fictions of the digital age because they resist the pull back into a disciplining and disciplinary milieu that would reduce them to a translatable value. That end is where they thrive; that is where they end.

3

"ARGO FUCK YOURSELF"

Iranian Cinema and the Curious Logics of Circulation

One time when the crowd chanted "Marg bar Amrika" (Death to America), Seyyed Mostafa—a clerical student visiting from Qom who wears his mustard-colored robes and a white turban, indicating his descent from the Prophet—turns to me and says, "You know when we yell that, we're not talking about the American people. We LOVE the American people. We're only talking about the government. That's the difference between Iran and the Arab countries. The Arab countries . . . their leaders love the American government, but I think the people hate the American people. We're the opposite."

WHEN *A SEPARATION*, directed by Asghar Farhadi, won the Best Foreign-Language Film Award at the 2012 Academy Awards, it was cause for widespread celebration in Tehran. Despite a vibrant debate about the controversial social drama prior to the awards ceremony, the response to Farhadi's Hollywood victory briefly bridged the divide between his film's former opponents and its champions in Iran.[1] A year later, when Ben Affleck's political suspense film *Argo* took home the 2013 Oscar for Best Picture, the reaction in Iran once again crossed social and political boundaries, but this time rather than exuberance there was general dismay—particularly about the film's representations of Iranians and recent history. The Islamic Republic promised to fund a remake, the Iranian government retained a French lawyer to sue Affleck in international court, and two academic conferences held in Tehran about Hollywood's "Iranophobia" garnered international press coverage.[2]

In both cases, cinema took center stage in the public discussions of relations between the two nations. In Iran, *Argo* stood for more than itself, as did *A Separation* in the United States. Political relations remained fraught through this period because of a stand-off in discussions of Iran's nuclear ambitions, unresolved tensions over the way Iran suppressed protests of the 2009 presidential election, and Iranian perceptions that the U.S. government, military, and entertainment industries were colluding to overthrow or suppress the elected Iranian government. *Argo*, set in 1979 during the hostage crisis, dredged up memories of older hostilities between the two nations and renewed American anxieties about Iranian perfidy and vice versa. *A Separation*, by contrast, not only was an individual triumph for its director but also represented the celebrated body of postrevolutionary Iranian "new wave" cinema—proving that great art is being produced in the Islamic Republic of Iran. As such, *A Separation* benefited from two decades of Western fascination with new Iranian cinema by film critics, scholars, and art cinema audiences and helped to popularize that interest to a broader American public.

The way both films were circumscribed and overwhelmed by international politics, however, demonstrates the limits to how cultural products can communicate to audiences in ways that might defy those politics. Both *Argo* and *A Separation* were apparently against the kind of polarization that appeared in the media discussion of their films in Iran and the United States. *Argo* opened with a left-leaning prologue in which American audiences were told that the United States had "engineered a coup d'état" that deposed democratically elected Prime Minister Mohammad Mosaddegh, "a secular democrat," and in his place "installed" Reza Pahlavi as shah, initiating an "era of torture and fear."[3] Despite some errors about Pahlavi (he was already shah when the U.S. coup was staged, and "Reza" is the name of his father; he is properly called "Mohammad Reza"), *Argo* thus provided the version of the painful events of 1953 that Iranians had long claimed but that the United States did not officially acknowledge until 2000.[4] For its part, *A Separation*, set in the present, revolves in part around an Iranian woman's desire to leave Iran because she feels that remaining there will limit her daughter's future. In this chapter, I give fuller readings of the films, arguing that *Argo*'s liberal opening prologue is undercut by Ben Affleck's recuperation of the U.S. Central Intelligence Agency (CIA) and the substitution of the heroic American male for a silenced Iranian female and showing how Farhadi's film allows for a more nuanced understanding of domestic Iran that emphasizes the ties and obligations that bind Iranians to their country and each other.

But to appreciate the meanings of cinema in Iran in the late twentieth and twenty-first centuries, it is not enough to look closely at the content and artistry of these particular films. In the long-standing U.S.–Iranian standoff, cinema plays a key and crucial role. What I call here the curious logics of circulation alter our understanding not only of the meaning of individual films but also more broadly of the way that cultural products function politically in the digital age. To put it simply, one cannot understand the meaning of Iranian films without attending to their circulation—what sorts of debates they occasion at home and how the international reception of them affects their meanings in Iran.

Some of the most interesting discussions of postrevolution Iranian cinema have encouraged us to consider the circulation of Iranian cinema abroad as part of the greater discussion of it, from Hamid Naficy's four-volume work *A Social History of Iranian Cinema* to Saeed Zeydabadi-Nejad's slim but excellent book *The Politics of Iranian Cinema* and from Hamid Dabashi's many writings on Iranian cinema both scholarly and journalistic to Negar Mottahedeh's monograph *Displaced Allegories,* which addresses the gendering of Iranian art cinema as women's cinema as a result of censorship restrictions.[5] Iranian cinema is so diverse, and there is so much of it, of course, that the films that do circulate internationally should be considered a limited subset, even if a particularly prominent part of the fuller picture. Hamid Naficy takes great care to categorize multiple genres and traditions within "Iranian cinema," including social dramas, art cinema, war films, documentaries, and films by women, most of which are not what Western audiences know or think they know about films from Iran.

In this chapter on Iranian cinema, I for the most part focus on what is often called "art cinema" precisely because it is the cinema that circulates internationally. In so doing, I am engaging an impressive body of scholarship and trying to bring Iranian cinema in as a key case for my larger argument. Discussions of Iranian cinema—a distinguished field unto itself—have had little or no role in American studies or comparative literary studies generally. Insofar as any readers of this chapter may be interested in Iranian film studies more broadly, I should point out that what I am doing differently here from some of the aforementioned works is engaging both American and Iranian films as they move through the United States and Iran and as they are taken up in both contexts. I agree with a key argument Zeydabadi-Nejad makes about the circulation of Iranian film: "the problematic of reception starts much earlier" than the moment that the film is viewed by an audience. He is interested in the relationship between filmmakers and state control and makes a key intervention when he argues that we should not see that relationship as fixed or binary; he insists that "negotiations of power and meaning [occur] at the level of filmmaking" itself.[6] In other words, Iranian filmmakers know (or think they know) what they can get away with and are particularly aware of the Iranian audience—including the censor—as they construct their films. This negotiation of course goes beyond the filmmakers, I argue, and includes a wide range of individuals involved with film, including those who comment on it, those who pirate films, and those involved in dubbing them. Scholars who have focused on Iranian cinema have been particularly attuned to the complex relationship of text to context, circulation to "meaning," and the multiple contingent meanings that Iranian cinema always engages. Indeed, these things are often points of contention and are perhaps impossible to escape.

In bringing a discussion of Iranian cinema into this book, however, I am addressing a larger audience than those focused on Iranian film. In comparative literature and in the transnational strand of American literary studies, those who argue that the meaning of the text can be identified by reading it closely clash with those who argue that whatever the apparent meaning might be, it is a distraction from the more important question of what the text does, how it circulates, and what form it takes. (I have suggested that cultural diplomacy is invested in these debates as well, though with significantly less theoretical nuance.) So there are those—most famously Franco Moretti, who has argued for a "distant reading" of literary texts—who would attend only to the circulation of the text and others, including Dilip Gaonkar and Elizabeth Povinelli, who would go yet further and focus only on the "circulatory matrix" within which a cultural product operates, explicitly denying what they call the "virtuoso reading" of the cultural object.[7] To this debate, I bring my discussion of Iranian films to how we might look closely at the way they negotiate complex publics *without* refusing a close reading of the text itself. Indeed, I argue that the close reading of the film and its engagement with its public is a way into a richer sense of how circulation implicates the text for a global comparative literary studies.

This chapter therefore challenges those in both academic and diplomatic realms who argue that cultural products such as film, literature, music, and art communicate simply in the past two or three decades, if they ever did before, and therefore are a useful barometer of the society from which they come or a means by which to convince foreign audiences to appreciate these products' cultures of origin. By "simply," I do not mean that such diplomats and critics consider films or literary works "simple" or "uncomplicated" but rather that they imply that there is a legible meaning; this meaning may require a critic to elaborate it for readers, but it is ultimately a single meaning rather than multiple, possibly contradictory meanings as the text is entextualized.

I take a circuitous path in presenting my argument, first examining *Argo* and *A Separation* and the discussion of them on both sides of the divide and then venturing through the film worlds of Tehran, including the digital piracy of Hollywood films, the way the long fascination with American cinema takes on its own meanings through exuberant dubbing, and the different meanings attributed to Iran's greatest auteur in the contemporary period, Abbas Kiarostami. My goal is to show how circulation explains Iranian cinema and, by the same token, how Iranian cinema explains circulation.

The stakes are important for comparative literary studies, American studies, and film studies on the level of methodology. My argument is that it is not enough to read a film closely on its own because its meaning shifts when we take its circulation into new publics into account. But here, as with the Egyptian fictions of the digital age, the misreading of the role of social networking software in the Arab uprisings, and our understanding of the Moroccan exception, a dimension of this argument goes beyond academic pursuits and exceeds the question of how to read the text in the contemporary period. So I hope to show at the same time what the "curious logics of circulation" mean to understanding cultural diplomacy in the digital age. Here, in the ongoing U.S. conflict with Iran that has affected the period during which this book was researched and written, the question of circulation is political as well as critical.

Cultural diplomacy traditionally assumes that the exchange of cultural products promotes better understanding and might even sway some foreign audiences to sympathize with the United States and that the primary challenge is getting foreign audiences to engage with creative works from afar. In the digital age, the realities are much more complex. Fueled by digital piracy, translation websites, and the Internet's porous boundaries, cultural products move quickly into locations their producers rarely imagined and are picked up by multiple new publics.

From a policy standpoint, cultural diplomacy will have to acknowledge and deal with the political impact of cultural "exchanges" that are not sponsored by the government but that have significant political ramifications. Of course, even here things get more complicated: at the 2013 Academy Awards, the much vaunted award for best picture was presented by none other than Michelle Obama herself via a video link from the White House. Iranians who had long declared that Hollywood was in cahoots with Washington—that the putative separation of entertainment from politics in the United States was a fiction—now had a pointed and incontrovertible bit of evidence on their side. If so, any new bit of cinema, whether Hollywood films that offended Iranians such as *300* (Zack Snyder, 2007), *The Wrestler* (Daren Aronofsky, 2009), and *Babel* (Alejandro González Iñárritu, 2006) or, more dangerously, hateful videos posted on YouTube such as *Innocence of Muslims*, now reflected on U.S. government projects.

BEN AFFLECK IN IRAN

A month before the 2013 Academy Awards, the following story appeared inside the front section of the *New York Times*: "Film to Present Iran's View of 'Argo' Events."[8] Written by the *Times* Tehran Bureau chief, Thomas Erd-brink, the piece reported on—but at the same time subtly mocked—the proposition that there might be an Iranian version of the story told in Ben Affleck's blockbuster, which had recently been nominated for best picture.[9] "Not much is known about the proposed movie," the *Times* reported. "But it is a sure bet that it will center on the official Iranian view of the 1979 hostage crisis." From the start, Affleck's film was posited as superior to the imagined Iranian film, not because of its artistry but because it supposedly offered an *unofficial* view—one outside of government politics presented by an individual artist working free of state-imposed constraints. An Iranian film version of the "Argo" rescue could only be compromised and ridiculous by this logic; by giving the official Iranian view, the imagined film would necessarily politicize the story. In contrast, Affleck's work is value free, not tied to the "official" U.S. view. How could a film made by a Hollywood celebrity be official, anyway?

The short article did eventually, almost grudgingly, admit that there may be more to the story. A few paragraphs down, Erdbrink wrote: "Iranian films . . . have attracted foreign acclaim." But as if recognizing the trap into which he had written himself, the *Times* writer stressed that the Iranian films celebrated in the West are independent, not official. The implication was that readers should not be distracted into thinking that an Iranian version of *Argo* might be any good. That may be true—films commissioned by governments are rarely works of lasting power (consider the films commissioned by the U.S. government during World War II). But what is important here is how the awareness of Iranian art cinema made its way into this article about *Argo*, which was after all an article about the conflict between the United States and Iran. The *Times* writer brought these disparate elements together—How could he not?—and made explicit the ways in which the discussion of film in Iran and American films about Iran have always also been about U.S.–Iranian politics since 1979 (or since 1953) until today.

Here, the *Times* bureau chief picked up something from the larger discussion of Iranian art cinema in the West: the way numerous American critics who celebrate Iranian films have posited that their originality emerges from the fraught relationship between film directors and the state. It doesn't matter how much Iranian cinema Erdbrink had seen. What does matter is that a logic from discussions of that cinema had made its way into his article.[10] According to that logic, state censorship creates a situation within which the genius of the Iranian film director can flourish even though by definition censorship limits the work of the Iranian auteur. If in the West the auteur director is generally understood to work against the prerogatives of capital and in tension with the industrial aspects of film production, in Iran the auteur is understood to work against the state.[11] In a later section of this chapter, I discuss how this logic works in discussions of Abbas Kiarostami, the most celebrated Iranian film auteur. But here note how in the *Times* article Ben Affleck's absolute independence is assumed and the invisibility of the marketplace and of Hollywood film formulas is left unremarked. Iranians, in contrast, would not and did not see Affleck as free from pressures placed on Hollywood by the state or as working outside American ideology, but that this position might have any credibility is unimaginable in the article printed in the *New York Times*.

In January 2013, when this article appeared, the idea that six weeks later the Oscar would be presented to the producers of *Argo* from the White House itself—with uniformed soldiers surrounding the First Lady—was also unimaginable to the Tehran bureau chief of the *New York Times*. And though for many Iranians the image of Michelle Obama naming *Argo* as recipient of the Academy Award for best picture confirmed precisely the collusion of the U.S. government and the powerful film industry, I will venture to say that it had little effect on American audiences. Did it really corrupt anything for them when the camera made that surprising and unprecedented shift from the stage of Hollywood's Dolby Theatre to somewhere within the White House? Would it have been any different if an Iranian film was awarded a top prize by President Mahmoud Ahmadinejad surrounded by the Revolutionary Guard? Yet the official imprimatur on *Argo* was acceptable precisely because any connection between Hollywood and the state is not in danger of being perceived. Perceived in the United States, that is. In Iran, it was definitely noted.

Argo was released on October 4, 2012—the same week that the Iranian rial dropped 40 percent in value, an enormous economic crisis that spurred significant protests in Tehran.[12] The relationship between domestic crises in Iran and international posturing is rarely noted in U.S. media, but we must recall that there is an economic context for the debate about the cinematic representation of Iranian–U.S. relations.[13] By rewriting the Iranian individual as an anonymous, mostly violent enemy of the United States, *Argo* unwittingly underwrote the continued sanctions against the Iranian state, which have had the gravest consequences on middle- and lower-class Iranians. By committing this representational violence against the individuality and subjectivity of the Iranian, therefore, *Argo* had and still has a very real effect on the lives of ordinary Iranians: it undergirds a context in which people in the United States are able to forget the pain of economic sanctions and the anxiety produced by continual threats of war. Further, by offering a heroic story of the "creative" and "nonviolent" work of a now good CIA, the film allowed an American audience to forget briefly the contemporary controversies over the use of torture by U.S. intelligence communities and to excuse retroactively the CIA's involvement in the 1953 overthrow of Mohammad Mosaddegh.

The film—part espionage thriller, part comedy—tells a lesser-known story about the famous hostage crisis. Based on actual events—though quite loose in their adaptation—the film depicts the rescue of six American consular workers who escaped during the 1979 takeover of the U.S. embassy by Iranian students. These six Americans fled to the residence of the Canadian ambassador Kenneth Taylor (as well as to the residence of John Sheardown, a Canadian immigration officer, though this detail is not included in the film), from which they were eventually retrieved by a CIA officer, who smuggled them out of the country using fake Canadian passports. The title of the film refers to the cover story used by the CIA to justify the presence of the six men and women in Iran: they were film artists scouting locations for a science fiction picture to be called *Argo*. A fictitious production company was set up in Hollywood in case anyone in Iran was looking. (They weren't.) Remarkably, this elaborate cover story is where *Argo* comes closest to historical reality.

Where it diverges most from the record is in its account of the role played by Tony Mendez, the CIA operative sent to "exfiltrate" the Americans, and nearly everything that happens once he arrives in Tehran, from a fabricated tour through the Grand Bazaar to an imagined scene at Mehrabad Airport in which Iranian police and passport agents detain the Americans, then release them, and finally chase them down the airport runway with guns drawn in a scene reminiscent of 1970s television (for me, the *Dukes of Hazard* came to mind). These scenes are what most Iranians objected to, for they portray Iranians variously as hapless and foolish (the government workers) or violent and faceless (regular Iranians). As one observer pointed out in the *Palestine Chronicle*, "'Argo' ultimately reinforces the binary opposition of a civilized West and a savage Iran. We hear a lot of Farsi in the movie, but only when Farsi is spoken by a Western character is the dialogue given subtitles. Farsi spoken by Iranian characters in the film is merely incomprehensible noise. Here the film accurately mirrors our contemporary reality, in which we inflict our discourse on Iranians, but are incapable of listening to theirs."[14] Although this description is a bit of an overstatement—two crucial scenes involving the Iranian housemaid provide subtitles to translate Farsi speech by Iranians—the general point is defensible.

The silencing of the Iranian subject is the crucial flaw of *Argo*. Iranian voices are not heard, or when they are heard, it is as "noise" (figure 3.1). Iranian subjects are pure sound, the beating of fists upon a car (in one particularly horrific scene, when Tony Mendez drives the six Americans through the streets of Tehran toward the bazaar, a complete fabrication from the historical record), or they are represented by angry rhetoric on news media. Gone from the film is the debate within Iran about the taking of American hostages; gone are the ideas and discussions of the radical students behind the takeover; gone is the debate in the region over whether to support the students or not; missing is the very real frustration of individual Iranians outside the activists' political actions; and missing are the frustration and fear among Iranian exiles in the United States.

How can a critical approach committed to circulation respond to this silencing? Here I propose two tacks: one we might associate with postcolonial studies, which here means focusing on an Iranian character silenced by the film; and one that in the edited collection *Globalizing American Studies*

FIGURE 3.1 Iranians as noise in *Argo* (Ben Affleck, 2012).

I have called a multisited, comparative method,[15] which here means follow-ing Affleck and his film to Tehran.

One Iranian character in the main arc of the film allows us a way out, the only Iranian character with a name who carries the burden of the si-lenced Iranian: Sahar—she has no last name in film or credits—played by Sheila Vand, an Iranian American actress (figure 3.2).[16] Sahar is the house-keeper at the residence of the Canadian ambassador. At great and obvious personal risk, she helps maintain the dangerous fiction that the Americans hiding there are in fact Canadian "houseguests." Sahar is featured in three brief but key scenes. In the first, the ambassador's wife, Dr. Patricia Taylor (played by Page Leong), has a brief conversation in Persian with Sahar dur-ing which the latter indirectly reveals she is aware of the fiction. In the second, Sahar silently witnesses the execution by authorities of an Iranian living next door, suggesting the personal risk she is taking. In the third, an Iranian officer questions Sahar through the gate to the ambassador's house, and she tells a lie that enables the fiction to continue. These scenes are by all accounts fictional,[17] as is the character of Sahar,[18] and therefore the final

FIGURE 3.2 Sahar, played by Sheila Vand in *Argo*.

image we have of Sahar as she escapes Iran by entering Iraq on foot across the border provides an unremarked upon but tangible sense that she is the remainder of the film. In other words, she is that which is left over, that which does not fit into the film's arc, that which is indivisible. The risk Sahar takes is thus noted but forgotten, and her fate is left to the imagination as she enters a country that will be a war zone for the next decade, arguably the last hot conflict of the Cold War (the Iran–Iraq War took place mostly in Iraq, especially on the border lands, from September 1980 until August 1988 and should be considered in the context of the overarching U.S.–Soviet conflict).[19] Sahar talks in this film, but using the distinction made famous by Gayatri Chakravorty Spivak, she is a subject who cannot speak—her language does not register. Her words are heard but only as they advance the plot for the American characters. Otherwise she is silenced, and like the erasure of Persian/Farsi language when it is not spoken by Westerners or when it does not advance their story line, Sahar remains only a trace.

It would seem to me reasonable to counter my argument by saying that Affleck gives us the minor character precisely to offer a critique of how the

United States takes advantage of Sahar (or some aspect of Iran that she represents). And yet the evidence to the contrary is overwhelming: the film consistently puts history, Iranians, and even the Canadian allies themselves under erasure but tells its viewers that what they are seeing is historical reality, even while it uses familiar Hollywood formulas to advance the action and enhance the drama. If Sahar appears in the film, in other words, Affleck distracts the film's audience from lingering on her or considering her fate. Instead, the film overwhelms its audience with carefully reconstructed sets, location shooting—the Grand Bazaar in Istanbul stands in for that of Tehran—comedic relief, action segments, and dramatic tension not between any of the Americans and Sahar, but between two American men: Tony Mendez (Affleck) and escapee Joe Stafford (played by Scoot McNairy).

Given the amount of fabrication in *Argo,* it is striking that the film emphasizes its own "absolute authenticity." It does so with such insistence, so much repetition, that Affleck reveals something like anxiety. Again and again he takes recourse in multiple ways to what I call "photographic realism" to circumscribe the critique of *Argo* in advance. He does so, first, by expending extensive effort to cast actors who look like the Western individuals they are meant to represent. Given that all the historical figures represented in the film are unknown to contemporary audiences, this is a strange choice. But the final credits include photographs of the real hostages, the Canadian ambassador and his wife, the original John Chambers (played here by John Goodman), and of course Tony Mendez—the only historical character whom the actor playing him does not resemble. Second, Affleck's exuberance with actual events of the so-called Canadian Caper is counterbalanced by his inclusion (again in the final credits) of historical photos from 1979 Iran that have been re-created in particular scenes in *Argo.* Third, as the Canadian press (but not the U.S. press) reported, Affleck rewrote the ending postscript after Ambassador Taylor complained about its inaccuracies, although the changes were limited to text that appears on screen at the film's end and does little to address the larger critique.[20] And finally, on the BluRay release of the film, which was moved up to the week prior to the Academy Awards while the film was still in American theaters (a marketing novelty), numerous extra features attempt to emphasize the film's historical veracity while downplaying its fictions, including interviews with historical figures such as Jimmy Carter and Kenneth Taylor (both edited not to appear critical of the historical inventions within the film) in a special feature documentary titled "*Argo*: Absolute Authenticity."[21]

Argo thus vacillated between this photorealistic idea of historical accuracy and pure invention. Shifting between comedy and action formulas (John Goodman and Alan Arkin's scenes in the former case and the airport scenes in the latter), the narrative arc takes over where the historical arc leaves off. Nonetheless, Thomas Erdbrink's article in January 2013 quoted none other than Kenneth Taylor, the former Canadian ambassador to Iran who is depicted in the film, to suggest that an Iranian approach would be "amusing." Taylor was elsewhere quoted as saying he was dismayed by Affleck's film, and the Canadian press was up in arms about the film, but the *Times* used him to belittle the argument against the film.[22] And rather than take up any of the notable controversies or the political dimensions of the story, the *Times* framed its piece around the provincial Hollywood dimensions: "A tough week for Ben Affleck just got tougher."[23] The reference was to the apparent dismay in Hollywood circles that Affleck had been passed over by the Academy for a nomination in the best director award category even though his film itself had been nominated for best picture, which received much more attention in the U.S. press than anything else.

The *Times* article was simply repeating a common approach for reporting on matters of Iranian popular culture: foreclosing the possibility of an alternative view of the U.S.–Iranian relationship even while reporting on it.[24] In other words, it reported on the very subject it went on to mock; it raised the topic and then withdrew it, not unlike the way in which *Argo* itself raises the idea of Sahar's subjectivity and then distracts viewers from considering it further. Furthermore, Erdbrink's lead—"a tough week for Ben Affleck just got tougher"—summoned up a second familiar pattern in U.S. media accounts of Iran: recasting the account of a transnational audience for an American cultural product in terms of its implications for a Hollywood star. (David Hasselhoff's notoriously awkward comments in the late 1990s trumpeting the alleged popular success of *Baywatch* in Iran is perhaps the most famous prior example: for Hasselhoff, in one of the more ridiculous comments of the decade, *Baywatch* represented "a cultural revolution.")[25] What is striking is that *Argo* operates in a similar fashion: its opening provides a potentially disruptive view of the Iran hostage crisis, but then the film pulls back from the alternative account to deliver a conservative version of the episode—the heroic act of a single individual, the CIA agent Tony Mendez, played here by the director Ben Affleck himself.

What allowed *Argo* to be so successful among major critics and academy voters in the United States was the suggestion of a liberal corrective—its opening—replaced with the reinscription of a palatable conservative story (the heroic act of a single individual, Mendez). At the same time, the exaggerated account of Tony Mendez emerging from the shadows of history merged with the Hollywood story of Ben Affleck leaving behind the shadow of his own prior history—the narrative that without his former collaborator Matt Damon, he was a lightweight—to emerge victorious in the land of motion pictures. As such, *Argo* and the media accounts about it continued a long tradition of Hollywood Orientalism wherein the heroic, lone individual takes on a corrupted world and recalled *Casablanca* (Michael Curtiz, 1942).

But what about the provocative, left-leaning opening? *Argo* opens with a capsule history of the events leading up to the hostage crisis that was sure to rankle both Republicans and many in the Iranian diaspora in southern California's "Tehrangeles": U.S. support for the shah's decadent and oppressive regime, overthrow of the democratically elected Mosaddegh, and the like. By 2012, though, this history was hardly revisionist. In March 2000, the Clinton administration had acknowledged the CIA role in the overthrow of Mosaddegh: Secretary of State Madeleine Albright apologized for events that took place during the Eisenhower administration. The next month the *New York Times* had published declassified records from the CIA under the Freedom of Information Act.[26] Stephen Kinzer's book *All the Shah's Men*, which recounts the story in gripping detail, was a national best seller.[27] Still, given the limits of public discourse in the United States, where Barack Obama's rumored Muslim lineage made talking tough to Iran a prerequisite to political candidacy, Affleck's segment on U.S.–Iran relations can still be seen as surprising or refreshing (and the reach of his film far exceeded that of even a national best seller, a presidential apology, or the circulation of the *New York Times*). The film, however, would substitute this attempt at setting the record straight with its own historical slight of hand.

Indeed by authorizing itself as historically reliable and Affleck himself as committed to "absolute authenticity," *Argo* could go on to take remarkable liberties with the record—especially the major role that the Canadian government played in rescuing the Americans.[28] The film makes comedy out of the idea of its own fabrication. The director of the fictional film within the film, played by Alan Arkin, doesn't know much about it. At a first reading put on to hoodwink the Hollywood press, a "real" journalist asks Arkin—playing the producer Lester Siegel, a composite character Arkin based on Jack Warner[29]—what the title *Argo* refers to. "I don't know," he says. "Argo fuck yourself." This pun on "Oh, go fuck yourself" becomes the film's tag line, which the three principle conspirators on the Hollywood end repeat to each other as joke and as code that they are in on the hoax that the fake film represents. But this tagline is as surely a message to the Iranian hostage takers as well and arguably to Iran as a whole—as well as to those, such as myself, who might critique the film!

In 2013 in the United States, *Argo's* promise of a liberal alternative to a more militarized version of U.S.–Middle Eastern history was the key to its success at the Academy Awards. The film that might have won, *Zero Dark Thirty*, was sunk in the weeks leading up to the awards ceremony by a public debate about its depiction of torture and whether director Kathryn Bigelow unwittingly expressed sympathy for the Bush administration's justification for torture. The uncomfortable feelings occasioned by Bigelow's film cathected onto the emerging discomfort on the American left for the Obama administration's increasing use of drones in the Middle East, the uncomfortable remainder of the president's victory in his November reelection.[30] As *Argo* emerged as the front-runner and then the winner for best picture, it seized upon a logic of creative nonviolent solutions to the problems of the U.S.–Iranian conflict. Screenwriter Chris Terrio delivered the summary of this position in his acceptance speech for the Oscar for best adapted screenplay: "Thirty-three years ago, Tony [Mendez], using nothing but his creativity

FIGURE 3.3 Poster for the conference "The Hoax of Hollywood," Tehran, 2013. Note the image from *Argo*.

and his intelligence, got six people out of a very bad situation. And so I want to dedicate this [award] to him, and the Taylors and the Sheardowns, and people all over the world, in the U.S., in Canada, in Iran, who use creativity and intelligence to solve problems nonviolently."[31] As the camera panned the audience at the Dolby Theatre, Hollywood celebrities nodded in agreement, apparently confident that they were helping to solve global problems with their own intelligence.[32]

In Iran, by contrast, *Argo* was seen quite differently. Two conferences, "Hollywoodism" (February 3–6, 2013) and "The Hoax of Hollywood" (March 11, 2013) were sponsored or supported by the Iranian government and included speakers from the United States, Europe, and Iran (figure 3.3). ("Hollywoodism" is an annual conference held to coincide with the annual Fajr Film Festival; this was its third installment.)[33] Speakers at these conferences addressed what participant Mike Gravel, former U.S. senator from Alaska (Democrat, 1969–1981), called "the cultural excesses of the motion picture and communication industry."[34] As can be gleaned from the abstracts published on the conference website and from press reports, the presentations at the 2013 "Hollywoodism" event ranged from reasoned critique to conspiracy theory (many of the speakers from United States, Europe, and Iran were political figures rather than academics). But rather than write off these conferences as mere counterpropaganda, as they were in Western media, or, worse, as anti-Semitic (the Anti-Defamation League called the speakers "a rogue's gallery of conspiratorial anti-Semites and anti-Zionists"),[35] we should use these conferences to listen to the ways in which Iranians respond to American films. In unofficial media, including Persian-language blogs, which do not generally tote the government line, *Argo* was no less criticized. For example, one blogger wrote about *Argo*:

> *Argo* is not the first and certainly not the only anti-Iranian film. In recent years, Hollywood has made many films against us, and despite all the advertising controversy, none could communicate with internal [i.e., Iranian] audiences. The reason is clear. The social atmosphere of the films are so far alien to the Iranian audience that they cannot be received by them. Even if someone has a problem with the government and political system, as an Iranian one cannot defend the positions created by these movies. Iranians in these movies are pictured so evil, dark, and false that every viewer realizes the depth of enmity and hatred toward Iran in them.[36]

The official Iranian position was that *Argo* demonstrated the Zionism of Hollywood, but those on the Iranian cultural left did not defend the film either. *Argo* was immediately available on the streets of Iran through pirated copies, but the commercial interest in the film did not mean that there wasn't a strong Iranian critique of it. As an Iranian film critic commented to me when I asked him if there might be an unofficial reading of the film less concerned with historical errors, "How can you *sympathize* with the action when you see yourself as the bad guy or the evil?" In an interview produced by BBC Persian (the Persian-language TV station based in London and much criticized by officials in Iran), Ali Alizadeh commented that "we are not its typical audience. We are viewing it as Iranians, and the pictures from the time of revolution are very sensitive to us." Later in the same interview, Alizadeh said: "What is absent from this film is the lack of Iranian people's suffering; it's only given as mere factual data in the first two minutes of the movie."[37]

Nevertheless, Iranian voices writing in Persian also defended the film. Tahmineh Milani, who has made films with feminist themes and was imprisoned briefly in 2001 for the theme of one of her films, claimed that *Argo* may not have been a particularly outstanding film, but it was "not anti-Iranian." Milani went so far as to suggest that *Argo* was "made to normalize the suspended Iran–US relations" and, despite a few excesses, depicted the "restless" days of the hostage crisis with calm. Milani discouraged her compatriots from politicizing its success at the Academy Awards. Hollywood "has the technical might" to make a truly anti-Iranian film "if it wants."[38]

Filmmaker Asghar Farhadi himself had an interesting perspective on the film. As a recent winner of an Oscar, he was invited to the 2013 Academy Awards ceremony, but he did not attend. Farhadi did not find *Argo* a worthy winner of the Oscar, calling it "a mediocre film cinematically [that] will be forgotten soon. But the image that it creates about the Iranians will stay with its audience and this is unfortunately very bitter." But he was also eager to dispel some Iranian conspiracy theories about the Academy Awards: "The academy members are not one body working under a horrifying controlled room aiming to damage other religions and cultures and foster one way of thought and life. This is part of the illusion that has been with us for long." He remarked that there might be "a few of the members who judge films through their ideological biases, political tendencies, or associational benefits," but he dismissed the conspiracy theory. He remarked that among the nominees for best picture that year, several were films about politics, specifying *Lincoln* (Steven Spielberg), *Zero Dark Thirty*, *Argo*, and *Django Unchained* (Quentin Tarantino). Farhadi explained the nomination of *Argo* on commercial grounds; its great success at the box office, he believed, forced a nomination and then the advertising campaign that ensued helped it along. "Why it was lucrative is obvious: constructing a heroic narrative, employing threaded clichés, use of superficial suspense, offering a limited, shadowy, one-dimensional image of its anti-heroes made it accessible to a public who is not expected to think through a film but be entertained by it."[39] Farhadi, as we will see in the next section, is a director who has given thought to what makes a film successful commercially as well as an art film director attuned to cinematic concerns.

This understanding of the social context for the Hollywood film is more sophisticated than simply saying that Hollywood narratives are interested only in box office receipts or that Washington and Hollywood conspire outwardly. Farhadi is recognizing that after the American century the vestiges of Cold War logics about Iran and the role of the heroic American in the world remain. But now because of the circuits of communication opened up by the digital age, it is no longer enough to be stuck in those logics. To move beyond them, critics working in American studies after the American century must follow texts where they travel to hear those voices whose commentary is now mostly excluded and who can help us disrupt the logics of the American century itself.

DECONSTRUCTING DEPARTURE

A year earlier, 2011, Asghar Farhadi's own film *A Separation* provided a dramatically different portrait of Iran and Iranian society. The film, in turn, was received and understood in divergent ways in the United States and Iran. There is much less fanfare for a foreign art film than for a blockbuster in U.S. media, of course; front-runners for best foreign-language film get significantly less comment than those for best picture. Nonetheless, the success of *A Separation* was an occasion for a range of American critics to take the time to discuss it, offering us a set of responses beyond the otherwise limited number of experts in the United States who comment on Iranian art films. Most who did so focused on the "humanity" of Iranians in Farhadi's film, which, critics suggested either implicitly or explicitly, might surprise American audiences. *Time* magazine's chief film critic Richard Corliss, for example, wrote: "*A Separation* is both Iranian and universal. The warring husbands could as easily be an urban American liberal and a rural fundamentalist."[40] Other reviews invoked the expectation of exoticism that

American filmgoers allegedly bring to watching a film from Iran and claimed that their preconceptions would be betrayed by the experience of viewing *A Separation*.

In Iran, the film was heralded as a masterpiece, though not without some controversy. Its success in the West was cause for celebration but also concern, as is often the case for Iranian art cinema. After being awarded the top prize for *A Separation* at the Berlin Film Festival (February 10–21, 2011) a year before receiving the Oscar, Farhadi was interviewed by Massoud Mehrabi in the Tehran film quarterly *Film International*. Farhadi was sophisticated and thoughtful about the success of the film at this important festival (it also took top honors for best actor and best actress), and the long interview begins with an extended discussion of the Western reception of his work. Though it was his second time presenting a film at Berlin, Farhadi noted his own surprise that the new film resonated with a foreign audience to such an extent; he had expected it to be too local to translate outside of Iran. He explained: "Some aspects of the story cannot be understood unless you know Persian and, therefore, I did not expect anything important would happen in Berlin." But it was precisely this attention to detail, Farhadi explained, that resonated with foreign audiences: "They said that they believed the film through details and told me that although those details were mostly local, it did not prevent them from understanding [the] . . . totality of the film." That said, Farhadi expressed to the Iranian interviewer his frustration that "every reporter was sure to ask a question about the situation in Iran and filmmaking conditions in addition to questions they asked about the film." Though it does not come up in the interview with Farhadi, it is notable that director Jafar Panahi has also been honored at Berlin; Panahi had been sentenced to a six-year jail term and twenty-year ban on filmmaking just two months earlier. Farhadi might not be expected to protest the censorship of Panahi in an Iranian publication, but he did go to lengths to point out the ways in which his own work is not meant to propose social reform: "I am a filmmaker who tells a story and poses question for which he has no answers. When I don't have the answers, how could I be a reformist? I think that this attitude to artists is outdated."[41]

A few months later Farhadi was subjected to a number of interviews in U.S. media and was no less expert at resisting American reporters' attempts to pigeonhole his work or his relationship to Iran itself. Most famously, in his much lauded acceptance speech at the 2012 Academy Awards, he said: "At this time, many Iranians all over the world are watching us, and I imagine them to be very happy. At the time when talk of war, intimidation, and aggression is exchanged between politicians, the name of their country, Iran, is spoken here through her glorious culture, a rich and ancient culture that has been hidden under the heavy dust of politics." Indeed, in the immediate aftermath of his victory, Facebook lit up with Iranians based in Iran celebrating the director and proclaiming their pride in his success. Farhadi dedicated his Oscar to "the people of my country, the people who respect all cultures and civilizations and despise hostility and resentment."[42] The first Iranian to win the Oscar for best foreign-language picture, Farhadi was the beneficiary of a long fascination with Iranian art cinema among American film critics. This fascination revolves around the relationship of individual creativity to the regime of censorship within which Iranian filmmakers work. In this respect, Farhadi played well both in interviews—where he skirted the boundary between the two opposing cultural regimes—and in his award-winning film itself, where the question of whether contemporary Iran limits the future of its youth and its citizens in general is raised and then dissected.

The film, whose original title is *Jodaei-ye Nader az Simin* (Separation of Nader from Simin), is a powerful exploration of marriage, divorce, parenting, Alzheimer's, class conflict, and gender relations in contemporary Tehran, and it is not difficult to feel that the academy might have chosen it as best foreign-language film on its own, irrespective of its Iranian origins. Yet the film is so deeply *about* its setting (using the distinction I clarified in chapter 2) that not to consider its Iranian origin would be disingenuous. To be sure, the critical discussion of it in American media could not ignore the way it bucks against Western stereotypes of Iran and Iranians. So to ignore the fact that this first Iranian film to win the Oscar carries with it the burden (and the benefit) of being Iranian would be critically irresponsible. As art films such as *A Separation* circulate in American theaters, they seem at first the antithesis of Iranian politics—philosophically rich, elusive, ambiguous. But then American critics discuss them in terms of the very politics they seem to evade or avoid, and the films are compared to and harnessed to the political conflict between the United States and Iran. As they circulate in media, then, the films are unable to escape politics. Farhadi is, it would seem, aware of this paradox, and without coding it into his film directly, he indexes it, which makes his film yet more appealing and rich.

A Separation puts the question of circulation itself in the foreground, where it means variously the ability or inability to leave Iran, the so-called brain drain of Iranian doctors and engineers, the strictures of class, the perils of age and senility, and, most of all, the ways in which marriage in general and marriage with children in particular limit the ability to act as a free and unfettered agent. The film begins with its two protagonists, Simin and Nader, a middle-class Iranian couple in their forties, facing an unseen judge who sits in the position where the camera is placed. Simin, played by actress Leila Hatami—who had become famous in Iran for her depiction of the title character in Dariush Mehrjui's great film *Leila* (1997), another movie about marital difficulties—is confident and cosmopolitan. Her husband, Nader, played by Payman Maadi (better known in Iran as a screen writer until he appeared in Farhadi's previous film, *Darbare-ye Eli* [About Elly, 2009]), also appears modern in both appearance and attitudes, though he is stubborn and arrogant as well. In this opening, Farhadi silently invokes Abbas Kiarostami's film *Namay-e nazdik* (Close-up, 1990) or at least recalls it; in both films, a judge is asked to arbitrate a central question (in Kiarostami's film whether Sabzian is crazy, in Farhadi's whether Simin is being reasonable). In *A Separation*, the film places the viewer in the judge's position from the start—the couple faces the camera directly as they present their problem to him/us (figure 3.4). This is different from Kiarostami's film, where the judge is viewed from across the room, an object among objects. The character of the judge or examining magistrate (played by Babak Karimi) returns later in *A Separation* and allows the film to take seriously the idea that truth—the various truths in circulation in the film, whether they

FIGURE 3.4 Simin (Leila Hatami) and Nader (Payman Maadi) face the examining magistrate in *A Separation* (Asghar Farhadi, 2011).

are Simin and Nader's or other characters' later—is constantly viewed from a perspective.[43] What makes this idea important given the film's own circulation through the world is the contrast between Farhadi's portrayal of Iran and Affleck's. Farhadi's Iran is one in which differing positions are considered, interrogated, and weighed. Affleck's model of engagement with Iran is one of tricking Iran, slipping one past Iran; that is what circulation means to him. Farhadi shows us how listening to the particularities of a situation, hearing it and considering it, gives a more nuanced judgment.

Simin wants a divorce from Nader because he will not leave Iran with her, despite their prolonged successful effort to obtain visas. Nader will agree to the divorce, but he will not allow his wife to take their daughter, Termeh, with her out of the country (under Iranian family law his permission is required). Nader's father, suffering with advanced Alzheimer's, needs him, he says. It is a simple but intractable problem. After she explains the situation to the judge, Simin turns to address Nader:

SIMIN: Your daughter or her future is not important to you?
NADER: Who said anything about our daughter? Why do you think
only you care?[44]

But the judge is quick to interrupt, bringing the conflict immediately to another register:

JUDGE: So the children living in this country don't have a future?
SIMIN: As a mother, I'd rather she didn't grow up in these
circumstances.
JUDGE: What circumstances?

Now, Simin looks down. She doesn't want to push the point; it is clear the judge will not side with her. The judge continues:

JUDGE: What circumstances? Is she better off here with both her
parents or there without a father?
SIMIN: That's why I want him to come.
NADER: I can't leave.

With this exchange, much more is unsaid than is said. Simin's downward glance, played subtly by Hatami, seems to suggest that the judge has pushed her to a dead end in the conversation. There is no way she can answer this question honestly, either as a character in this scene or as an actress in Farhadi's film. This is, of course, a fictional scene in front of a fictional judge, but it indexes a real system in crisis. The conversational dead end suggests an afterlife for the film: Will this exchange jump from fiction to real life? In other words, will it bring political trouble for Farhadi? (Jafar Panahi explores this case in *In film nist* [This is not a film, 2011], in which Panahi plays with the legal restrictions imposed on his ability to make a film and makes a film about the film he is restricted from making.)[45] Unlike Ben Affleck's *Argo*, *A Separation* makes no pretense to be "based on a true story," but it is the deep resonance of what Simin refers to as "circumstances" that alerts us to danger.

The film's indexical relationship to contemporary Iranian society was picked up in Iran, where viewers commented that *A Separation* has a powerful immediacy. One Iranian blogger who named herself Aram wrote a piece she called "Who Represents What in *A Separation*?" She found each of the characters of the film to represent aspects of life in contemporary Tehran:

> Nader represents the Iranian community which is struggling on the one hand with traditions and on the other hand with modernity.
>
> The grandfather is representative of traditions in the community. His Alzheimer's is our historical memory. It is neither forgettable nor can he stand on his feet without the community.
>
> Simin represents Iranian modernity. She is the one who tries to make the community believe the necessity of her cause, i.e. migration.
>
> The pregnant woman stands for the religious views in Iranian society. She wants to help carry the load of tradition (grandfather) but gets caught in the questions of purity/impurity and becomes a new problem for the community.
>
> Her husband is a representative of social biases and prejudices.
>
> Termeh is representative of the future stuck in the struggle between modernity, tradition, and religion and the film ends with her inability to choose.
>
> The little girl is the representative of the present. Younger than everyone, she is constantly reporting and painting the events.[46]

Aram's sense that Farhadi was creating an allegory of contemporary Tehran is perhaps overdetermined, but she does pick up on the film's direct, almost second-person address to its audience suggested by the opening scene.

The film remains close to the primary couple, their strife, and the way it affects their daughter, Termeh (played by Farhadi's own daughter, Sarina Farhadi). With this main story line, the director intertwines a dramatic story about the poor, traditional young woman who is hired to take care of Nader's father when Simin moves out.

For those who had seen Farhadi's earlier work, it is clear how *A Separation* picks up and builds on his acclaimed film *Chaharshanbeh souri* (Fireworks Wednesday, 2006), another powerful exploration of marital strife, children, and class conflict. In its own way, *Fireworks Wednesday* is also about circulation. Traffic, marital stasis, and class immobility are associated with one another, and the notorious difficulty of moving through downtown Tehran in an automobile at rush hour is a key plot device. In this earlier film, a young woman from a lower social class is brought in to work as a temporary housemaid for a middle-class married couple and serves as witness to her employers' foibles. Roohi, the housemaid (played by Taraneh Alidoosti) is preparing for her own marriage when she is hired to clean up a household on the verge of collapse. Her employer, Mozhde (played by Hedye Tehrani), suspects her husband, Morteza, of having an affair with a neighbor and enlists Roohi to help her gain evidence. But Mozhde is so obsessive and anxious and the evidence against an affair seems increasingly convincing that the audience comes to side with the husband and to believe that Mozhde's suspicions are unfounded. (The fact that Mozhde is correct about Morteza comes as a shock, which the film withholds masterfully.) And as in *A Separation*, there is the turning over and over of bits of evidence, amateur interrogations of people in a household that seem to hold the truth of domestic disputes.

In *A Separation*, a lower-class domestic worker is again at the center of the action. Here, the worker, Razieh (played by Sareh Bayat), is already married and has a young daughter, whom she brings along to work with her. We learn that she is pregnant with a second child. When the job of caring for Nader's father, who is suffering with Alzheimer's, proves more difficult than she expected, and when it requires her to bathe him, Razieh decides to give up the job so as not to break any Islamic moral codes. But she attempts to pass the job along to her own husband, Hojjat (Shahab Hosseini), somehow without Hojjat finding out that his wife has taken a job (or bathed an old man) without his knowledge or permission. Before Hojjat can assume the job, however, Razieh works one last day, during which she leaves the grandfather alone in order to see a doctor about the baby she is carrying. She is not back in time for the return of her employers, who find the old man tied to a bed (so that he does not wander off), tangled and on the floor, having rolled off the bed. A dispute ensues, and Razieh falls or is pushed by Nader (a key distinction in the film). She subsequently has a miscarriage, and the action of the film turns from the conflict between Nader and Simin over leaving Iran to the conflict between Nader, Razieh, and Hojjat about whether Nader is responsible for Razieh's miscarriage and the conflict between Nader and Simin about the way Nader is handling the conflict with Razieh and Hojjat. Fueled by Shahab Hosseini's electric performance in the role of Hojjat, the tension escalates to a seeming breaking point.

Despite the layering of themes between the two films, with *A Separation* Farhadi's achievement is to create a social drama that travels across and outside of Iranian social contexts in ways that *Fireworks Wednesday*, in spite of its dramatic power, does not. I watched the 2006 film after having seen *A Separation*, and as I did so, I found myself wondering about their similarities. How can we understand the international success of *A Separation* compared to the relatively local circulation of *Fireworks Wednesday*? I hypothesized that the storyline of *Fireworks Wednesday* may be too anchored to an Iranian holiday, the Wednesday before Nowruz, around which the action takes place (and upon which the plot relies), for foreign audiences to appreciate. Some of the anxieties Mozhde expresses about her husband's infidelity rely on Iranian customs and concerns that do not translate as easily (the neighbor Mozhde suspects runs a beauty salon in their apartment building, is unmarried, and lives by herself, all of which cause concern among the neighbors). *A Separation*, by contrast, replaces these local details with an internationally comprehensible set of concerns—Alzheimer's, divorce with children, and so on—without completely foregoing "local" details, which allows the film to remain marked as Iranian for foreign audiences.

In the opening scene with the judge, the suggestion that Simin and Nader had gone through the steps to leave the country or circulate outside of Iran would have local meanings—I mean here national or Iranian—*and* simultaneously index or double the global circulation of the film itself. For Iranians living in diaspora in the West, an important part of the chain of circulation, both local and global resonances would be noticeable. (We see a similarly complex set of references to the local Iranian context and the global circulation of a film in the film *Kasi az gorbe-haye irani khabar nadareh* [No one knows about Persian cats, 2009], directed by Bahman Ghobadi, a film about Iranian indy rockers trying to get out of Iran while making a film that can only pose difficulties to their future, which I come back to later.) So what is *local* is the urgency Simin feels in attempting to resolve her dispute with Nader before their visas expire and how the impossibility of stating in a film that she wants to emigrate translates into the way she drops her eyes when questioned by the judge about the "circumstances" of contemporary Iran. What is *global* is the suggestion of a circulation beyond these local circumstances.

But the dichotomy I am setting up here turns out to be a trap because *A Separation* goes on to deconstruct the idea of leaving Iran to better one's circumstances. It does so through an elaborate exploration of social obligation: not only to one's family and parents but also to society at large. Farhadi's film suggests that departure from local circumstances can never come without a sense that one has abandoned the most difficult aspects of life itself. Nader is not the hero of the film because his stubbornness and inability to communicate with his wife temper his admirable sense of responsibility toward his father, yet his comment to Simin is nevertheless damning: "Your whole life, instead of solving problems, you've either run away or raised your hands and given up. Just say why you want to leave this country. You're afraid to stay." Departure is impossible without irresponsibility, a forgetting of those who cannot remember for themselves (the father who suffers from Alzheimer's). Simin's heroic ability to stand up to Nader and to the judge in the opening—the repression of her sense that her daughter's future would be better served outside of Iran—is undercut.

Thus, the film's ending poses a mysterious, allegorical challenge. The final scene of the film brings Nader and Simin's daughter, Termeh, back into the judge's chambers. With the conflict between her parents and Razieh and Hojjat resolved, Termeh is given the opportunity to choose which parent she will live with. Their separation is no longer temporary; divorce is now certain. The judge asks her if she has made a decision. "*Baleh*," she replies in the affirmative in a soft voice. "Do I have to say it now?" she asks, with tears streaming down her cheeks. Nader and Simin are asked to leave so that she can speak to the judge alone.

The camera follows her parents out to the hallway. They sit apart from one another in a municipal building where numerous others wait their turn. The hallway is noisy and crowded, full of life but also full of unhappiness. The wait is interminable. In the background, there is more arguing down the hallway, a minor disturbance, the courts where people are always sitting around, an argument down a hallway, a baby crying in the distance.

As the scene extends, it becomes apparent to us that we will not know the resolution. Nader looks stubborn; Simin looks at the floor. Both are beautiful but unreachable to each other. In a sense, to know whom Termeh chooses to live with would be politically explosive, but it is moreover an impossible choice. It is and it is not a metaphor for Iran and the United States or for Iran and itself. There is no solution. Of course, that is Farhadi's point: not the impossibility of allowing Termeh to leave Iran, symbolically, by choosing the mother, Simin, but rather the impossibility of there even being a choice.

A Separation was difficult to resolve for critics and audiences in the United States. American reviewers were sometimes confused about aspects of Iranian society depicted within it, and American journalists asked Farhadi again and again about Termeh's decision. The great achievement of the film, however, is how truth, responsibility, and finally morality are tied up with circulation itself. The truth of whether Nader caused Razieh's miscarriage is elusive, just as the truth regarding whether Morteza is having an affair is elusive in *Fireworks Wednesday*; both rely on details that are seen as if through a prism. Both conflicts and both questions do come to a resolution (Morteza *is* having an affair, and Nader did *not* cause the miscarriage, or at least probably not). But multiple perspectives and incomplete questions, none of which converge, are at play in coming to these conclusions. In this sense, *Argo*'s neat ending represents a polar opposite: the hostages escape just in the nick of time; the plane takes off from the runway just out of the reach of the Iranian security forces. Farhadi's film could never be this neat in its conclusions.

It is this mobility of meaning that makes much Iranian art cinema intriguing to viewers in the West. As indicated in the following sections, this openness has led some critics to fill in the blanks with political stereotypes—in other words, Orientalism. But doing so is an error, and I want to insist that circulation itself is the rubric through which we will best understand Iranian art cinema.

Jean-Luc Nancy picks up on this point in his writing on Abbas Kiarostami, in which he remarks that mobility is a key characteristic of this filmmaker's work.[47] I explore Kiarostami's work further later, but for now let me state that when critics and philosophers have embraced Iranian art films for a certain mobility, they tend to mean the indeterminacy of the text itself. If there is a tendency to read Iranian art cinema in relationship to poststructuralism, this tendency is delimited by the way that politics surrounds the discussion of Iranian cinema. Farhadi's attempt to evade politics or to deconstruct the politics invoked in the opening scene of the film is undercut by the way the film is entextualized in an American context. (Thus, Farhadi's statement at the 2012 Academy Awards about the Iranian people was picked up and repeated by Western media.) And in the same light but from a completely different perspective, Iranian reception of the film was never far from the question of how the film was faring internationally. Debates in Tehran about whether *A Separation* should be the Iranian nominee for the Academy Awards were less about its quality and more about precisely what it was that was circulating abroad. Some defenders of the film pointed to its humane treatment of the grandfather with Alzheimer's and argued that Farhadi presented Iranian values and "an Islamic philosophy [that] is ethical, religious, and divine" to its audience, as Ezatolah Zarghami wrote in *Hozeh News*; others could only see in *A Separation* a film "standing for [Western] values, and they are mocking us. . . . [It is a film] in line with the animosity of these countries toward us," as pro-Khamenei director Jamal Shourjeh commented in *Tehran Today*.[48]

Now of course, circulation and the contingency of meaning are a condition of film itself, inscribed within it, if only we learn to take that engagement of a public, of multiple publics, into account. We recognize that directors such as Farhadi and Kiarostami know from the start that they are addressing multiple publics at once: Iranians in Iran, the global Iranian diaspora, those who attend international film festivals or frequent art houses and commercial cinemas and so engage with the various media associated with all these different venues. Ben Affleck, in this light, is addressing a more limited public, even if that public includes many millions more than those who will see works by Kiarostami or Farhadi. But Affleck is not really considering the Iranian (or even the Canadian) response. His is a more local film with a huge global audience.

METHODOLOGICAL PARENTHESIS

How might we get beyond this binarism? Are there ways to escape the critical loop that American film critics seem to be stuck in—celebrating Iranian films in the very political terms that have apparently been refused or rejected by those films? On the other side of the ocean, how can Iranian audiences and commentators ignore the Western response to some of their greatest cultural exports?

My own interest in the mobility of film, its circulation, has required a more active research protocol. My commitment to Iranian cinema and my frustration with the terms in which it is discussed led me to Iran. And traveling to Iran to research its cinema opened up my sense of it dramatically, leading me not only to understand better the place of art cinema in the various film communities of Tehran but to discover a rich terrain of creativity I would never have otherwise known about—Iranian dubbings of Hollywood films using computer-generated imagery (CGI).

The larger project of this book—or one of them—is to inspire research methodologies for texts and cultural forms in circulation. Research methods are personal, to an extent, and any good anthropologist knows that you make up a lot of them as you go along. But for Americanists, there is little impetus to leave the United States, especially for Americanist literature and film critics writing about texts from the United States. The next section provides an account of what happened when I set out to track down Kiarostami in Tehran and instead came across a figure I least expected to find.

WATCHING *SHREK* IN TEHRAN

Downtown Tehran, February 2009: impossible traffic, the energy of 9 million Iranians making their way through congested streets, the white peaks of the Alborz Mountains disappearing shade by shade in the ever-increasing smog. The government has declared another pollution emergency, and the city center is closed to license plates ending in odd and even numbers on alternate days. The students at the university where I am teaching a graduate seminar on American studies are complaining openly about the failures of their elected officials.

Nahal and I are sitting in a café off Haft-e Tir Square.[49] She is smart and dynamic, a graduate student and freelance journalist who is quick to criticize the U.S. government and the perfidy of CNN. When I mention that a few days earlier I had overheard Friday prayers and was taken aback by the chanting of the phrase "Marg bar Amrika!" (Death to America), she retorts: "But you call us the Axis of Evil!"

Our conversation turns to the movie *Shrek* (Andrew Adamson and Vicky Jenson, 2001). Nahal loves *Shrek* so much that she has seen the first installment of the DreamWorks trilogy "at least thirty-six or thirty-seven times." Together we have been shopping for copies of the various Farsi-dubbed versions, in particular the elusive "illegal" versions. In downtown supermarkets, in small DVD stalls on Kargar Street or Enqalab Square, in shopping malls in elite north Tehran, and in the markets of grimy south Tehran, we inquire and follow various pathways, many of them dead ends.

It is I who have insisted on tracking down dubbed versions of *Shrek*, though I didn't return to Iran planning to do so. I came here interested in figuring out what Iranians really think and say about Abbas Kiarostami, but as I engaged in what I thought of as fieldwork in transnational film studies, I was struck by how ubiquitous pirated versions of *Shrek* and other

FIGURE 3.5 Scenes from *Shrek* in the food court at Jam-e Jam Mall, Tehran.
(Photograph by Brian Edwards)

CGI Hollywood films are in Iran. Not that anyone said so, and many in
Iran resisted my interpretation, although the evidence seemed overwhelming to me. The image of Shrek is, it seems, everywhere in Tehran: painted on
the walls of DVD and electronics shops, featured in an elaborate mural in
the children's play area of the food court at the Jam-e Jam Mall (figure 3.5).
While in a car I once passed a five-foot-tall Shrek mannequin on the sidewalk; like his fellow pedestrians, he wore a surgical face mask to protect
him from the smog.

Nahal explains, "You know, it's not really the original *Shrek* that we love
so much here. It's really the dubbing. It's really more the Iranian *Shrek* that
interests us."

The Iranian film industry has a long and illustrious tradition of high-
quality dubbings.[50] In the postrevolution era and with the ensuing rise of

censorship, dubbing has evolved to become a form of underground art as well as a metacommentary on Iranians' attempt to adapt and in some way lay claim to the products of Western culture. A single American film such as *Shrek* inspires multiple dubbed versions—some illegal by local standards, some not—causing Iranians to discuss and debate which of the many Farsi *Shreks* is superior. In some unauthorized versions (which are more difficult to find), various regional and ethnic dialects are paired with the diverse characters of *Shrek*, the stereotypes associated with each accent adding an additional layer of humor for Iranians. In the more risqué bootlegs, obscene or off-topic conversations are transposed over *Shrek*'s fairy-tale shenanigans.

Despite knowing all this, I still ask Nahal, "Why *Shrek* of all things?" Or why, more generally, are Iranians so taken with American CGI films coming out of studios such as DreamWorks and Pixar? Is it the racially coded weirdness of *Shrek*'s cast of characters that somehow speaks to Iranians? Does Shrek himself symbolize the repressed id of people living in a sexually censorious society? Or are Iranians simply attracted to the impossible lushness and the tactile pleasures of American CGI technology itself?

But Nahal finds my questions beside the point. Our *Shrek*, she tells me, isn't an American film at all.

Perhaps I should have been asking instead, What does it mean that Americans and Iranians make such different things of each other's cinemas? I had come back to Tehran to try to make more sense of these cultural readings and misreadings and in particular to try to better understand the debate in Iran over Iranian directors such as Abbas Kiarostami, who are lionized in the United States but not (so I thought) generally admired in Iran. Kiarostami is the reason why Iranian cinema is upheld—in France, the United States, and elsewhere—as the greatest since the French New Wave brought us Jean-Luc Godard, François Truffaut, Jean-Pierre Melville, and Eric Rohmer. His success in the United States paved the way for Asghar Farhadi.

And yet to many people within his own country, Kiarostami, as one Iranian film critic said to me, is considered "a crime against the cinema of the world." How could such disparate truths coexist?

I arrived in Tehran at an auspicious time for filmgoers—February marks the beginning of the annual Fajr Film Festival, which includes multiple competitions (the national and international competitions as well as those for documentaries, shorts, Asian cinema, and "spiritual films") as well as retrospectives and screenings of classic films. But more importantly, the festival is the only time the censors allow all new Iranian films to be screened; only after the premieres will they determine which of these new films can be shown in wider release. The festival is thus a precious ten-day window of unrestricted viewing.

During my time in Tehran, I run with a film crowd. My colleague Hamid Naficy has put me in touch with Houshang Golmakani, the editor of the important film journal *Mahnameh-ye Sinema'i-ye Film* (and its English-language version *Filmmag*), who in turn puts me in touch with a young film critic named Mahmoud. Mahmoud and I speak on the phone before we meet. Mahmoud wants to take me to an unusual place. He says: "I think it will be very interesting for your research."

The next morning I find Mahmoud outside the Bahman Cinema wearing a Woody Allen trench coat.

"Let's walk," he says . "Ali is waiting for us."

Ali, Mahmoud tells me, has a sizable—and illegal—collection of classic Hollywood films, lobby cards, and posters, though that only begins to describe what I would soon encounter. Apparently, it is illegal for "nonofficial" people to own 35-mm films at all. Also, much of what Ali owns are considered "immoral" materials: a poster of a semiclad Marlene Dietrich in *The Garden of Allah* (Richard Boleslawski, 1936) can get you into serious trouble.

"Ali is the Henri Langlois of Iran," says Mahmoud. This reference to the famed creator of the Cinémathèque française (the archive in which Langlois preserved miles of footage from destruction during the Nazi occupation of Paris and later from oblivion) points as much to Ali's daring as to his near obsessiveness. And Ali has taken risks, to be sure: twice he has been arrested and sent to jail. When he was arrested in the early 1990s, the Islamic Republic confiscated a truckload of tins of film. Mahmoud estimates three thousand canisters of film were lost; fortunately, Ali had many others hidden elsewhere.

As we walk through the grime of downtown Tehran, Mahmoud talks of his other film critic friends who have been sent to jail. "The authorities accuse the critics of advertising Western values with their reviews," says Mahmoud. "These films have sex in them. They tell us, 'You are advertising sex.'"

"Is the government particularly sensitive to cinema?" I ask

"Indeed, more so than to music and literature," he says. "It's risky to be a film critic. They can't keep up with the blogs, but they read the print magazines"—in particular the half-dozen weekly film magazines plus the couple of daily newspapers dedicated to cinema.

According to Mahmoud, the censorship rules governing what is allowed onto Iranian screens are haphazard and idiosyncratic. One day the Ministry of Culture and Islamic Guidance will allow a film, but the next day the Supreme Council of Clergymen (an unofficial group that Mahmoud calls a "powerful, mafia-like organization") may reverse the ministry's finding, and the picture will be banned. "The president of Farabi [the Iranian Cinema Foundation] produces a movie, and then his own ministry will ban it, and it disappears forever."

Mahmoud curses the system, complaining about rules that keep changing, the unpredictability and willy-nilly aspect of what will get censored and what makes it through. He shakes his head at the absurdity of the government's fear of film. At least in the Soviet Union, he says, Russians could screen films to their students at the universities. Here, no.

I struggle to keep up with Mahmoud's quick pace. As if to underscore his indictment of the government's haphazard and idiosyncratic censorship methods, he leads me past an endless string of street vendors offering pirated DVD copies of banned movies. Back in the United States, it is almost time for the Academy Awards. Here on the streets of Tehran, I buy copies of many of the contenders for $1.50—*Benjamin Button*, *Slumdog Millionaire*, *Frost/Nixon*, *Revolutionary Road*.

We finally arrive at Ali's apartment. He invites us inside what seems less a home than a storage space—posters stacked against the wall of a cramped sitting room, lobby cards piled in a cluttered kitchen, bags and bags of film canisters arranged haphazardly in the hallway. Ali's bedroom is a crumbling crawlspace lined with metal shelves. Most of his bathroom is given over to film canisters, with only a tiny bit of real estate allowed to the toilet and the curtainless shower.

Ali is about sixty and wears a plaid shirt under a well-used tweed jacket. He is quiet; his face is worn; his eyes turn down at the edges. He has lived through a great deal. But he is at ease amid his treasures. We make our way through the full apartment, half a floor below ground. There is no place to sit. It takes some time before Ali warms up to talk.

He tells me that he started collecting early and explains his clever methods of subterfuge. When Hollywood films were screened throughout Iran under the shah's regime, they were licensed for a brief run, after which they were returned to the studios' Iranian headquarters in Tehran. But rather than pay to ship the bulky prints back to the United States, the studios allowed the film stock to be destroyed in front of witnesses. (The preferred means of destruction was to take an ax to the reels.) Ali, who worked as a projectionist, substituted worthless copies of easily accessible Iranian films for the Hollywood pictures, then secreted away cans holding the more valuable films by United, Paramount, Disney, and other studios.

He keeps his collection—worth millions of dollars, according to Mahmoud—scattered in a number of locations south of downtown, basement apartments and storage rooms. Ali pulls out catalogs showing prices being paid at Sotheby's for the posters he owns. "Here look: $10,000."

Over the years, Ali has come to serve as a valuable resource for the film communities in Tehran and as such occupies a strange place both above and below the government's radar. He tells me of the day in the 1950s when he met director William Wyler, who had come to Iran for a screening of his film *Roman Holiday* (1953). The Tehran branch of Paramount couldn't get its hands on a copy of the film in time, and someone thought to contact Ali. He supplied his copy for the screening. He continues to provide rare films for Iranian film students and scholars, and his screenings are reminiscent of the ones with which Langlois inspired the French New Wave.

Mahmoud tells me, "Everybody knows Ali in Iran, but nobody knows where his archive is."

The following day Mahmoud introduces me to Kamran, a critic who, Mahmoud claims, knows Iranian cinema better than anyone.

The three of us meet at Jam-e Jam Mall; walking among the high-end stores and Western-style cafés, I feel as if we have blundered into another world. We sit in the basement café, where we can smoke. Kamran asks me which film theorists I respect most, and then he grills me on their fine points better than my own graduate students in the United States can. But I am most curious to learn what Kamran makes of Abbas Kiarostami.

Kiarostami, born in 1940, is the director of forty films, one of which, *Ta'm-e gilas* (Taste of cherry), won the Palme d'Or at Cannes in 1997, launching his international celebrity and bringing postrevolution Iranian cinema into global focus. In Iran, he is seen as an art director whose films are far removed from politics or any sense of contemporaneity, inhabiting instead a more mythical and contemplative place. In *Taste of Cherry*, a man drives around Tehran looking for someone to help him commit suicide, stopping to chat with pedestrians and workers at construction sites, the dialogue becoming more and more philosophical. In *Bad ma ra khahad bord* (The wind will carry us, 1999), a fictional film crew visits a remote town to await the death of an ancient (ever unseen) woman, after which some sort of ceremony will take place. In *Khaneh-ye dust kojast?* (Where is the friend's home? 1987), an eight-year-old boy living in a village far removed from urban life attempts repeatedly to return a notebook he took home from school by mistake. Kiarostami's reputation in Iran is surely affected by his popularity in the West and by how French and American film critics extrapolate from his films certain assumptions about Iranian society. For some, Kiarostami's celebration abroad is reason to cherish him more. For others, his international fame is a reason to be doubtful of him; his prominence reinforces their belief that Kiarostami is just another pawn in the West's media game of demonizing Iran. Some even suspect that he may be capitalizing on it.

Such skepticism is hardly unfounded. When Deborah Solomon interviewed Kiarostami in 2007 for her weekly page in the *New York Times Magazine*, eleven of the sixteen questions published were explicitly about politics, Islam, violence, and repression; two were implicitly political; only the final three left politics behind, but they were flippant and short ("Do you always wear sunglasses?"). What is yet more striking is that Solomon herself pointed out that Kiarostami's filmmaking is hardly political: "It's odd that your films would be viewed as subversive, when they're more philosophical than political and abound with picturesque views of the countryside." And yet she or her editors apparently couldn't restrain themselves from a political interview.[51]

Few people I spoke to in Iran think of Kiarostami as subversive or as anything but an art film director. Most think he is overly feted in the West to the neglect of other Iranian directors. And that of course makes him, unwittingly, a political director. Alas.

Consider how this logic runs through even sophisticated discussions of Kiarostami in the West. Joan Copjec, a distinguished psychoanalytic film critic of a Lacanian bent, has written at length about Kiarostami. She positions her critique in the context of assumptions about the fundamental difference of Iranian cinema: "Iranian cinema is an exotic experience for audiences accustomed to Hollywood-dominated cinema. Not just for obvious reasons but because the obvious—the foreign locations and people, everything we actually see on screen—is produced by a different distribution of the visible and the invisible and an alien logic of the look."[52]

Copjec's take on Kiarostami crystallizes just how his films are seen in such a deeply political light in the West—and also how this vision is so alluring. These alien people with their alien logic have, she writes, "a different distribution of the visible and the invisible." This claim worries me because what Copjec does not see—"the hejab covering women that obscures them from the sight of men to whom they are not related" (11)—leads to a celebration of an "alien logic of the look." Despite her intention to champion Kiarostami's work, her gesture is an unwittingly exoticizing one. Thus, Kiarostami's becomes a cinema that anyone with Orientalist urges—from the browsers of Anthropologie clothing catalogs to the addicts of the *New York Times* Sunday travel section to the fedayeen of Samuel Huntington's book *Clash of Civilizations* (1996)—can cherish.

Thus, when Copjec goes on to posit Kiarostami's subtle "cinema of respectful reserve and restraint" and the way his camera seems to "separate itself from the action by inserting a distance between itself and the scene and refusing to venture forward into the private space of the characters," it is in the service of her argument that Iran is an "all-exterior world" (29).

Her Kiarostami is "uniquely interesting" (29) because he finds an original way to reinsert interiority and privacy into a "world" that cannot have any or cannot be depicted as having any because of the all-encompassing *hijab* she sees covering it. And this allows her to forward Kiarostami's vision of Iranian culture against the manifold misreadings of Muslim societies by the U.S. government (from the horrors at Abu Ghraib to the post–September 11 wiretappings), all of which, Copjec suggests, are based on a misreading of Islamic society as based in a culture of "shame." But she collapses far too much, and the burden is too heavy on the artist. What she calls the "Islamic system of modesty" (12) is hardly the same across all parts of the Middle East, across Arab and Iranian, with regional and sectarian particularities and differences enveloped in a phrase. To be sure, the Bush administration's reliance on Raphael Patai's intellectually corrupt book *The Arab Mind* (1973)—with its shaky distinction between "guilt cultures" and "shame cultures," where the former is associated with "advanced" societies and the latter with "primitive" Arab ones—led to some of the worst American excesses after September 11.

Yet here is where Copjec's act of politicizing a nonpolitical filmmaker starts to become not only problematic but also misleading. To claim that "woman must be secluded from the sight or touch of unrelated men" is a bit exaggerated when it comes to Iran, or at least what I have experienced in Tehran. Needless to say, there are many women—and men, too—in Tehran who believe in modesty, which is a precept of Islam. But it is not unusual to see, as I did one evening in a restaurant on Valiasr Avenue, an Iranian woman wearing a form-fitting white-leather jacket—covering her arms and her hips, as Islamic code dictates—but also white leggings, tall boots, and a scarf that looped up and over blond, highlighted hair and perfect makeup. The outfit or the elaborate hairdo was hardly unique, and the Iranian fascination with plastic surgery bespeaks a notable immodesty. And when I was invited to a party in North Tehran, I watched as the proper Islamic dress that female guests wore on their way to the party was shed at the door to reveal miniskirts and backless tops on braless young women, and the festivities included illegal music, contraband alcohol, as well as heavy flirting, contact between the sexes, and dirty dancing. Even among the nonelite and working class, female friends and students of mine often made a point of shaking my hand (against convention), lifting their head scarves to reveal their hair, and even showing me cell phone photos of themselves uncovered. Let me just say this: Joan Copjec describes an Iran that I have read about but that I only "saw" before I got to Iran. And although my experiences in Tehran are surely limited—my travel elsewhere in the country has been restricted to only three or four cities—the alien logic of the look on which Copjec bases her essay is belied by the profound cosmopolitanism of Tehran in the digital age. Whether it is the unofficial but authentic Gap store on Gandhi Street (with merchandise smuggled in from Dubai and the United Arab Emirates) or the Internet-fueled familiarity with visual and aural culture from Hollywood, New York, and Tehrangeles, global Tehran is hardly as Copjec imagines.

Yes, walk in downtown Tehran, and you will see the *hijab*, the chador, covering much of a woman's body, though again it depends on where you look and at whom you're looking in downtown Tehran. And yes, a woman in a white-leather jacket can seem provocative because of the contrast with what is mandated and what is common. But in their homes, Iranians are watching DVDs of Hollywood films, downloads from websites created everywhere, Facebook pages, lively Iranian serials and comedies, and, if they want to and have a satellite dish (which almost everyone does, even though they are technically not permitted), sexy music videos from Lebanon and unrestricted porn from the Persian Gulf. Everything is here, people like to say, just in the right place. You need to know where to look for it.

Read Copjec's essay out of context, in other words, and you may get the wrong idea about Iran and its cinema: "the look of desire around which Hollywood-dominated cinema is plotted had to be forsaken, along with the well-established system of relaying that look through an alternating pattern of shots and counter-shots and the telling insertion of psychologically motivated close-ups" (12). There is a sophisticated psychoanalytic argument about shame in Copjec's essay, and Hollywood-style representations of desire were indeed rejected in the first phase of Iranian cinema immediately after the revolution.[53] But one does not get a sense of historical contingency in her argument; all postrevolutionary cinematic representations collapse together. The postrevolutionary period in Copjec's essay is as timeless as it is in Azar Nafisi's account of it in *Reading* Lolita *in Tehran* (2003). Copjec's account doesn't square with what one sees in mainstream Iranian films that don't make it to the festival circuit or in daily life in Iran.

Back in the basement café at Jam-e Jam Mall, Kamran refers to a witty critique made by Khosro Dehghan, an Iranian film critic and screenwriter, to explain what is wrong with Kiarostami: "Remember the gun made out of soap in Woody Allen's *Take the Money and Run*? That's what Kiarostami's films are like. Eventually it will rain, and the gun will melt away."

As films such as *Shrek* and *Taste of Cherry* make their way across the ocean to new interpretive communities, they not only accrue different political meanings but also become different things. The Iranian *Shrek* and the American Kiarostami do not represent in their new homes what they represent in the worlds where they originated. In fact, the American Kiarostami is just as American as the Farsi-dubbed *Shrek* is Iranian. In each location, they become convenient foreign elements against which domestic film production can more clearly distinguish itself as domestic. This process runs counter to the logics by which both Copjec and fearful Iranian clerics—and indeed champions of U.S. cultural diplomacy—operate.

When U.S. State Department officials imagine that the export of Hollywood film and American pop music can be simple weapons in the battle for the "hearts and minds" of other societies, as many champions of "cultural diplomacy" have argued during the past decade and a half—just put them out there, and they will detonate—they suffer from a Cold War hangover. When Iranian clerics wring their hands that Hollywood movies will corrupt Iranian youth just by their captivating presence and so attempt to squeeze them out of circulation, they are only looking at the flashy posters and not at the more subtle ways in which films make their way in the world. Neither group of officials is seeing how these foreign products signify within a much richer cultural context and resonate in ways that their producers could hardly have predicted. This is what is unseen to those who fail to recognize what anyone who watches a movie beyond the DVD case or reads a book beyond the cover knows implicitly: the film or the book becomes your own. The Iranian *Shrek* is, after all, Iranian.

ENDS OF CIRCULATION:
THIS IS NOT A CONCLUSION

A generation ago Iran's supreme leader Ali Khamenei addressed the effect of the Western discussion of Iran's art films at the expense of its "revolutionary" cinema (by "revolutionary," he meant forwarding the values of the Islamic Revolution). Hamid Naficy points to the way in which Khamenei complained about Western film festivals; for the supreme leader, the celebration of directors such as those I discuss in this chapter was akin to cultural invasion: "How can you ignore what they do to our films, plays, and children's fare? How can you say that they are not political? . . . I predict that one day international organizations will award a Nobel Prize to one of these so-called cultural figures—anti-Islam and antirevolution figure—to raise their status in the world and to isolate the revolutionary figures. Is that not cultural invasion?"[54]

If you have read this far, you know that I have used the phrase "ends of circulation" in multiple ways. In my discussion of Magdy El Shafee in the previous chapter, I discussed the ways cultural forms such as the comic book "jump publics" to places where they are no longer legible. There, an "end of circulation" is a rejoinder to those who think of transnational circulation as the infinite circular return of images, texts, and so on in some heroic understanding of the pleasures and positive aspects of globalization.

What is clear to me, however, based on the time I have spent in Iran, is that a much simpler version of the "end of circulation" is in play. It is, quite simply, the inability to go back to Iran for many Iranians who have left it, whether of their own volition or under duress.

In the popular memoirs by Iranian Americans published in the past decade or so, there is a continual theme of captivity, lack of circulation, and in-betweenness. This theme ranges across generations, from writers such as Haleh Esfandiari, a scholar and head of the Middle East program at the Woodrow Wilson Center in Washington, D.C., who was incarcerated and then published *My Prison, My Home: One Woman's Story of Captivity in Iran* (2009), to Roxana Saberi, an Iranian Japanese American journalist nearly four decades Esfandiari's junior (Saberi's father emigrated from Iran to the

United States, where she was born and raised), whose memoir of her own jailing in 2009 was published as *Between Two Worlds: My Life and Captivity in Iran* (2010). Without spending the time here to take such memoirs apart and examine them for what Ali Behdad and Juliet Williams have called "neo-Orientalism"—propagated by "Middle Eastern women and men who use their native subjectivity and newfound agency in the West to render otherwise biased accounts of the region seemingly more authoritative and objective"—or, worse, for what Hamid Dabashi has called "comprador intellectuals,"[55] I merely note the way that *lack* of circulation functions as an element that New York publishers can exploit as well.

Hamid Naficy, the great critic and historian of Iranian film, has made of his own exile a brilliant theory of diasporic longing in *An Accented Cinema*, and the long, fifty-page preface to his magisterial four-volume work *A Social History of Iranian Cinema* is a memoir of time in a long-lost Iran, filled with nostalgia, out of which a reading of Iranian cinema emerges. Hamid Dabashi has done similar things in his own writings on Iran, such as relating the poignant memories of his childhood in Abadan in the preface to *Iran: A People Interrupted*.[56] When Dabashi connects this nostalgia to his work as an academic in New York at Columbia University—as he does in the same book when he recounts the story of an Iranian woman living in upstate New York who writes him to recommend a Persian poem for an upcoming wedding—again a way of reading Iran as a people and as a history *interrupted* emerges.

The anthropologist Michael Fisher has identified the peculiar terms by which much exile from Iran, experienced as an interruption, operates. Fisher notes that much is not forbidden but also is not permitted in Iran. Discussing a film that came out in 2004—the controversial satire *Marmoulak* (The lizard; Kamal Tabrizi)—as he was finishing his own book, he explains: "The film was shown on the big screens only briefly and was then withdrawn. It was not banned, nor was it released, but was available on the street in VCD [video CD] format. Neither banned nor not banned, said one of my new acquaintances, just like everything else in Iran."[57]

Contemporary Iranian filmmakers in exile and those preparing to leave Iran have played on precisely this paradox in their works. Jafar Panahi works it into *In film nist* (This is not a film), the first film he made (or didn't make) after his notorious blanket censorship by the Iranian government. In December 2010, Panahi was sentenced to six years in prison and a twenty-year ban on making films, writing scripts, traveling abroad, or giving media interviews in punishment for "colluding in gathering and making propaganda against the regime."[58] He lost his appeal in October 2011. In the meantime and in apparent flagrant violation of the ban, he made *This Is Not a Film* with Mojtaba Mirtahmasb, which is part documentary and part extended interview with the feeling of a reality show. The product was smuggled out of Iran on a USB memory stick hidden in a cake, whereupon the film premiered at Cannes. Mirtahmasb, who operated the camera and who briefly appears in the film, was himself later arrested as well.[59] When *This Is Not a Film* was released, the question of whether Panahi had broken the ban was of course pushed. *This Is Not a Film* plays continually on the question of the film's eventual circulation, which activates everything we are seeing. Is sitting around Panahi's apartment a crime, we wonder? Not until it is filmed. What if Panahi picks up an iPhone and makes a video? What if the camera is set down on the kitchen table? A young man working in Panahi's apartment building knocks on the door and comes across Mirtahmasb filming Panahi; he is excited to appear in the "film," and Panahi follows him into the elevator as he does his rounds, picking up garbage from each floor in the building. We wonder: Is the young man aware of Panahi's sentence and the implications of allowing himself to be filmed?

What is at play here is Panahi's inability to make films, of course. But to put it a different way, *This Is Not a Film* is a complex consideration of the individual's inability to circulate in contemporary Iran. Jafar Panahi laughs at himself when he realize his impulse is to say "cut" after finishing a statement—in other words, to direct the film in which he is appearing. From off camera, Mirtahmasb tells him that he can't say "cut." He has been prohibited from directing films or writing screenplays but not (necessarily) from acting or from talking about a screenplay he has written. As a result, we get an intriguing film that ultimately revolves around the discussion of a film that Panahi cannot make. He describes the film; using tape on an Oriental carpet in his apartment, he marks out the small room in which his protagonist would live. He shows us a photo of the two women he was going to cast.

But he also sits on his laptop trying to browse the Internet, frequently coming upon censored sites. Everything is blocked, he says, and what is not blocked has no information. He talks on the phone with his lawyer about his appeal and receives depressing news. Clearly upset and worried, Panahi hangs up and tries to shift gears and talk about his film. He discusses scenes from his earlier work, played on a flat-screen TV in his apartment, which we are allowed to view in close-up as he discusses them. This combination offers a good illustration of Zeydabadi-Nejad's argument that the conditions of reception are inscribed in an Iranian film before it is even seen, and here it seems to extend to the way Panahi reads his own earlier work. He puts the earlier films back into circulation, a new circulation here in the present. Are they the same films they were originally, re-viewed in the context of *This Is Not a Film*, or are they new films in their repetition, now filling the screen, by a man who can't otherwise direct actors? As Panahi reviews these scenes, he now expresses a fascination with moments that exceed his direction and that exceed the script. In the first clip he shows from his 1997 film *Ayneh* (The mirror), the child actor Mina Mohammad-Khani breaks the fiction of the scene she is in—set on a bus—by demanding to be let off, removing her head scarf, and stopping the bus. The scene he shows from the well-known film *Talaye sorkh* (Crimson gold, 2003) captures a moment when the actor playing Hussein, the pizza delivery man (Hussein Emadeddin), does something with his eyes that Panahi said no one expected or had seen him do before, which is the moment of art—unexpected and uncontrollable—that exceeds Panahi's direction and *Crimson Gold* itself.

Despite speaking in support of Panahi after his arrest, Hamid Dabashi has called *This Is Not a Film* and Panahi's subsequent work *Parde* (Closed curtain, 2013) "self-indulgent vagaries farthest removed from [his earlier] masterpieces." Dabashi offers these two films by Panahi as examples of the impasse of contemporary Iranian cinema, which he feels has reached a "tragic ending," the assessment of a critic who was one of its chief celebrators. Dabashi praises Kiarostami for the wisdom of "skirt[ing] politics" and "thus safeguard[ing] his cinema": "one hundred years from now, the best of Kiarostami's cinema will still mesmerize, baffle, and reward, when many other politically potent filmmakers will scarce be remembered." Dabashi criticizes Panahi, Mohsen Makhmalbaf, and Bahman Ghobadi, all of them celebrated internationally, and sends off a warning shot for others, such as Bahram Beizai, director of *Bashu, gharibeh-ye kuchak* (Bashu, the little stranger, 1986), who left Iran and moved to Los Angeles. Or, as Dabashi—who lives and works in New York—puts it, Beizai moved to "the heart of the infested environment of the most useless and pestiferous Iranian community, to which the ugly faces of the *Shahs of Sunset* [an American reality-TV program] does perfect justice."[60]

The Irish director and film commentator Mark Cousins has suggested—in a documentary interview by young Iranian filmmaker Ehsan Khoshbakht entitled *A Journey Through Iranian Cinema with Mark Cousins* (2012)—that the youngest generation of Iranian filmmakers are turning away from the work of the great directors from Iran that captivated the world cinema scene. Speaking with Khoshbakht about Iranian cinema of the past decade, Cousins says:

> Just like France in the sixties, just like Germany in the eighties, the younger filmmakers are so desperate to react against what they think is the old fashioned way, the *cinema du papa*, the orthodox way of doing it, so many filmmakers say "we cannot stand the films of Abbas Kiarostami, we want to do Tarentino, or something different. We want more speed, speed, speed." That's fine within the context of Iran. Because of course if you're rebellious at all, if you're innovative at all, you don't want to do the same as the people who came before. There's just a danger is that because they're so close to the great approach of Iranian cinema, they forget that no one else is doing it. They don't notice how distinctive those great Iranian films were in the nineties. . . . Rebellious young Iranian filmmakers, yes be rebellious but don't underestimate the greatness of Iranian cinema that came before you.[61]

If Cousins and Dabashi are correct, what I am calling ends of circulation might mean that a certain period in Iranian "art" cinema—of the

Kiarostami, Farhadi, and Samira Makhmalbaf tradition—is ending or has ended even as we describe it. If so, it is not only or not necessarily for the reason Dabashi claims—getting too caught up in political critique or protest—but rather because the peculiar conditions within which it thrived have now ceded to a different set of relations. The politics is still relatively the same, but the technologies and the new publics they have helped call into being can no longer hold that engagement in the same way. What will follow this "end" of Iranian cinema is not for me, here, to predict.

In the era of reality TV, of websites that are linked to webcams and provide windows on daily life, and of the ubiquity of iPhones that film everything, perhaps we can wonder whether Panahi's film about a film is a "film" at all. A similar case transpires with *No One Knows About Persian Cats*, which I mentioned earlier in this chapter. I find Bahman Ghobadi's film less compelling as a work of cinematic art but still interesting to think with, and it received a wide viewing in the United States. *No One Knows About Persian Cats* is about leaving Iran, about the public that one engages in Iran and then leaves behind or loses in transit. The film depicts the indy rock scene of Tehran and a fictional couple who in seeking exit visas through illegal means engage in a concert series to raise the funds for the fake documents. What is interesting in this film is that the audience for the groups being depicted is one that engages the foreign form, American indy rock music, but that the musicians cannot bring this foreign music with them outside Iran, where it will die.

JERRY LEWIS IN IRAN

People circulate, or they don't. Films circulate and are dubbed into new texts. And all along the encounter of individuals with films is both personal and social—an act of individual creativity that is also circumscribed by social history and politics.

Abbas Kiarostami has depicted the encounter of the individual with film in this way: "Originally, I thought that the lights went out in a movie theatre so that we could see the images on the screen better. Then I looked a little closer at the audience settling comfortably into the seats and saw that there was a much more important reason: the darkness allowed the members of the audience to isolate themselves from others and to be alone. They were both with others and distant from them."[62] It is a gorgeous quote that captures the scene of film not only as social but also as private. Today, however, we must also consider that films are passed on pirated DVDs and VCDs, downloaded both legally and not, consumed on laptops in apartments on moving airplanes or on iPads and smart phones. Films, even those seen in the increasingly rare circumstances of a darkened room filled with stadium seats, travel in ways that affect their meanings.

The curious logics of circulation of film in Iran and of Iranian film in the United States must account for these multiple pathways and temporalities. What happens when those pathways and temporalities are thematized in film itself?

Mehrnaz Saeedvafa is an Iranian filmmaker who lives and works in Chicago, where she teaches and writes about film. Saeedvafa's forty-minute documentary *Jerry & Me* (2012) treats her youth in Iran, when as a teenager she fell in love with Hollywood movies in the years before the Islamic Revolution. As the filmmaker describes it, her fascination with Hollywood was part of a longing for a place she didn't know. For her, the films of Jerry Lewis, dubbed into Persian, were especially irresistible: "[When I was] a child, Jerry's films inscribed a seductive image of America in me. The America that Jerry showed me was modern, fun, and colorful." But Hollywood, Lewis's films in particular, also touched a dissatisfaction or discomfort she felt with her own identity. Backed by a scene from Lewis's movie *The Nutty Professor* (1963, a parody of *Dr. Jekyll and Mr. Hyde*), Saeedvafa's voice-over shifts gears: "[In America] everything was possible, including changing your identity—a hidden wish that I had as a teenager: to drink a potion and turn into a happy white woman."[63] Now, after decades in Chicago and after having made several of her own films, Saeedvafa explores her nostalgia for that lost relationship—innocent and even naive—to American film.

What Saeedvafa's film contributes to the larger discussion of this chapter and why I want to conclude with it have to do not simply with how it shows that Jerry Lewis could mean something different to a teenage Iranian girl than to Americans. That art means different things to different audiences across space and time is a truth of the way cultural production circulates. Rather, I am struck by the way *Jerry & Me* intertwines Saeedvafa's changing perceptions of Jerry Lewis and other Hollywood film icons together with an exploration of the specificity of Persian-language dubbing and the process of viewing these Hollywood films in Iran. The conditions of circulation of American cinema in Iran supplemented the films themselves and Saeedvafa's subjective experience of them and made them something quite different from what they were when they began. In other words, both the films themselves—as texts—and the way the conditions and contexts of viewing them combined made these American movies what they were for young Mehrnaz.

Saeedvafa explains in the voice-over narration: "I grew up watching a lot of Hollywood films, all dubbed in Persian. In movie theaters that had Western names like Empire, Radio City, Golden City, Niagara, Paramount." Archival photos and footage of glitzy cinema houses with Farsi and English names bright in neon show us an image of a Tehran under the shah that might be New York or Las Vegas of the same period. But if the cinema houses resembled and sometimes replicated urban American spaces, the experience of watching the films inside was decidedly Iranian. Saeedvafa gathers numerous clips from the films of the era and brings us into the Tehran cinema houses to discuss how they seemed to her then: "The first time I saw people kissing was in the movies. . . . I'd close my eyes out of shame or hide under the seat until the scene was over. The quiet intimate kissing scenes were the noisiest in Tehran. The deprived working-class male audience would whistle and shout and blurt mocking words like 'Leave her alone . . . you're killing her . . . *velesh kon, khafash kardi*' [Let her go! You are suffocating her!], turning them into funny scenes." To illustrate such a kiss in her film, Saeedvafa includes a scene from *Rio Bravo* (Howard Hawks, 1959): a kiss between John Wayne and Angie Dickinson. The dialogue of the scene is dubbed into Persian (Saeedvafa has added English subtitles to translate the Persian dubbing back to English for her audience). Wayne is playing Sheriff John T. Chance, and Dickinson the woman referred to as

"Feathers." (Wayne's dialogue is dubbed by Iraj Doostdar, Wayne's regular voice in Iran.)[64] The scene quoted here begins with a kiss between Wayne and Dickinson, which in the original takes Wayne's character by surprise—Dickinson kisses him again, and he finally responds. After this exchange, Dickinson tells Wayne that he should go back to his work. Wayne starts to leave the room, then turns back to Dickinson to say something. He is still flustered by the kiss, apparently, and in the original scene as directed by Howard Hawks he shrugs his shoulders—momentarily speechless—and utters a meaningless sound before bolting out the door.

In the Persian dubbing, however, Wayne is given words where in the original he is grasping for them. John T. Chance turns back and says to Feathers: "La ilaha illa allah" (There is no god but God). Saeedvafa explains: "Funny words . . . were inserted during the dubbing." She leaves it at that, but we can say a little more. "La ilaha illa allah" is, of course, one of the most important statements in Arabic (or Persian). It is Arabic language, the centerpiece of the proclamation of Islamic belief (the *shahada*) that any Muslim knows and that is part of the call to prayer announced by the muezzin/moazzin (Arabic, *mu'adhdhin*; Persian, *mo'azzen*). As Iranian filmmaker and critic Ehsan Khoshbakht describes this use of the Arabic words in an Iranian context in this scene, "We use that expression in overwhelming situations (with a touch of humor)."[65] In any case, given that this sentence is inserted in the dubbing where the original has no words at all, we can call this an example of *exuberant* dubbing, which brings the otherwise foreign settings and relationships of *Rio Bravo* into an Iranian idiom. In this way, the inserted dialogue functions in the way the twenty-first-century dubbings of *Shrek* add locally inflected phrases or referents. In the context of those noisy theaters, the extra words and Iranized dialogue work against the escapism of the Hollywood picture. In both the original and the dubbing, John T. Chance is unusually flustered, to the point where he doesn't know what to say. In one case, he says nothing; in the other, he recites the profession of faith, sardonically perhaps. The meaning is the same. The meaning is completely different.

For Saeedvafa, after her obsession with American movies and upon moving to the United States, the real America could only be a disappointment.

Khoshbakht has compared Saeedvafa's documentary to other cinematic memoir films by Iranian exiles nostalgic for the film culture of prerevolutionary Iran, which offer a "subjective history of film culture in Iran." Khoshbakht finds value in these reminiscences but also considers them marked by a disabling melancholy: "Such melancholic documentations of the past echo the feelings of a generation lost, misplaced and confused after the revolution; people who are utterly unable to resituate themselves in the new post-Revolutionary nation and after the trauma of an eight year war."[66] Indeed, Saeedvafa's film is painful to watch. Just as she searches her past for clues into her vexed relationship to Iran after the revolution, she searches her self as she confronts her love for Jerry Lewis. She goes so far as to teach a course on "the art of Lewis" to provide a Middle Eastern perspective on his work.

In a final scene, these two worlds come together. Jerry Lewis himself comes to Columbia College in Chicago in 1996, where she teaches. The grand actor, the icon she had cherished for decades, is right there on stage, being interviewed by one of her colleagues. Lewis is charming and takes on and sheds his screen persona. What's more, he explains his own humor as connected to personal suffering, both as a Jew and on behalf of the suffering of Jews. Saeedvafa can identify; the resonances for her are deep.

She can identify, that is, until Lewis makes a surprising comment. In the process of telling a story, he makes an anti-Arab remark. He is talking about the poor reception Hollywood writers gave him after his initial success writing, directing, and starring in his own films. Lewis says that at a party he went to at the time, a group of writers looked at him like a bunch of Arabs who "knew what *he* was" (i.e., a Jew). He thinks the repetition of a negative stereotype about Arabs is safe in this audience, or perhaps he doesn't think at all. There are scattered laughs, but the joke falls flat. What's worse in terms of *Jerry & Me*, which till now has at times felt like a love letter, Saeedvafa feels alienated, even betrayed. She explains her own reaction: "When Jerry made that comment about the Arabs, he broke the image of himself as an outsider that he portrayed in his films, an image that I always identified with. That's probably why I couldn't talk to him."

In the aftermath of the on-stage interview, a turn opens things up to a different future. One member of the audience, who identifies himself as "an

Arab," stands to address Lewis during the Q&A: "My name is Hakim. . . . I'm probably the only Arab in the bunch. [Big laughs and applause.] Yeah, and I was actually enjoying everything you were saying up until the joke. [Laughter.] I thought, OK, we all have our dark side. [Applause]." Jerry was reflective, Saeedvafa says, though she doesn't tell us if he replied substantively to Hakim's comment. But the frame is broken; Lewis is no longer an icon who stands for her desire to be someone other than herself or with whom she can share a humorous response to common suffering. The icon with whom she had betrayed her homeland ends up betraying her. Still, she continues to ponder the effect of his films and years later develops a course on his art.

But Hakim's comment, as I hear it at the end of Saeedvafa's documentary, offers a different potentiality that is not otherwise explicit in her film: an unpredicted future personified in the young Arab addressing the old American icon who has just disparaged Arabs. This is the excess that exuberant dubbing and noisy theaters promise, which is the overarching theme of this chapter. The comment captured in Saeedvafa's film, as it turns out, was uttered by a young man who would a decade later turn out to be an important film director himself. As I watch *Jerry & Me* on my laptop, I recognize the voice of Hakim Belabbes, the Moroccan director who appeared in chapter 1 of this book (it was he who asked me in the Rabat classroom about *Innocence of Muslims*).[67] His comment to Jerry Lewis was made seven years before his first feature *Threads* (2003), which I discuss briefly in chapter 4. Belabbes earned his master's in film at Columbia College in 1993, and when Lewis visited in 1996, he was in his midthirties. Here in an Iranian woman's film, Belabbes, the Moroccan filmmaker who had moved to Chicago, encounters Jerry Lewis, whom Saeedvafa, the Iranian filmmaker who had moved to Chicago years earlier, could not yet exorcise. Belabbes's generosity—"OK, everyone has his dark side"—is a different response to the same betrayal that could bring Saeedvafa and Belabbes together at that moment, along with the many others in the room who applauded his remark. And that sense of betrayal can lead out to the vastly different kinds of works that these two directors from different backgrounds would end up doing.

What is true here, as in the multitude of other examples I have given in this and earlier chapters, is that the logics and contexts of circulation lead texts and their readers and viewers to places that would hardly have been imagined, even by the most capacious imagination, as they were created. Whether it is *Shrek* in Tehran or Jerry Lewis on a Chicago stage with Iranian and Moroccan interlocutors, we must adjust our perspective fundamentally to begin to glean the meanings of American cultural products out in the world as they are remade again. After the American century, close reading must include the process of following texts and films and cultural products through the curious logics of their circulation, however distant that may take us.

4

COMING OUT IN CASABLANCA

Shrek, Sex, and the Teen Pic in Contemporary Morocco

*Screening of Leïla Kilani film ʿAla hafa/Sur la planche [On the edge]
at the 7ème Art in Rabat, November 2012. The look of the film is tight,
dark, oppressive—more than anything it captures and creates the sense
of enclosure in a life, in a class, in misery. To me, the* look *is a form in
circulation, and the format is familiar (starting with the end, then an
extended flashback). . . . But the language takes it off the circulatory path.
It's in [Moroccan]* darija *of course but filled with slang, Tanjawi
[Tangier] dialect, language of the street. Sadik told me he was often
reading the French subtitles to understand. The character Badia speaks so
fast. . . . I found it compelling. Others apparently did too: it won the
grand prize at the National Film Festival and is featured in this month's*
Cinemag. *But the audience at 7ème Art seemed not to agree. Maybe
twenty to twenty-five people were at the screening—so dark, hard to
say—in groups of two to five. Three different cell phone conversations
took place during the film; not short ones either, with no effort to
whisper—in one case the guy kept raising his voice to be heard over the
film. People complained the first time but then just waited. And when the
film was over, a young man shouted, "Jabouna an-nassu": "They brought
us here to sleep."*

I N THE LAST WEEKS OF 2012, a new film sparked a vibrant public debate in
Morocco—certainly not the first time a movie had commanded such
attention and surely not the last in this dynamic nation of 30 million
people. The discussion was reminiscent of other similar disputes from the
past decade: the debate over Laïla Marrakchi's film *Marock* in 2006, the

public coming out of novelist Abdellah Taïa in the same year, the airing on YouTube of a video of an alleged "gay wedding" at a private home in Ksar el Kebir in November 2007, and the open picnicking of a group of activists during Ramadan in 2009.[1] In all these cases, sides were drawn between those defending putatively traditional values and those who—their opponents suggested—had been seduced by foreign corrupting forces and who were now introducing those "foreign" elements into Morocco. This time the debate was provoked by a film by Lahcen Zinoun, a director in his late sixties better known as a dancer and choreographer. The film, *Mawchouma* (translated for the Francophone market as *Femme écrite* [A written woman]), was showing in selected cinemas in Morocco's major cities. The problem was basically that Zinoun included shots of a naked woman.

At first blush, the controversy seemed ready made for a cultural critic trying to understand and explain the latest incarnation of social attitudes about gender, sexuality, and Moroccan identity in the early twenty-first century as well as the ways in which the transnational flows of images and ideas about modesty and the body from East and West come together in a land long considered a crossroads. Focusing on conflicts in the realm of cultural production has long been a preferred approach to untangling sociocultural complexity and one I have leveraged earlier in this book.[2] Indeed, in November and December 2012, I was trying to finish my research from the previous summer when I had gathered a substantial amount of material on young Casablancan authors and artists, around whom I had planned to write this chapter. But I sensed that I needed an anchor on which to build the chapter, and I considered whether the debate over *Mawchouma* would work. I stopped by Mohammed V University and gave the talk that led to the discussion about *Innocence of Muslims* I describe in chapter 1.

As I began to follow the controversy around Zinoun's film, I decided that the more interesting story—the more important critical angle—was elsewhere, heated as the discussion was. After all, the positions taken in the debate about *Mawchouma* were somewhat predictable, from those who championed the director's artistry and his right to express himself to those who thought he had offended Moroccan and Muslim values with "pornographic" themes. All interesting and revealing but not surprising.

Further, as is often the case in Morocco, the most extended discussion of Zinoun's film was limited to the cultural and financial capital Casablanca and to a lesser extent the political capital Rabat in large part because almost all Moroccan publishing and media are centered in the Casa–Rabat metropolitan area. Within that space, the debate was restricted to a particularly small subset of those who pay attention to contemporary culture and contribute to the discussion of it. I don't mean to say that no one elsewhere in Morocco was aware of the controversy, but it was not something that people were debating or discussing in the cafés and classrooms in Fes, from which I had just traveled, or in Marrakech, where the film had not been included among the Moroccan selections at the annual Festival International du Film de Marrakech. *Mawchouma* was showing in only one cinema in the country at that moment and only briefly.

A real conversation, however, was taking place online, especially on social networking media such as Facebook. There both fans and artists involved in the film itself debated, criticized, and defended the director, the actress, and so on in a way that I had seen before among Moroccan users of Facebook. Despite the large gathering of film enthusiasts present in Marrakech, it was online that the discussion took place. The film festival in Marrakech was strictly controlled in terms of schedule and audience, rendering what should have been a great public event in Morocco's second-largest city into a private affair.

In other words, what was more interesting than the particulars of the discussion about this particular film was Moroccans' ability to have the discussion and the means of access to that discussion, both of which had changed notably with the massive arrival of social networking software in Morocco. Access to the Internet itself has a history in Morocco, of course, and implicates class and gender differently from how it does in the United States. Since the late 1990s, cybercafés have been ubiquitous in Morocco and widely used. When they arrived on the scene, they were soon socially acceptable places for young Moroccan women to patronize and use, in notable contrast to cafés (i.e., shops serving coffee and tea) and cinemas, except perhaps in the more privileged neighborhoods of Casablanca and Rabat. By the early 2000s, Internet access was inexpensive, even for children of the lower middle class (sometimes even free during late-night hours). Although the rapidly improving level of access to the Internet was also changing in Egypt and Iran, all three countries are particular in the way and manner that their young people access the Internet—when, where, how—which leads in part to the particularities and real differences in how Moroccans and Egyptians used the same social networking software. Young Moroccans I spoke to about Egyptian use of social media were mystified that Egyptians liked Twitter and claimed that Moroccans were much more interested in Facebook. They had theories about why this was so (for instance, they emphasized Moroccan notions of community, which Facebook seems to emphasize more than Twitter). Also, cybercafés have never seemed as prevalent in Egyptian cities as they are in Moroccan cities. The increasing presence of smart phones in the second decade of the 2000s may obviate the need for the cybercafé. Either way, we must not forget the first decade of access to this software in Morocco. (Smart phones are still expensive in Morocco at the time this book goes to press, and many Moroccans, especially those of the lower-middle, working, and lower classes, use cell phones for texting and speaking to friends but go to computer screens to access the Internet and Facebook.)

One need not restrict the issue of Internet access and use to North Africa. In the United States, public and semiprivate discussions about literature and film are arguably more democratic because of social networking. Media scholars have argued that the ability to interact with and comment on works of literature, television, and film has made creators and innovators out of consumers of culture. Alex Galloway, one of the most innovative of such theorists, has drawn our attention to what he calls the "interface effect" and pointed to a striking rearrangement of how individuals engage not only with technology but also with each other.[3]

Can the same be said of Moroccans? Do the insights derived from observing American users of new digital technologies apply in such a different socioeconomic and political context? What does the use of social networking media in Morocco mean when we juxtapose it against low literacy rates in the country, and what do the energies to be found in such discussions mean when we compare them to low cinema-going and book-buying rates in

Morocco? Does the way that Moroccans engage in such debates help answer the question that many were asking in late 2012 and still ask as this book goes to press: Why had the so-called Arab Spring bypassed Morocco?

It is tempting to pursue such questions. In the years since September 11, 2001, and with renewed energy in the wake of the Arab uprisings a decade later, many have been looking not only for predictions about the future of places such as Morocco but also for a more rigorous attention to youth culture in the region. The sense that the world is transforming around us because of the rapid changes in technology and related software that connect individuals allows for a fresh look at a region that for too long has been assumed to be outside of the forward progress of time. Morocco has undergone important social changes in the past decade or two as a result of a combination of transformations from within and the impact of events and developments from without. From the transition to the rule of young King Mohammed VI (known locally by the hip moniker "M6," with the number pronounced in French) in 1999 after nearly four decades of reign by his father, King Hassan II, to the arrival and massive acceptance of digital technologies across the country, the past decade and a half have apparently ushered in a new Morocco.[4]

Americans should not assume, though, that greater access to public dialogue through digital technologies and a younger monarch taking the reins of the kingdom necessarily have led to a Morocco in which Western values or a pro-American position is ascendant. During much of the same period, U.S. policies have been especially unpopular in Morocco and, from many Moroccans' perspective, have fractured a historic friendship on all but the official level. During George W. Bush's administration, the global crackdown on terrorist networks had a powerful effect on Morocco as the kingdom partnered with the United States, frequently using the premise of routing out terrorists to settle domestic political scores. The U.S. military invasion of Iraq was criticized in Morocco, as it was elsewhere in the Arab world, even though many Moroccans considered Saddam Hussein to be a murderous despot. Arab and Muslim solidarity with Iraqi victims of the U.S. invasion encouraged Moroccans to sympathize with Iraqis and against Americans, especially as media coverage of the invasion by Arab news outlets depicted hostile attitudes toward Muslims and Islam among Americans. Satellite dishes, called *parabols* in Morocco, are ubiquitous and inexpensive, and television viewership is high, with transnational Arabic-language news sources such as al Jazeera and al Arabiya watched widely.

Nonetheless, American cultural products, cultural forms, and formulas have been extremely popular in Morocco and would seem to have had a significant effect on Moroccan cultural production itself. Moroccan cinema, both popular and art cinema, has visibly adapted Hollywood formulas and "look." Hip-hop has also become popular, and a generation of Moroccan rappers have used the form with a combination of highly local language and referents.[5] Moroccan discussions of sexuality and women's rights have often taken up Western models for talking about identity, even while disputing the ways in which Americans understand Moroccan identity and sexuality. In the realm of consumer culture, the famous Moroccan souk (*suq*) has been increasingly displaced by shopping malls and public spaces not only in the cosmopolitan capital cities of Casablanca and Rabat but even in the imperial cities of Fes, Marrakech, and Meknes. Higher education on the university level has been struggling with government-imposed reforms (themselves under pressure from International Monetary Fund directives), and American-style models for organizing curricula and degree programs have steadily been unseating long-held French models.[6]

What does the apparent contradiction between a Moroccan embrace of American educational and cultural forms and an increasing rejection of U.S. politics mean?

I argue that even though Moroccans identify many of these forms in circulation with the United States (even when the forms may not be explicitly American), they dissociate them from their putative culture of origin and do with them what they will. In other words, tempting as it might be to see films such as *Mawchouma* and *Marock* as taking up Western concepts of liberation and using them to open up Moroccan society to questions of "freedom" or equality, we should be aware that something else is going on.

In Morocco, as elsewhere in the Middle East and North Africa, outside cultural forms are taken up by local artists and authors, but they are recalibrated or reconfigured in ways that render them unfamiliar or incomprehensible to observers from the outside culture. This reconfiguration is not simply a question of a different language or local meaning that detaches the form in circulation from its own content. Rather, the Moroccan use of the Western form in circulation scrambles our sense of what those forms mean in their original context. It produces a version of what the late Miriam Hansen called a "global vernacular."[7]

Moroccans so often make everything from Arabic language to popular culture their own with a creativity at once local and vivid. It is well known among Moroccans that their own work does not travel particularly well on its own. Moroccan Arabic is not understood by Arabs beyond the Maghreb and the North African diaspora. The phrase "ends of circulation" has a final and particular meaning in this country at the edge of the Arab world, the land of the farthest west.

The Moroccan case matters to this book for two reasons. First, with it we have yet another model for understanding and employing circulation to add to the repertoire of critical rubrics necessary for the new comparative literature and new approaches in sociocultural anthropology. And second, we understand some aspects of contemporary Morocco more fully if we recognize this era's engagement with the outside form and distinguish it from the ways in which Moroccan cultural producers engaged French language and culture during the colonial and early postcolonial periods. Postcolonial criticism, strictly understood, is limited in helping us to understand the richness of these new situations. Moroccan filmmakers and writers since at least the 1980s have leveraged American works against French models because the American model is considered freer from the political oppressiveness of the former colonizer.

In my earlier work, I have asked whether circulation allows us to appreciate the strategies of contemporary North African cultural production with more nuance than does postcolonial theory, which seems generally to be better suited to the concerns of works from the 1950s through 1980s. For example, I followed *Casablanca* the movie (Michael Curtiz, 1942) to Casablanca the city and found that Moroccan director Abdelkader Lagtaa disoriented the meanings of the Hollywood film for his own purposes while making the film *al-Hubb fi Dar al-Baida* (Love in Casablanca) in 1991.[8] At that point, the Warner Bros. film *Casablanca*, despite its stereotypes and Orientalism, might seem to a Moroccan director less noxious than French representations of Morocco because of the less fraught political relationship between the United States and Morocco in the early 1990s.

In the twenty-first century, however, as Moroccan attitudes toward the United States have become increasingly negative, the presence and popularity of American cultural forms do not necessarily implicate collaboration.

And so, rather than deconstruct the rich debate around *Mawchouma* in the winter of 2012–2013, I want to step back a few years to examine three turning points in the twenty-first-century Moroccan encounter with American forms and cultural products. Each of these turning points occasioned public discussion and significant debate and helps us to understand the most recent occasions for renewing that debate. And we must continually insist on attending not only to the meanings of these films, fictions, and other Moroccan cultural products but also to the social spaces in which they operate and make meaning. Doing so may mean thinking about Moroccan cinema in the spaces where it is viewed, from the illegally reproduced DVDs and VCDs to the mostly empty cinema houses where phone conversations compete with the soundtrack (as in my experience of watching *'Ala hafa* in Rabat). And it means understanding that private encounters with novels by Abdellah Taïa or with films seen on laptops take place within a vibrant public debate that surrounds those private moments.

This chapter focuses on three episodes that advance this claim and that congregate around questions of gender and sexuality. First, I discuss the peculiar case of a Casablanca video pirate named Hamada and some of his work from 2003 to 2005. Then, I provide an extended discussion of Leila Marrakchi's film *Marock* and the debate around it. Finally, I discuss the work of openly gay Moroccan writer of fiction Abdellah Taïa. Any of these works and other newer works of Moroccan literature and cinema can be read and interpreted outside the framework I am proposing, but what I think makes them all especially worthy of attention is how they index—usually silently but in ways that resonate with local Moroccan audiences—foreign, recognizably American forms and formulas for representing identity yet do so in ways that detach them fully from their source.

"WA HAID AL MILOUDI": *SHREK* IN CASABLANCA

The central idea for my work of the past decade came to me by accident— an overheard comment at a private social gathering in Rabat. It was March 2004, and I had just given a lecture at Mohammed V University drawn from the last chapter of my first book, which I was then in the process of completing. My host, Hasna Lebaddy, then the chair of the English Department at Mohammed V, held a small reception at her home after the lecture. Perhaps a dozen of her colleagues were there, and we sat around the perimeter of a room chatting over pastries and cakes. During a lull in my immediate conversation, I overheard a guest across the room ask her neighbor whether she had yet seen the newest "Miloudi." The question received an especially positive response.

I interrupted to ask who Miloudi was. My colleague started to answer, but the other interrupted: "You won't understand this." I was, I admit, a little insulted, but I also took the remark as an intellectual challenge.

I pressed the question. I would simply have to experience Miloudi, she told me. My Moroccan colleague told me to go to the Rabat *medina*—that is, the walled portion of the old city, where much commerce is done—and walk down Mohammed V Avenue to the end, where the electronics *suq* was to be found. There, I would find several stalls where pirated DVDs, music CDs, and VCDs were sold. If I asked for "Miloudi" at any of them, the shopkeepers would know what I was talking about, and I would be able to purchase a creative work difficult to describe. It would probably just confuse me.

I succeeded in locating the disk without too much trouble. Video CDs were then a popular format in Morocco; with only 700-megabyte storage on a CD-ROM, however, the quality was notably poor, and the video jumpy and often pixelated. When I inserted the CD into my laptop, I encountered a curious work by a video pirate-artist who identified himself as

"Hamada." (His name, email address, and a cell phone number appear on a banner that runs across some of the video tracks.) Hamada and his collaborators had reproduced digital video clips from familiar American films using CGI and sitcoms and had dubbed them with Moroccan popular music and in some cases Moroccan dialogue. "Albums" of a dozen or so such tracks had been compiled, put on VCDs, duplicated, and sold for about $1 each (figure 4.1).

In 2004, Hamada's work was popular among young, urban Moroccans, selling thousands of copies and sometimes playing on screens in cafés. His most popular work, the one he came to be identified with, paired a clip from DreamWorks animated film *Shrek* (Andrew Adamson and Vicky Jenson, 2001) with a *chaabi* song that begins "Wa haid al Miloudi wa haid ah." The video is of a dance number in *Shrek* with the familiar character Donkey singing into a microphone while other characters dance (figure 4.2). The music paired with this visual was a song by the Moroccan pop star Adil al Miloudi, here performing an exuberant piece in which he continually names himself and calls attention to his own drug and alcohol use. The song was already well known, but the juxtaposition of song and video, apparently perfectly synced but obviously not made for one another, endlessly entertained Moroccans in on the joke.

Although Hamada includes on his CD the banner with his name and cell phone number and makes the claim "All Rights Reserved," the success of this particular piece was such that most of his future compilations were referred to as "Miloudi" (one that I bought on a subsequent trip back to Morocco later the same year demonstrates that they were released as a series). But others referred to them as "Cheb Hemar," using the word *cheb* for *rai* or other pop stars in North Africa and the word for "donkey," apparently referring to the donkey in *Shrek* featured in the dubbed video "Wa haid al Miloudi."

Hamada's creative work—or, more accurately, the Hamada phenomenon—deserves our attention here because of the original way this artist took up a foreign text—an American text at that, none other than *Shrek*—and shaped it into a work of Moroccan art. Hamada was surely not the first to do this, and over the years that I have spoken about his works, I have been

FIGURE 4.1 Covers of Miloudi VCDs. (Photograph by Brian Edwards)

FIGURE 4.2 Hamada's *Shrek*–Miloudi work.

sent links or video clips of *Shrek* paired with songs from multiple national contexts. (Despite my discussion of *Shrek* in Iran in the previous chapter and a great deal of searching, I have never found an Iranian parallel.) Hamada's version has always seemed the best to me, and it sparked an unusually popular phenomenon in Morocco. But Hamada's originality is not, after all, my primary concern here.

Hamada's "Wa haid al Miloudi" video is perhaps the paradigmatic example of circulation in the way I have been describing it throughout this book. Despite the building body of criticism of Moroccan literature, film, and visual culture, Hamada's work has been neglected. To my mind, it is among the more innovative. It reflects in advance the ways in which film directors from Laïla Marrakchi and Faouzi Bensaïdi to Nour-Eddine Lakhmari and Leïla Kilani would pick from American cultural forms and formulas as they created original Moroccan films. The starkness of what Hamada did makes it particularly compelling.

How should we make sense of his work? One option emerges from a short discussion of it in a prominent Moroccan culture magazine, the weekly *TelQuel*, whose reporter tracked down Hamada in May 2004, at the height of his fame. Maria Daïf interviewed Hamada, then about twenty years old, and one of his collaborators (identified as "Majd") in the coastal city of Kenitra. The interview is useful in particular because Hamada, understandably wary of the press, left little trace before he disappeared from view. In the brief *TelQuel* interview, Hamada explained how the project had begun six years earlier, in 1998, when to amuse himself he dubbed a scene from Disney's animated film *The Jungle Book* (Wolfgang Reitherman, 1967) with *chaabi* music. In that clip, included on the Miloudi VCDs, Mowgli and his animal friends from the jungle dance to a Moroccan popular beat. Hamada's friends loved the work, and he put it on the Internet, which had been introduced in Morocco just a few years earlier, in 1995, and in limited fashion. *TelQuel* does not go over the technological aspects of Hamada's limited circulation except to say, "It was not until the VCD boom that 'his clips' could make the tour of the country." Hamada explained: "I understood then that I didn't have to put everything up on the web. Others downloaded the clips and sold them. I earned nothing."[9]

Daïf herself focuses less on the ways the changing technology impacts Hamada's work itself or its circulation within Morocco and more on extrapolating a traditional sense of the work's meaning. Writing while Hamada's works were still new and fresh, she concludes that they are best understood as the expression of youth who don't see themselves reflected in Moroccan cinema and films: "What do young people do when they don't recognize themselves in television dramas, Moroccan films, or Moroccan TV? They appropriate images from elsewhere and adapt them to their daily life and their language."[10]

In some ways, this statement could describe the editorial mission of *TelQuel* magazine in the first decade of the 2000s, whose motto was "Morocco as it is" and which was consistently courting trouble with the kingdom for pushing at the boundaries of what could be said and for defending cultural renegades. So it is little surprise to find this conclusion in the article on Hamada or indeed that the magazine thought to profile him. Here the understanding is that what Hamada is doing is finding a form to express Moroccan reality via the work of appropriation and adaptation. Fair enough, except that the concept of appropriation the article mobilizes runs against the journalist's own sense of the work's underlying realism.

Daïf writes: "You won't hear [the dialogues and songs Hamada used] on Moroccan TV because they are too politically incorrect (they swear, speak of girls, hashish, money, and unemployment, the life of youth in the neighborhoods, to summarize). That's why these dubbings are successful, in addition to the fact that the 'décalage' (Matrix speaking Marrakech dialect, for example) is hilarious."[11] (This is my translation from the French. Daïf uses English to express the idea of political incorrectness; in the original she writes, "parce que trop politically not correct.")

Without analyzing Daïf's own reading of Hamada any further, we can note that she hits on a key aspect of Moroccan appreciation of his work: the humor or hilarity of what she calls the work's "décalage." What she means by the term *décalage* is the awkward or jarring juxtaposition of Moroccan dialect and Moroccan popular music with visuals from global media, in particular films with Hollywood high production values, which Hamada favored, such as *Shrek*, *The Mask*, any Disney film, and *The Matrix*. Of course, the high resolution and high production values of these film clips would be mostly lost in the transfer to VCD, where they would pixelate and jump. But they could still summon up a feeling of *décalage*, as Daïf put it.

Décalage is a notoriously difficult term to render into English with precision because it has multiple meanings. Brent Hayes Edwards has given us the most brilliant and extended discussion of its signification and the ways in which diasporic artists communicate via or across experiences of *décalage*. In his essay "The Uses of Diaspora," Edwards writes:

> [*Décalage*] can be translated as "gap," "discrepancy," "time lag," or "interval"; it is also the term that French speakers sometimes use to translate "jet lag." In other words, a *décalage* is either a difference or gap in time (advancing or delaying a schedule) *or* in space (shifting or displacing an object). . . . The verb *caler* means "to prop up or wedge something" (as when one leg on a table is uneven). So *décalage* in its etymological sense refers to the removal of such an added prop or wedge. *Décalage* indicates the reestablishment of a prior unevenness or diversity; it alludes to the

taking away of something that was added in the first place, something artificial, a stone or piece of wood that served to fill some gap or to rectify some imbalance. In other words, *décalage* is the kernel of precisely that which cannot be transferred or exchanged, the received biases that refuse to pass over when one crosses the water. It is a changing core of difference; it is the work of "differences within unity," an unidentifiable point that is incessantly touched and fingered and pressed.[12]

When Edwards invokes the phrase "differences within unity," he is referring to Ranajit Guha, who uses the term *décalage* "to indicate a structural overlap or discrepancy, a period of 'social transformation' when one class, state bureaucracy, or social formation 'challenges the authority of another that is older and moribund but still dominant.'"[13] Here, then, via Maria Daïf's sense that what makes Hamada's work intriguing and hilarious is that which she names *décalage*, and through Edwards's rich critical etymology of the term, we can open up the discussion of Hamada a bit further.

The so-called *décalage*—let us also call it the "disjuncture"—in Hamada's tracks work against the realism that *TelQuel* otherwise attributed to it. In other words, if the magazine saw Hamada's appropriation of Hollywood film clips as the result of his inability to find himself and his peers reflected in contemporary Moroccan cinema, there was also a greater and not so literal disjuncture. That which we could call the disjuncture, both temporal and geographic, between the soundtrack and the visual is the active space of possibility. It is that which is difficult to translate. But that space of disjuncture or experience of *décalage* is what makes Hamada crucial. Huge numbers of Moroccans got it. My colleagues at the party in Rabat were not confident that I ever could.

Playing with Brent Edwards's use of Guha, we might be tempted to say that there was a structural discrepancy between what Hamada was doing in the Moroccan cybercafés in the Global South and what the high-paid CGI mavens in the DreamWorks studios were doing in the West when they created *Shrek*, a sort of appropriation in a postcolonial sense. The risk that the West would recognize Hamada's work as resistance (i.e., piracy) was always there, which is why Hamada had to stay incognito when the *TelQuel* journalist tracked him down. But we should insist on not losing or forgetting the more exuberant aspects of the project—its hilarity. Many Moroccans expressed to me a sense of joy in the juxtapositions Hamada staged. When I pressed them further, they rarely stated that Hamada stole from the West and made an American product "Moroccan" but rather commented that the unexpected juxtaposition of the global and the local provoked an immediate and visceral reaction. That's an important distinction.

We can go one step further by looking closely at Hamada's most famous product itself—the *Shrek* piece reproduced on several of Hamada's albums—for Adil al Miloudi's lyrics are not without significance, of course, for the product as a whole. Hamada created the juxtaposition and did the digital work to bring Adil al Miloudi's song together with the *Shrek* dance number.

The lyrics are straightforward but also elusive. It is a party song, where the singer is high on drugs.

> Take a line and sniff it
> And you will be so happy.
> Look at Miloudi
> He has taken drugs
> And now is on the ninth cloud.[14]

But then the singer appears to want not to be on drugs—to sober up:

> I'm afraid lest I get drunk, lose my mind
> And be bad to you.
> So I'd rather drink milk.

The music is exuberant, pulsing, catchy. And then the lyrics repeat, with the first refrain in which the singer is on drugs returning after he has already renounced them. Perhaps most intriguing and difficult to translate is the opening line: "Wa haid al Miloudi wa haid ah," which I discussed extensively with Sadik Rddad and Mostafa Ouajjani, Moroccan colleagues who helped me transliterate and then translate the elusive lyrics of the song. It is an invocation—a naming—of the singer himself but also a renouncing of his name. The term *haid* means "to go away." And because the dubbed track by Hamada is known as "Miloudi," this evocation-rejection seems all the more interesting. Sadik Rddad says it means something and nothing at all.

Its hilarity, let's say, is just this naming and then anonymity, the way Hamada brings forth Shrek and then brings forth Miloudi. It is a work that takes one of the most familiar icons of Hollywood film, *Shrek*, and makes it Moroccan but then plays off its foreignness at the same time. In this way, the work is illegible to an American audience. Its potent expression of *décalage* remains in the gap. Is it piracy? Is Hamada joking when he reserves his rights to this product? Does anyone in Hollywood care?

These questions were left unanswered, of course, while Hamada produced his massively popular VCDs. Moroccans were consuming his work, though Hamada himself was not profiting financially from his stunning success (his VCDs were easily pirated and resold by others). But just as Hamada was doing his original and unusual work, a young Moroccan filmmaker living in France, working in film more traditionally understood, was about to upset everything again.

MAROCK IN MOROCCO: ROCKING THE CASA

"The film of all the taboos," it was called by its sympathizers. In the late spring of 2006, a controversial new film titled *Marock* was all over the Moroccan papers and culture magazines. Made by a twenty-nine-year-old Moroccan woman named Laïla Marrakchi, who had left Casablanca for France a decade earlier, the film was released in Morocco on May 10, 2006, a year after it had premiered at the Cannes Film Festival and a month after its general release in France. These dynamics—a director with a Moroccan upbringing but a French address and a film about Morocco with French funding and a European provenance—would haunt the film. In Morocco, its arrival on local screens was heralded with the sort of media coverage of an American *succès de scandale*, with the free publicity from excessive news coverage obviating the need for paid advertising. Indeed, multiple parallels could be made to Hollywood films, both within the film itself, its Hollywood look and American teen movie soundtrack, and in its wide distribution via both formal and informal circuits. Soon after its run at cinemas in Casablanca, Rabat, Fes, and Marrakech, contraband copies of the film were available for sale on the sidewalks of Moroccan cities, where it stood alongside pirated copies of Hollywood blockbusters such as *Syriana, Jarhead, Munich, Ice Age 2*, and *Cars*, to name those with the broadest informal circulation in June–July 2006.[15] But if part of the surprise about *Marock*'s reception in Morocco was just how Hollywood it all seemed, the controversies it provoked in Morocco revolved around the representations of Moroccan particularity within it.

Marock, Marrakchi's first feature, builds on a theme she explored in her first film, a twelve-minute short called *L'Horizon perdu* (Lost horizon, 2000), about a young man broken by life in the Tangier *medina* who leaves Morocco for Spain in clandestine fashion. In the case of *Marock*, however, the protagonist's departure from the homeland is deferred for a full ninety minutes and comes at the conclusion of a coming-of-age tale. Though the protagonist in *Marock* is no less broken by her milieu than the protagonist in the short, her elite socioeconomic status is never in jeopardy, and the emigration is legal and transparent (the last spoken word of the film is the passport control officer's demand, "Passport," which causes no anxiety). Nearly everything that precedes this final word justifies the departure, which comes both as a relief and as the tearful leave taking from adolescence and Morocco alike. The seventeen-year-old female protagonist's departure from Morocco was not, however, what made *Marock* controversial, even though the film associates Morocco itself with adolescence and departure from Morocco with the process of maturing. (To be sure, the film's detractors repeated the fact that the director herself had emigrated from Morocco to France.)[16] Rather, the provocations were the director's frank portrayal of premarital sexuality among elite Casablancans and her flaunting of religious and cultural conventions.

Three plot strands in particular stood out: the open refusal of the protagonist, Rita (Morjana Alaoui), to fast during the month of Ramadan, when the film is set; Rita's mockery of her brother, Mao (Assad El Bouab), at prayer; and her open affair with a Jewish teenager, Youri (Matthieu Boujenah), an affair that is apparently consummated sexually. As the last plot element suggests, the frank treatment of teenage Moroccan sexuality and a disregard for the sanctities of religious tradition are in *Marock* deeply intertwined. Across the board, the moment in the film that most disturbed commentators was an intimate scene between Youri and Rita, the two entangled in each other's arms, kissing in an isolated seaside shed. Youri, following Rita's eyes to the silver Star of David he wears around his neck, removes the chain and places it around the Muslim girl's neck. "This way," he says, "you won't have to think about it."[17] The film's defenders, such as the liberal cultural magazines *TelQuel* and *Le Journal Hebdomadaire*, both of which featured it on their covers and dedicated long articles to it, found this scene the most difficult aspect to watch in its disregard for religious decorum.[18]

Its detractors used the moment as evidence that the film was part of a Zionist plot and were quick to discredit the director. Strong criticism was delivered to Marrakchi in person in Tangier, where the film was screened at the national film festival in December 2005, and online, where an active discussion about the film took place among the Moroccan diaspora in France on its French release in February 2006, taking Marrakchi to task for claiming to speak on behalf of the young generation of Moroccans.[19]

In the public debate that ensued upon the film's general release in Morocco, *Marock* and Marrakchi herself quickly came to stand for multiple positions—freedom of speech, the young "rock" generation, intellectual and artistic honesty, and humanism, on the one hand, but disrespect for Moroccan tradition, diasporic elitism cut off from the homeland, neocolonialist pandering to Europe's Islamophobic preoccupations, and savvy self-publicity/provocation, on the other. These positions are not mutually exclusive, but the debate needs to be understood first.

The anxieties that *Marock* provoked were intense across the cultural and political spectrum. Whatever the validity of the critiques of the film's aesthetic quality[20] or whatever the anachronism of the film's attempt to offer a national allegory of twenty-first-century Morocco via a tale of departure (which recalled mid-twentieth-century modes of the late-colonial and early-postcolonial period), *Marock* struck a nerve. And if Marrakchi herself predicted that it would do so in a statement made in France before the film even got to Moroccan screens—a comment that in itself of course antagonized—her success in making this prediction is no less important to understand.

Marock makes vivid a variety of intertwined features of urban Morocco at a key turning point in the decade. It was one of the first feature films in Morocco to operate within diverse Moroccan media worlds, which I argue it both anticipated and helped to create. It was a film designed for the big screen in traditional cinema houses, of course, but it was more often viewed on pirated DVDs, shared via YouTube uploads, and discussed and debated online by a young public in Morocco and in the diaspora in France. This wide debate was an effect not only of its controversial and contemporary theme but of its addressing a public that has deep ties to Morocco as well as either transnational experience (the Moroccan diaspora in Europe) or transnational aspirations (urban Moroccan youth). If Laïla Marrakchi hit a nerve with her film, it was not simply because of the film's explosive subject matter. Rather, she located and created a public whose nerve was ready to be struck. *Marock* was thus a harbinger of the new pressures on the Moroccan nation of the digital age.

Shana Cohen and Larabi Jaidi's description of the Moroccan encounter with globalization, published in the same year as *Marock*'s release, 2006, is useful in recalling the moment in which Marrakchi was intervening. In *Morocco: Globalization and Its Consequences*, Cohen and Jaidi give an account of the interplay of economic and political pressures from outside and the protean forms that the Moroccan kingdom assumed in responding to the pulls and pressures of development.[21] They argue that Moroccan youth have retrenched into apathy and apoliticism, despite an environment that seems poised toward political inclusion. For Cohen and Jaidi, Moroccan youth can be seen in terms of what Susan Ossman has called the "lightness" of bodies in her own important study of the transnational circulation of forms of beauty between Casablanca, Paris, and Cairo, published at the beginning of the new millennium.[22] And though Cohen and Jaidi focus on economic and political processes, they suggest some of the forms of cultural production that may be implicated by attention to Morocco's complex relationship to globalization when they pay brief attention to an anonymous Moroccan rapper in the diaspora who challenges from afar the cultural contradictions of Moroccan national culture. Marrakchi's film depicts a segment of Moroccan youth who are apathetic and locates an outside form or look to tell their story. It was both aspects of *Marock* that were provocative.

Marock was one of several Moroccan films that in the first half of the 2000s engaged the state of the Moroccan nation under a new set of arrangements that were no longer burdened by postcolonial anxieties.[23] Films as varied in their themes and artistic ambitions as *Baidaoua* (Casablancans; Abdelkader Lagtaa, 1999), *Ali Zaoua* (Nabil Ayouch, 2000), *Khahit errouh* (Threads; Hakim Belabbes, 2003), and *Le Grand voyage* (Ismael Ferroukhi, 2004), all of which commanded attention in different Moroccan and diaspora publics, were concerned with what place Morocco and Moroccan culture might have in a global setting in which ideas, products and commodities, lifestyles, and technologies had complicated what was once, perhaps, a more simple binary (France–Morocco). I say this without meaning to reduce colonial (and postcolonial) Morocco to a binary, either internally with respect to French division of Arab and Tamazight cultures, languages, and populations or globally with respect to the changing position of the United States toward Morocco (and that of Morocco toward the United States) in the late-colonial period and the first two decades of the postcolonial period. As I have argued elsewhere, from the arrival of American troops in Morocco in November 1942 and certainly after Franklin Roosevelt's participation in the Casablanca Conference in January 1943, a vivid and visible triangulation of paradigms became available in Morocco, within which the American position might offer liberty from the French; the promise/threat of American commodities was the harbinger of this new paradigm.[24] To say so is not to confuse the American "alternative" as liberating, though that was the frame within which Roosevelt spoke to Mohammed V, but rather to identify it as an arrangement that would threaten to place Morocco in the time lag of American neoliberalism *avant la lettre*. But even if we agree that the postcolonial period itself be reconsidered outside these binarisms, we must still note the shift by the end of the 1990s into a new set of concerns and ways of engaging with social collectivities in Morocco.

Marock was made in 2005 but set in 1997; it is thus sensitive to the moment before cell phones and the Internet pervaded daily life in Morocco but no less attentive to the new circulation of cultural objects in that setting, and Marrakchi and the film's producers were acutely aware of the use of new technologies to market the film. In 1997, the opposition came to power in Morocco—the so-called government of alternance, a solution to the series of large and sometimes violent demonstrations against the legislative government in the 1980s and early 1990s. But after the death of King Hassan II in 1999, the stability of the monarchy was achieved in part by addressing the worst repression of the preceding years—through a truth-and-reconciliation process, the release of political prisoners, and the opening of press freedoms. These actions were not only necessary but also perhaps served to distract the Moroccan public from the opening to the world outside that new technologies of the digital age were forcing (from the fax machine and satellite television in the first half of the 1990s to the Internet and cell phones in the last years of the 1990s and in the early 2000s).

Films from the late 1990s through the mid-2000s leading up to *Marock* took up the theme of circulation in various ways and help us to see how a variety of interrelated aspects of movement and communication reflect on each other. Lagtaa's film *Baidaoua*, for example, thematizes censorship and Morocco's morality police (who represent the lack of free circulation). His protagonist's desire to procure a restricted book anchors the film's action. Lagtaa was less interested in the newer technologies (such as the fax machine) that were already putting pressure on state censorship in the early and middle 1990s and more in exploring questions of stasis and immobility as a challenge to contemporary Morocco. The book Salwa wants is available in France, and to procure it may require her to leave the country, but in another scene an Islamist teacher instructs his pupils that the Qur'an is good for all times and places. Lagtaa suggests that circulation—the circulation or censorship of a book—returns Morocco to contemporary temporality, whereas a more fundamentalist strand of Islam in Morocco conjoins stasis and being out of time.

Other films seized on the intervention of technologies in altering the nation's spatial and temporal bases, which would soon be apparent when cell phones became massively available in Morocco. Ismael Ferroukhi's film *Le Grand voyage*, a road movie from Paris to Mecca, portrays the cell phone as a technology that challenges the authority of face-to-face contact and symbolizes the generational gap. Hakim Belabbes's film *Khahit errouh* (Threads), an experimental, avant-garde film, associates the ruptures of generational and diasporic change, of its shift in setting from Chicago to Boujjad, and perhaps of its own avant-garde fragmented technique with the interruption of the telephone, a technology that both connects and ruptures. And *Ali Zaoua*, a greatly successful film both locally in Morocco and internationally, demonstrates in two ways a sense that the world of young street children may be seen in relationship to the technologies and economic forces of globalization. Nabil Ayouch's framing device for his tale of Casablanca street children is to show Moroccan media depicting these marginalized youth to the larger nation, suggesting both the social stratification to be found in Casablanca and the media worlds located there. But *Ali Zaoua* is notable among Moroccan films of the decade in its use of digitally generated animation to depict what these children imagine. The street children of *Ali Zaoua* are caught in social and economic stasis, but their imaginations allow them to circulate outside their immediate circumstances. Ayouch thus seizes on a metaphor that Moroccan sociologist Said Graiouid would pick up on in his own research on social exile and virtual escape in Morocco. Graiouid's ethnographic research in Moroccan cybercafés found that otherwise hopeless youth were chatting with Moroccans living in diaspora and engaging in "virtual h'rig" (referring to the illegal form of emigrating—literally, "burning").[25]

With these descriptions, I do not mean to imply that the question of the nation is not central to many of these films. Yet even narratives that are centered around the nation or a critique of the nation must be considered in the changed framework within which the nation operates, globalization.[26] For *Marock*, sensitive to the global movement of ideas, images, bodies, and commodities (to say nothing of politics and technologies), awareness of this framework is crucial to judging the film and whether Marrakchi's national critique is anachronistic or daring or both. In *Baidaoua*, awareness of this context allows us to see how the film is concerned primarily with circulation, whether one can move socially, across borders, within a city or not. In *Ali Zaoua*, taking this in another direction, social immobility is contrasted with the mobilities represented by media and digital animation. To shift the conversation to "circulation" is in part to register frustration with a logic that insists that all Moroccan cultural production forever after 1956 is in reference to France and to insist that other concerns and other networks have in fact taken center stage in recent years.[27] *Marock*'s intertwined set of concerns include questions of circulation, diaspora, cultural clash, friction with (or rupture from) Moroccan traditions, which together suggest that the analytics of postcolonialism do not apply here *even though* postcolonialism may be the register within which Marrakchi imagines the narrative resolution of her film via Rita's departure from Morocco to France.

But *Marock* is notable, too, for the way in which American objects, songs, and a "Hollywood look" run through it when the film otherwise is not geographically or politically concerned with the United States. Here we have a vivid example of how Moroccan cultural production in what I call the "digital age" or, alternatively, the "age of circulation" is animated by a different set of concerns than the concerns that were dominant during the postcolonial period. Maghribi cultural production during the first three decades of the postcolonial period, which commenced in Morocco with independence from the French protectorate in 1956, frequently exhibited an anxious relationship to French history, culture, and language—major examples include Abdelkebir Khatibi's novels *La Mémoire tatouée* (Tattooed memory, 1971) and *Amour bilingue* (1983; *Love in Two Languages* [1990]) as well as Abdellah Laroui's work of revisionist history *L'histoire du Maghreb* (The history of Morocco, 1970). By the 1990s, however, the concerns of younger Moroccan writers and filmmakers seem to have moved beyond the classic postcolonial concerns and taken up a new set of themes I associate with circulation, both literal (migration, travel, expatriation, etc.) and formal. We see an engagement with circulation earlier in cinema (for example, in Abdelkader Lagtaa's film *al-Hubb fi Dar al-Baida*) than in Moroccan literature, perhaps because influential American cinematic representations of Morocco (such as *Casablanca*) were an early harbinger of the later geopolitical order that would follow the colonial era. The interest in circulation as a theme can be traced through Moroccan literature beginning in the second half of the 1990s (e.g., Aicha Ech-Chana's socially committed documentary text *Miseria* [1996] and Soumya Zahy's novel *On ne rentrera peut-être plus jamais chez nous* [We will perhaps never return to our homes, 2001]). Writers of the various Moroccan diasporas—such as Abdelkader Benali, writing in Dutch in Holland; Laila Lalami, writing in English in the United States; and Tahar Ben Jelloun, writing in French in France— were sensitive to the theme of migration and return, as might be expected. Benali's novel *Bruiloft aan zee* (1996; *Wedding by the Sea* [2000]), Lalami's first book of fiction *Hope and Other Dangerous Pursuits* (2005), and Ben Jelloun's book *Partir* (2006; *Leaving Tangier* [2009]) all narrate tales of Moroccans in motion to and from Europe.

Marock is less aesthetically or narratively original than these works. Lagtaa's *Baidaoua*, which summons an innovative visual technique in the service of a complex narrative exploration of circulation, is significantly more original from an aesthetic point of view, and Benali's *Wedding by the Sea* is formally exuberant and linguistically inventive. But *Marock* is nonetheless successful in making clear the forms of social organization produced by and within the age of circulation.

In its coverage of the debate over *Marock,* the maverick weekly *Le Journal Hebdomadaire* staged a debate between Bilal Talidi, a representative of the Islamist Parti de la justice et du développement (PJD), which had called for banning the film, and Abdellah Zaazaa, the leader of a network of Casablanca neighborhood associations, Réseau des Associations de Quartier du Grand Casablanca, and representative of a liberal, secular position. In the debate, printed in the pages of *Le Journal,* the question of aesthetics became a screen against which to argue larger questions about Moroccan society. Talidi, who had published an editorial against *Marock* in the paper *Attajdid,* claimed in the pages of *Le Journal* that "one should not judge a film without watching it." His indictment of the film was, in this venue, pitched in terms of aesthetics: a "maladroit" use of French and Arabic, an "extreme lightness of plot," and a lack of "dynamism, drama or life"; for him, *Marock* was closer to a documentary than to a "true film." Zaazaa, in contrast, resisted the analysis of the film's language or aesthetic quality and launched his own defense of it on political grounds. The film's ability to "trace Moroccan realities," in particular, justified its screening in Morocco, and he called attention to the ways in which its opposition was manipulating the film for its ulterior motives of creating a "state of law" (*état de droit*). But he, too, made recourse to aesthetic judgment. He noted: "I saw the film in the company of my wife. We left struck [*boulversés*] by how well it had traced Moroccan social realities. The story pleased me in every way."[28]

The point that Zaazaa had seen the film in the company of his wife was clearly part of his implied defense. If *Marock* posed a challenge to "traditions of the country," "religious values," and the "fundamentals of Islam" (as religious politicians had suggested, including those who did not call for its censorship, but rather for a national boycott of it),[29] Zaazaa claimed that the film could educate the Moroccan conjugal couple on the new realities of Moroccan society. But Talidi called Zaazaa on the latter's expression of "pleasure" on seeing the film, which Talidi said was not an "objective response" and therefore to be discarded. He claimed such objectivity for his own analysis of the film; Zaazaa's pleasure was subjective.

Marock, the viewing of *Marock*, the response one had to the viewing of *Marock*, and what the nation's appropriate response to *Marock* should be in 2006 became fraught places to debate the status of national culture itself. Talidi's comment about Zaazaa's pleasure begs the question of an "objective" reading. How do we read this film? Can an "objective" reading of the film by a representative of a political party stand in for that of a citizenry?

Talidi and Zaazaa notably agreed that *Marock* offered a representation of Moroccan reality, though they did not call attention to their agreement on this question. For Talidi, *Marock* was more documentary than film; for Zaazaa, it was a shocking representation of a reality he recognized but about which he knew nothing. Their implied disagreement was over what role the elite and westward-looking Moroccan youth of *Marock* might have in the society at large. It is the teen look of the picture, inscribed within a style deeply redolent of American cinema, that was perhaps the most upsetting, though these terms were not used in the debate. PJD's call for the film to be banned drew on the law's defense of "sacred values and good morals." Therefore, the question of whether the film was Moroccan or not could be linked to whether it should be banned under Moroccan law. Marrakchi's Moroccanness or her Frenchness was itself a cipher for a question of *style* and what I call the film's "look."

On the level of style, *Marock* itself exhibits the circulation of an American look, which is doubled by the film's interest (both visually and in the narrative) in American commodities. This interest is the threat that is harder to speak of, but the one that made the PJD position ultimately anachronistic, as other commentators realized. Mohamed Ameskane, representative of the Union pour un mouvement populaire (known best by its abbreviation, UMP), stated in the same pages that the film could be boycotted "if it were judged contrary to our principles. [But] one must sign up for this new world, the world of the Internet and of globalization."[30] Seen in this light, many Moroccan commentators' resistance to *Marock* should be regarded as aligned with an anxiety about globalization, and the championing of it on grounds of free speech can be viewed as a celebration of the open borders (of both information and trade in commodities) associated with globalization. My point is not to take a side but to show that *Marock* heralds but does not initiate a new stage in Moroccan cinema. From *Marock*, we can look backward to see this interest in circulation in a number of places and forward to the works that would come, such as those with which I began this chapter. But first we must describe how a "look" circulates.

The story *Marock* tells is familiar enough to those who have watched Hollywood teen romances, and on the level of plot it borrows from a number of Hollywood films and TV serials. To say so is not to denigrate it per se—nor is it a compliment on artistic grounds—but rather to note why the familiarity of the formula might itself be so bothersome to some Moroccan critics such as Talidi and also why for others it immediately raised the question of protection on the grounds of free speech. The circulation of this look operates on both the level of plot/scenario (which allowed politicians to target the film) and the level of the film's visual and aural registers (which politicians did not invoke). *Marock* borrows what we can call, following Miriam Hansen again, a vernacular familiar from Hollywood cinema, in this case the teen romance, and brings it into Moroccan circulation. That combination of a familiar look and the familiarity of a Hollywood formula, the problem-picture-cum-teen-romance, emerges as the most interesting form of global culture in circulation in this film. But we can also note the many explicit indications of global circulation in the film: the music, apparel, food, products, and commodities that animate the world of these Casablancan youth. If these youth look to Europe for their futures after the baccalaureate ("bac") exam, the commodities, products, and culture that they consume are for the most part American. More accurately, these objects of consumption are global and are generally rendered in global English, both of which are associated with the United States irrespective of the national origin of the cultural product or artist.

Marock is a teen pic, which seems at once a comfortable and uncomfortable way to describe it, given that the phrase implies an American relationship to the family and society that was and is not the norm in Morocco. In other words, without the particular identity of "teens" that we know in the United States, which is not universal, you can't have a "teen pic." However, as *Marock* itself demonstrates, not only does "teen pic" sound appropriate as a way to describe the film, but the film so successfully mobilizes this style to describe a social milieu that it effaces for its non-Moroccan audiences much of the particularity of Moroccan adolescence. Such particularity is swept away by *Marock*'s depiction of a world of discos, parties, romance, and preparation for a life after high school that will be spent in France. Whatever the accuracy of this representation of the young elite of Casablanca, it is clearly not the life enjoyed by most Moroccans. (Juxtaposing *Ali Zaoua*, with its representation of the poor homeless children of Casablanca, and *Marock*, the two Moroccan films of the first decade of the twenty-first century with the largest international success, would be provocative.) With poverty and social class for the most part dispensed with by *Marock*'s fascination with the elite, the problems that remain in the social problem aspects of the film are those presented by Moroccan society itself. Perhaps, then, it is not surprising that the solutions to those problems are also brought in from abroad (American music, for example, and the characters' choice to depart from Morocco). The way the Hollywood "look" functions, therefore, is to naturalize the import of foreign solutions to domestic problems and to make domestic recalcitrance to them seem itself foreign or anachronistic. That is, the film's adoption of an American vernacular, within which the social problem of a romance between a Jewish young man and a Muslim young woman may be overcome naturally by the power of love (and romantic comedy as a genre), was a solution that made most Moroccans' difficulty in imagining it seem irrelevant or retrograde. Indeed, the film ends in tragedy with respect to the love story, not the comedy it has suggested, which we may see as the translation of the vernacular to local realities. This relationship to the Hollywood vernacular is the deep level on which Marrakchi's outsider perspective functions, and, though unnamed by its opponents, it produced the relationship to Morocco that many found bothersome about the film—and that titillated others. Without the language to discuss this vernacular as that which was foreign to the Moroccan film, however, the debate revolved instead around the question of Marrakchi's roots as a Moroccan and the route she took to France as ways to prove that she and therefore her film were not after all "Moroccan." This approach, it should be clear, was a dead end.

The story is a simple problem tale set during the month of Ramadan. Rita is a high school senior; it is the year of the baccalaureate exam, a year that in her circles is spent studying, partying, listening to music, and thinking about the next stage of life. For Rita and most of her friends at the privileged Lycée Lyautey, the next stage of life often means leaving Morocco for Europe (though not in all cases); the present is generally met with abandon. Drinking alcohol, smoking hashish, flirting, and being sexually active are the norm for weekend nights, which are spent racing around in sports cars between nightclubs and homes without parents, where prostitutes may be called in for quick fixes for the boys. Rita's brother, Mao, has returned home from London for Ramadan, and from the start we can see that he does not approve of Rita's milieu. We see Mao praying, to his sister's surprise, and wearing a close-cropped beard; he is clearly disturbed by the frivolities of his old circle of friends. He rarely comments directly, except to Rita, who he says looks like a "whore" because of the makeup she wears. At a party, Rita falls for a young man she has observed at a nightclub. She learns his name (Youri) through a mutual friend and bets her friends that she'll have him by the end of Ramadan. The problem, though, is not whether she can or will have him—there are meaningful glances between them from the start that make this clear—but what it will mean if she does.

Youri is, after all, a Moroccan Jew, and although this detail seems to bother no one too much in the present (except Mao, who is teased by friends and reports it to his parents), the fact that these young people's future is always on their minds poses the question that Rita rarely asks herself: Can this relationship have a future? Learning about Rita's social life from Mao, Rita's parents ground her until the bac is over and done with. But she escapes, consummates her affair with Youri, passes her bac, and worries about what to do with her romance if it cannot be shared openly. She suggests to Youri that he could convert to Islam; he suggests the same to her about Judaism. No sooner have they discussed these options than Youri is killed in a car crash. Rita, distraught, retreats into herself. Her brother apologizes for his part in her unhappiness. They reconcile. Two months pass. Rita leaves for Europe.

The plot is fast and efficient. The film is visually sensuous; its world is socially vapid. Rita, played by a newcomer to the cinema whom Marrakchi plucked from Paris and who admitted in interviews to being from the same elevated Casablanca class that is depicted in the film, is attractive and starry-eyed. (Morjana Alaoui was in fact a student at the American University in Paris when Marrakchi cast her in her first film role; after passing her bac in Morocco, she had lived in Florida. Her own pathways neatly demonstrate the triangulation of the colonial, postcolonial, and global that I have discussed.) She is also barely clad much of the time, in-close fitting tank tops and boxer shorts, in a string bikini another time, or faded Levis, costuming choices that are both part of the film's verisimilitude in representing the young Casa elite—from press photos and in film festival appearances, it was striking how much Marrakchi herself looked and dressed like her own characters[31]—and part of Marrakchi's juxtaposition of the visual appearances of the libertine Casablancan youth and the more traditional members of the community.

The most famous example of this juxtaposition appears in the film still that was circulated as part of the film's publicity and featured on the cover of *TelQuel*. In the still, Rita wears skin-tight shorts and a cotton camisole, hand on hip, navel exposed, and stands over her brother bowing in prayer.

In the film's scene, she provokes him: "Are you sick or what? What are you doing? Did you fall on your head?" Then, more aggressively: "Do you think you're in Algeria? Are you going to become a fundamentalist [*barbu*]?'" The pose, reproduced on the cover of *TelQuel* next to the words "the film of all the taboos," presents a vivid example of the changing look of young women in Casablanca not only in terms of clothing and brands but in terms of body size and type itself (figure 4.3).

During the period in which *Marock* is set, the late 1990s, sociologist Fatima Mernissi was writing columns in the Casablanca-based women's magazine *Femmes du Maroc* that remarked on the generational shift of young Moroccan women increasingly toward Western body types as models of beauty; Mernissi lamented this shift as she called for Moroccan women to resist the emaciated "waif" look of then prominent models such as Kate Moss.[32]

Mernissi's comments on the ways in which Moroccan women's body types could represent a form of cultural circulation and Susan Ossman's subsequent ethnographic work that charted the transnational circulation of Western models of beauty and body type open up the ways in which we can discuss the Western look of *Marock*, both in terms of the individual actors, their bodies, and their clothing and in terms of the cinematic vernacular that Marrakchi mobilizes. It is, after all, the look thus conceived that is the most immediate presence of America in a film that only once invokes the United States as a geopolitical entity (and then quickly dispenses with it as a place where the characters know "no one"). Nevertheless, America plays a major, if imagined and silent, presence in the film. *Marock* thus presents itself to us not as a film that is postcolonial but rather as one that inhabits the era of circulation in an interrelated series of ways. Before we come back to the literal markers of this presence of global culture, we need to return to the more slippery question of what I have referred to as the film's Hollywood "teen pic" vernacular.

In several essays, the late Miriam Hansen presented a powerful argument that broadens our understanding of what she calls the "vexed issue of Americanism" for transnational cinema studies—namely, the ways in which "an aesthetic idiom developed in one country could achieve transnational

FIGURE 4.3 The provocative cover of *TelQuel*, April 29–May 5, 2006.
(Reproduced with permission of TelQuel Media)

and global currency."[33] Her focus was on the circulation of the classical style of Hollywood cinema produced during the dominance of the studio system, roughly from 1917 to 1960), and on the ways in which that style has been translated and differently understood in a variety of other national cinemas—most notably Shanghai cinema. There are at least two lessons from Hansen's rich work that I want to apply here. First is her analysis of the way in which classical narrative Hollywood cinema masks the "anachronistic tension" of its "combination of neoclassicist style and Fordist mass culture" (66). The anachronism of classical cinema is that it took on neoclassicist aesthetics (it is readerly and transparent and has linear narratives, coherent subjects, and so on) even while it was an art associated with the new and the modern, both as a new technology and with respect to the Fordist mass (cultural) production perfected by the studio system. By naturalizing its own form of narrative, Hansen argues, classical Hollywood cinema developed a rhetoric that could in fact articulate "something radically new and different under the guise of a continuity with tradition" (67). Part of what is articulated is the very messiness of Fordism and modernity itself, with its various forms of structural and literal violence and how (certain) individuals could find a place in that system. Hansen's second lesson, then, follows from the first and is related to my discussion of circulation: that Hollywood cinema traveled so well and so much better than other national cinemas because of the way it "forg[ed] a mass market out of an ethnically and culturally heterogeneous society, if often at the expense of racial others" (68). This "first global vernacular" worked because classical Hollywood cinema mobilized "biologically hardwired structures and universal narrative templates"; mediated competing discourses on modernity and modernization; and "articulated, multiplied, and globalized a particular historical experience" (68). Hollywood cinema found its way influentially into other national cinemas not because classical cinema universalized the American experience but rather because it was translatable. "It meant different things to different publics, both at home and abroad," Hansen writes (68). On the level of reception, the Hollywood films and that which might be taken from them (their rhetoric) could be changed, localized, and adapted.

What I want borrow from Hansen's work is her discussion of the contradictions that the classical style masks and allows as well as her sense of how that particular conjunction itself is particularly well suited for global circulation. With these notions, we can revisit the discussion of "cultures of circulation" that Benjamin Lee and Edward LiPuma advance and balance the temptation to read for meaning with attention to what Dilip

Parameshwar Gaonkar and Elizabeth Povinelli call the "circulatory matrix."[34] *Marock*'s engagement with a Hollywood vernacular—no longer the classical vernacular, pure and simple, though at most times borrowing from it—allows it to smooth over some of the more troubling aspects of economic globalization that affect the world behind that which is represented in the film. The film does repeatedly attend to class and economic differences, even while too comfortably keeping them at the margins. But this smoothing over of the crises of economic globalization happens naturally, as it were, in the fluid way in which *Marock* adopts the cultural style or look of the Hollywood teen pic. In other words, the ways in which the film may be seen in terms of "globalization" are multiple and reinforce one another: the circulation of the Hollywood vernacular and the fascination with American cultural products and commodities serve both to double the elite characters' ability to circulate across national borders and to efface the ways in which the Moroccan underclass may not. When Rita's friend Asmaa (Razika Simozrag) tells Mao that she will not be relocating to Europe after the bac because her parents don't have the means, he does not know what to say. Mao's surprise—"je [ne] savais pas," he mutters and looks down—is echoed, as it were, by the film's inability to dwell on those who do not circulate. Though the film notes these individuals who represent dead ends, it cannot itself resist always remaining in motion.

Marock, to be clear, is most fascinated by upper-middle-class teenagers in Casablanca, a group whose own ability to circulate is strikingly more capacious than that of other Moroccans. This is a point the film does suggest, most vividly in a climactic scene when Rita denounces her parents for paying off the family of a young poor child whom Mao apparently struck with his car and killed at some time in the past. Although the film does offer sympathetic portraits of working-class Moroccans as minor figures (most often as servants, by which it offers an additional critique of upper-middle-class Moroccan family values), its portrait of Morocco is clearly delimited to a small portion of the population. That it did apparently speak to a much larger public than it represents, though, should not be doubted, in part perhaps because of its own subtle critique of class dynamics, but otherwise because of the apparent translatability of some of its characters' aspirations to other social classes among Moroccan youth. Nevertheless, the visual pleasure the film takes in depicting the sumptuous residences, cars, parties, and bodies of Casablanca's elite allies it with the Hollywood teen pic and not with class critique. To be sure, *Marock* is not a critique of globalization, either economic or cultural.

The immediacy and power of the Moroccan debate around *Marock* with which I began this discussion, then, can be seen as the resistance from Moroccans left behind by those very processes of globalization, both cultural and economic, that Marrakchi's film represents and enacts. Hansen's crucial point that the classical style was anachronistic because it was neoclassical and modern—which I would recast as "preposterous," meaning simultaneously "before" and "after"[35]—may be applied to Marrakchi's translation of the Hollywood teen pic. In this sense, *Marock* is a film that struck many Moroccan viewers as new (Zaazaa's comments given earlier), and yet it is a film that is clearly nostalgic for a different form of looking at and being in the world, a world before the advent of digital technologies. *Marock* offers the newness of a modern Morocco, engaging the putatively taboo topics of teen sexuality and interreligious relationships while playing a reassuringly retro soundtrack—some of the songs featured most prominently are "The Power" by Snap! (1990); "Rock 'n' Roll Suicide" by David Bowie (1972); "Shake Your Groove Thing" by Peaches and Herb (1978); "Sad Soul" by Ronnie Bird (1969); and "Junk Shop Clothes" by the Auteurs (1993). This retro soundtrack hints at the retrograde anachronism of Marrakchi's resolution of her tale. The nostalgia for a world before digital technologies overwhelmed daily practice substitutes for or overlays smoothly, as I have suggested, an allegory of the Moroccan nation for the more complex situation of contemporary Morocco in the age of circulation. That is, the way in which *Marock* proposes itself as something radically new on the Moroccan cultural scene and then delivers in multiple ways something more comfortably nostalgic is the way in which its look and soundtrack betray the trap that the film slips into: the idea that national allegory provides an adequate mode within which to comprehend twenty-first-century Moroccan reality.

In *Marock*, the interplay of the new and the nostalgic is associated throughout with the Hollywood look. The camera savors the streets, the exteriors and interiors of the wealthy Anfa neighborhood of Casablanca, to a slow sensual rock-and-roll soundtrack. Even to those who have been to privileged neighborhoods of Casablanca and Rabat, the scenes depict an almost impossibly wealthy milieu. *Marock* includes several scenes that do nothing to advance the plot but that are nonetheless crucial to comprehending its meaning: a car chase through the streets of Anfa; young people sitting around swimming pools, nightclubs, and outdoor cafés. They curse, they drink alcohol, the young men harass the female maids. The film's global audience and its Moroccan audience alike are in a familiar world, but one not familiar from film images of Morocco in general or of Casablanca in particular. It is instead a world familiar from TV and Hollywood images of Beverly Hills. The language of the film is for the most part French (only the servants speak in Moroccan Arabic), a choice that Marrakchi defended on the grounds of realism.[36] If this is a more accurate representation of the bourgeoisie, the verisimilitude also comes packaged within the look of a foreign film, and that is precisely the point. Patrick Antona, a French interviewer, asked if the (limited) amount of Arabic used in the film would limit the film's accessibility, presumably to French audiences.[37] If to some younger Moroccan audiences, the film brought together a Hollywood look with Moroccan actors and backgrounds, to the French interviewer the global circulation worked in a different direction—the occurrence of Moroccan Arabic stood out.

What the exchange between Antona and Marrakchi reveals, almost painfully, is how Marrakchi's choice to write out Moroccan Arabic and with it the bulk of the Moroccan population (save the elite of Casablanca) follows the directives of globalization as a form of economic distribution. This silent translation of Moroccan Arabic is the flattening of language so that it might circulate more easily; it is the reduction of local/national particularity to global "value."[38] By claiming that her choice to render so much of her film in French was based on realism, Marrakchi not only reveals the partial nature of her regard of contemporary Morocco but also demonstrates her intention that her film *stand in* for the Moroccan nation. The moments in *Marock* that gesture toward those who are left out of its perspective are thereby deleted (or put in parentheses) as illegible and thereby irrelevant.

That the film imagines itself as an allegory of the nation is clear from its title, which plays on the French name for Morocco, "Maroc," but with an added *k* to suggest contemporaneity via the reference to rock music. Organizing its narrative around its protagonist's coming of age as she butts up against the recalcitrance of her own society invokes a well-worn formula. But if *Marock* claims contemporaneity, it is unable to offer more than a repetition of that oldest of postcolonial narrative resolutions: the protagonist's departure from a nation that cannot contain her enlightened consciousness. This resolution, however, exceeds the cultural conditions of the moment being represented in that departure and travel itself do not have the status they once did—particularly not for Rita's class. Departure from Morocco, therefore, cannot equal renunciation or enlightenment without eliminating the very contemporaneity that the film wants to claim. The import of what I consider an anachronistic formula to resolve the film narrative suggests how important nostalgia is for Marrakchi in the attempt to efface that anachronism (or the audience's awareness of it). Further, it suggests why the category of circulation, the film's obsession, is a contested one. Not surprisingly, circulation operates or signifies multiply within the film.

Contested interpretations of circulation within *Marock*—those uses that Marrakchi makes of it versus how I think the idea of circulation offers an analytic tool by which to suggest the anachronistic limits of her project in national allegory—demonstrate Hansen's point about the way in which global vernaculars can mean different things to different audiences. As a way to further elaborate this point and to move toward a conclusion of this analysis of the film's relationship to circulation, the car race scene is perhaps worth a second look, precisely because it is so formulaic and unoriginal. There is little apparent importance to the scene other than that it appears in a Moroccan film at all. Youri has Rita in his car and races two other cars driven by his buddies, each of which is stocked with a young woman in the passenger seat. Youri of course wins the race because of his daring, cutting down a side street recklessly; that he will eventually die in a car crash is clearly signaled. The scene's very banality makes it interesting for our purposes; it is literally about circulation in two ways that French language makes possible:

1. There are no cars on the streets of Anfa, presumably cleared by Marrakchi and her crew; as an audience, we never fear that a car will appear out of nowhere. We are in a pure space of cinema. The racing cars can circulate on a road without traffic.

2. The Hollywood B-movie staple is here represented in a Moroccan film. It is not the first car chase in a Moroccan film, surely, but here the chase signals the *circulation* of the Hollywood vernacular (of the teen pic, of the banal movie, of the picture in which "true love" forged between a young man and a young woman across the space of a passenger car can cure all social ills).

Indeed, in its very familiarity from Hollywood films, *Marock*'s car race scene evokes an earlier scene in the film in which the fact that the free circulation of automobiles is inhibited allows for romance. If the car race seems to invoke Hollywood, the earlier scene invokes Morocco in its attention to social details or at least to the Morocco of the haute bourgeoisie. What happens is this: Rita is being driven home from school by the family chauffeur when they come across Youri's car and his family's driver, broken down at the side of the road. Rita (or rather her driver) offers Youri a ride home, which allows the couple to make eyes at one another and begin their romance. This scene works within the teen-pic vernacular, but it also localizes it to its own particular class and national location. That Youri's car is not in circulation, suffering a moment of Moroccan technological breakdown, should be juxtaposed with the rapid and easy circulation in the car race scene and highlights the way a global vernacular (Hollywood via the car race) can be used alongside a local one (the details of the breakdown).[39] The fact that this scene allows Rita and Youri to enjoy the later car scene (the race) in which their love is symbolically consummated (as it will be sexually consummated later) will in turn produce a second Moroccan response that forces a temporary end to circulation: when Rita's parents discover that she has been seeing Youri, they confine her to their enormous house. Her own social circulation is cut off, at least until she passes her bac exam, when she may continue her circulatory trajectory toward Europe. The car chase, banal and not visually compelling, thus can be understood as the key to the ways in which circulation operates multiply in *Marock*.

If driving around in cars—racing, being driven to and from school, drinking and driving—is an important component of the film's grammar, *Marock*'s obsession with the circulation of commodities provides the conjunctions in those sentences. The technology of the automobile, which allows the characters to circulate physically, is paired with the commodities that allow for virtual movement. In the world of *Marock*, pirated Hollywood films get delivered to your driveway by video rental agents with their inventory in the trunk of their cars, and friends from Miami send you authentic New York Yankee caps. These products not only lubricate the social relations of the characters' interactions but also sometimes provide the film with spoken or visual words that echo the cinematic vernacular I have discussed. Words, products, and phrases on T-shirts offer further verisimilitude in Marrakchi's representation of her milieu. But they eventually jump right off the screen. My eye is drawn to the American T-shirts paraded through *Marock*. "Hopper for State Senate," reads one that Youri wears; "Where in the Hell Is Slippery Rock?" reads another. Why have the characters wear shirts with these particular phrases? Are they markers of distinction, like Driss's (Rachid Benhaissan) cherished New York Yankees cap, tossed around the swimming pool away from its owner's grasp? Our eyes are drawn to English-language phrases on the characters' clothing, clothing that may or may not be authentic imports, just as the detached signifier of American phrases (often with spelling or grammatical errors) appears on clothing for sale throughout Moroccan cities today.

For the bulk of the film, these phrases and the commodities they decorate serve merely to echo and solidify the theme of circulation I have identified. But in one of the final scenes, there is a twist. Youri's death in a car crash, though apparently accidental, occurs shortly after Rita and he have discussed their society's unwillingness to sanction an affair between a Moroccan Jew and Moroccan Muslim. Mao is the character who most assumes the guilt of this societal intractability because it is he who seems most disturbed by the affair and informs his parents about it (Mao also assumes this guilt symbolically because he struck and killed a boy with his car before the film narrative begins, and the compensation for this killing has not been yet satisfied). After Youri's death, we are forced to watch the impossibly painful melodrama of a high school girl mourning the death of her boyfriend. There is nothing that can be said, and the film is silent—without words. That is, until Mao comes up to Rita's rooftop perch and reconciles with her. When he arrives, he is wearing a T-shirt printed with the word *America*, a small heart dotting the *i*. There is no justification in the plot for his wearing of such a shirt (Mao supposedly lives in London), and it is unlike anything he has worn before. In fact, it seems impossible to imagine the character Mao wearing this particular shirt. But his shirt, which speaks before he does, suggests something about the depth of the apology he is making and underlines his implied renunciation of the intolerance he showed earlier toward Youri's religion.

The suggestion this T-shirt makes is complex, especially given the associations in Morocco (and elsewhere in the Middle East and North Africa) of the United States with strong support for Israel. The America of the showcased cultural products and the film vernacular is now the America that loves the departed Youri, and the film thus offers a liberal sentiment toward tolerance and inclusion as its solution to its central problem. It is important to note that America is not a place that the characters imagine going to literally—it is mentioned once, as a place not possible. Rita had asked Youri what he will do after passing the bac exam. He says that his parents want to go to America, but he knows "personne" (no one). His knowing no one is modulated by his parents' suggestion that America is the place where they, as Moroccan Jews, will go to after he graduates from high school. The lost potential of Youri's circulation in America is named by Mao's shirt: of course, Youri will not circulate in America because he is dead. Thus, the T-shirt initiates its own conversation about the possibility or impossibility of circulation for Moroccans along the multiple registers I have been naming.

The appearance of the startling T-shirt here demonstrates how Marrakchi associates the circulation of commodities with her own national allegory. "America" on the T-shirt signifies the tolerance that the film argues Morocco does not have but should learn to have. The T-shirt—the last of the global commodities to make a cameo appearance—also suggests how Marrakchi anachronistically combines the national allegory form and the resolution she arrives at for her allegory (departure) to grapple with a Morocco already within the grip of globalization. The Morocco that she represents in *Marock*, that is to say, is already within what I have called the "age of circulation," in which national allegory must be insufficient. Thus, despite the fact that Rita is in tears when Mao (wearing "America") embraces her, that her friends are in tears as she leaves Morocco for France, and that the price for both scenes is the death of Youri, the film makes it possible to see Rita's departure for France and reconciliation with her brother as a particular form of comic resolution. This resolution should be disturbing. Indeed, *TelQuel* called it a "happy end," using the American English expression (missing the gerund ending), and claimed that this reconciliation between siblings without religious conversion is the final "taboo" the film breaks.[40] *TelQuel* was one of *Marock*'s greatest champions precisely on the basis of the film's willingness to challenge Moroccan taboos, so the ease with which the magazine's editors slipped into the epistemological trap of falling for Marrakchi's national allegory may be explained, yet again, by the peculiar seduction of the film's vernacular.

As *Marock* circulated from Paris to Cannes and from Tangier to Casablanca and the streets of Fes, where I bought a pirated copy on the sidewalks of the *ville nouvelle*, it was following yet another trajectory than the one it depicts. (I later bought a legal copy of the film when it began to be distributed in Canada and France.) The trajectory of the film's circulation in 2006 was much more complex than the representation of a young woman taking an airplane from a Casablanca that has disappointed her to a Paris that offers her escape. Discussions of the film raged on the Internet and in blogs and chatrooms from Bladi.net to Islamist sites (where Marrakchi's alleged support of Danish newspapers publication of cartoons depicting the Prophet was marshaled against her in one strand of discussion). The space in time from 1997, the fictional world of *Marock*, to 2005, when the film was made, is immense. And to imagine a social world of elite young Moroccans that does not involve mobile telephones, text messaging, and Internet-enabled video chatting seems as nostalgic as the classic rock and disco sounds that fill the film. To be sure, Marrakchi chose this time period in part because it approximated the time of her own adolescence in

Casablanca, as she stated in interviews, but also because she knew that these dominating technologies would soon alter the social environment within which an individual's relationship to the collective takes shape. This brings the lessons of cultures of circulation back together with the debate that Marrakchi's film engendered in 2006. If Marrakchi's and *Marock*'s Moroccanness was up for discussion, the location of the Morocco in which that debate might take place was no longer immediately clear or perfectly bound. In the coming years, with the increasing impact of digital technologies and software, such as YouTube, in Morocco, it would become yet more unbound. The case of Abdellah Taïa, which I turn to now, would bring together aspects of the debate over *Marock* and the ways in which Hamada played with a set of American cultural products and made them his own.

ABDELLAH TAÏA: THE COMING OUT OF MOROCCAN FICTION

Abdellah Taïa is the most interesting writer to emerge from Morocco in the twenty-first century, and, next to Tahar Ben Jelloun, he is quickly becoming the best known. This is so not just because he is the first Moroccan public figure to identify himself as homosexual or because he has become something of a media celebrity or even because he has inspired a generation of still younger Moroccan writers to find their voice and helped several of them to get published. He is important for all of these reasons, of course, especially from the perspective I have taken in this book, concerned as I am with how creative works inhabit the social worlds within which they function. But from the start of this discussion about Taïa I want to state simply that his literary voice is distinct, vivid, and original in Moroccan literature. Beyond all of the discussion and debate around his work and personal life and beyond his public statements, his writing itself is compelling; it holds up well on rereading. In 2012, he published his sixth book of fiction, the novel *Infidèles* (Faithless), which followed his award-winning

novel *Le jour du roi* (The day of the king, 2010) and four other books la-
beled variously *roman* (novel), *récit* (first-person narrative), or *livre* (book):
Une mélancholie arabe (2008, *An Arab melancholia* [2012]), *L'armée du salut*
(2006, *Salvation Army* [2009]), *Le rouge de tarbouche* (The red of the fez cap,
2005), and *Mon Maroc* (My Morocco, 2000). He has also edited and con-
tributed to two collections: the book *Lettres à un jeune marocain* (Letters to
a young Moroccan, 2009), which had a significant circulation in Morocco,
and a special issue of the Tangier literary journal *Nejma* entitled "Jean Genet
un saïnt marocain" (2010). I discuss some of his writing more closely later,
but because the relationship of Taïa's creative work to the context within
which it operates and the discussion of it is particularly intimate, it is there
I want to begin.

This most interesting of young Moroccan writers—he was born in
1973—makes vivid the circulation of Western models and ideas about sexuality inside Morocco as well as the limits of those models. Taïa's career is
intertwined with *TelQuel*, where he has been championed and which he has
himself used to further his literary career, and the way both have leveraged
Western models of sexual identity in the effort to open up Moroccan discussions of personal freedom is crucial. Further, Taïa's case offers a useful
way to engage and move beyond Joseph Massad's much debated argument
about the way the "Gay International" framed sexuality in the Arab world.
In brief, Massad argued that Western proponents of gay rights in Arab
countries had adopted a "missionary role" in the way they advocated for and
understood (homo)sexuality outside of the West, tending to universalize
their own experience. Massad critiqued the "orientalist impulse" in their
particular focus on Arab Muslim countries: "The[ir] larger mission . . . is
to liberate Arab and Muslim 'gays and lesbians' from the oppression under
which they allegedly live by transforming them from practitioners of
same-sex contact into subjects who identify as homosexual and gay." Borrowing from Michel Foucault's notion of the incitement to discourse in *The
History of Sexuality*, Massad asserted that the Gay International "both produces homosexuals, as well as gays and lesbians, where they do not exist,
and represses same-sex desires and practices that refuse to be assimilated
into its sexual epistemology."[41]

Although I will not rehearse the debate that ensued—Massad provoked a firestorm—I want to invoke it here because Taïa is my last example of what I call an "end of circulation." Here, Western constructs of homosexual identity jump publics as Taïa both participates in this discourse and then refuses it. The way Taïa engages Western models of sexuality ultimately detaches those models from the source, even though some of his most ardent Moroccan champions (and certainly his Western ones) have consistently tried to keep him within the discourse of the homosexual, which he selectively adopts as well. To be sure, many in the West—notably his publishers—have been trying to absorb his work and what it means back into a familiar idiom. For example, the American editions of two of his works translated into English, *Salvation Army* and *An Arab Melancholia*, note on their back covers that he is the "the first openly gay autobiographical writer published in Morocco," a characterization that has aided his rising popularity in the United States. (Note the awkward phrasing of this construction, though, which suggests its own breakdown.) The French and Moroccan editions do not use this formulation, though the most recent of Taïa's books published in France calls him an "icon" in Muslim countries, praised by youth and "modernists."[42]

Taïa's case may be the most complex of those I have taken up in this book because of the variety of forms and texts in circulation that come together in his work and life and the way he apparently picks up and sheds the identity attributed to him. Unraveling the strands of influence, deciding where one begins and ends, is difficult. For one thing, Taïa's fiction is notably autobiographical. In *Mon Maroc, Le rouge du tarbouche, L'armée du salut,* and *Une mélancholie arabe*, the first-person narrator is called "Abdellah Taïa" or simply "Abdellah"; the narrator's mother has the first name of Taïa's own mother, "M'Barka"; the young Abdellah of the books grows up in Salé, as did Taïa himself. Further, Taïa's public statements and press interviews often replicate or approximate the voice he uses in his first-person fiction. Here we have an author who apparently seamlessly blends his life, his work, and his public. (Even his professional emails affect the signature style of his literary work.) In order to discuss responsibly the literature signed by Abdellah Taïa, therefore, we must engage the context of its circulation. But from the standpoint of literary criticism, Taïa is elusive in part because of the way he moves between text and context. His sentences are open and mobile, and his literary themes are frequently about movement, constrictedness, and circulation.

A short story by Taïa was included in a 1999 collection copublished in France and Morocco, *Des Nouvelles du Maroc* (Stories from Morocco),[43] and the monograph *Mon Maroc* was published by Séguier in 2000. But it wasn't until the publication of *Le rouge de tarbouche* in late 2005 that he started to attract significant attention in Morocco.[44] To anyone who was reading his fiction, it was apparent that Taïa had been sexually active with other young men (one of the stories in *Mon Maroc*, "La poubelle des Américains" [The garbage heap of the Americans] leaves little doubt about what the ten-year-old Abdellah has done with a sixteen-year old neighbor boy, and that it is not the first time the first-person narrator, Abdellah, has done this).[45] But the number of readers of literary fiction in Morocco, especially fiction written in French, is small, and his first published stories attracted little attention.

A short article in *TelQuel* in January 2006, however, picked up on the sexual aspects of his work. Discussing *Le rouge du tarbouche* in the context of the Taïa's biography, journalist Chadwane Bensalmia wrote: "Two shadows hovered over these small obsessions: his childhood dream to make movies and a deep fear of his family's reaction when they discovered the secret of his homosexuality."[46] There it was, the explosive statement that would be picked up in the Arabic-language press, magnifying its reach, broadening its circulation, and setting the stage for copies to be delivered anonymously to members of Taïa's family (who did not know about his private sexual activities). Looking back three years later, Taïa commented that this short article changed his "status from 'the new hip Moroccan writer' to the 'new hip *gay* Moroccan writer.'" He went on: "At first people were talking only about the books and after that they were talking [about] the books and homosexuality."[47] Although this is true, it is also the case that there wasn't substantial discussion of Taïa's fiction before he was outed in *TelQuel*. The public discussion of Taïa's work was thus framed by *TelQuel* as gay fiction from the start.

In the original *TelQuel* article, Bensalmia discussed the frank sexuality found in *Le rouge du tarbouche* and posed the question why the author wrote it: "Is it an act of witnessing, a testament, a therapy? Abdellah Taïa rejects any label: 'It's simply the revelation of a reality of Moroccan society that I never came across in any literature.'"[48] Now, my claims that *TelQuel* framed Taïa as a gay author from the start of its coverage of his work and that the magazine's coverage was crucial to his fame are not intended to dismiss Taïa's own self-portrayal but rather to note how that portrayal is framed. In 2007, in the wake of the Ksar el Kebir affair, which I discuss later, Taïa will say, "I am a homosexual," but here his statement—"the revelation of a reality of Moroccan society that I never came across in any literature"— diverges from the magazine's use of him.

Taïa's comment opens up two aspects of his work that overlap but deserve their own treatment. First, of course, male–male love and physical intimacy between men were real and present in Morocco before he started writing, and in his writing he was revealing something that exists. Second, in authoring his books, he was adding something new to the body of Moroccan literature or literature about Morocco. Let me take these two aspects separately for a moment. In the first, Taïa implies that his fiction has a relationship to social reality and that his writing achieves a sort of realism. Describing his work as social realism would likely come as a surprise to his readers. True, there are scenes in his most autobiographical works that evoke his own youth in a large family in Salé, the harsh realities of the Moroccan street, sexual abuse, and other grittier aspects of urban Morocco. But Taïa's literary style is not realist, in either tone or the resolution of his scenes or how he transitions between episodes. His writing has evoked comparisons to dreams and cinema. The prominent Moroccan literary critic Abdellah Baïda, for example, has rejected the idea of Taïa's work as realist, comparing his writing style in *Le jour du roi* to a dream ("one enters into *Le jour du roi* the way one enters into a dream, imperceptibly") and noting that his depiction of themes of ignorance, poverty, superstition, prejudice, injustice, and absurdity is "far from the dry and cold tone of a sociological discourse, opting for fluidity of time and space."[49]

When I reviewed the English translation of *Une mélancholie arabe* for the New York–based magazine *Bookforum* in 2012, I suggested that Taïa's interest in cinema played itself out in his fiction: "As Taïa's life unfolds, the retelling of it is not quite the reordering of a life's experiences to make sense of it as in therapy. Rather, the way he crafts his stories, layering them, coming back to obsessions, is more like a filmmaker's montage, with flashbacks, voice-overs, and characters who blend into each other. Indeed, Taïa encourages us to see his novel as a film: The ambition to make cinema is what leads him to Paris and, later in the novel, to Cairo, where he participates in another project in exploring the melancholia he sees all around him."[50] Taïa's cinematic realism—or, rather, the way his writing evokes cinema—brings us back to his comment about what was missing, what he hadn't encountered, in literature about Morocco. Taïa suggests not that his writing is the expression of an identity—for example, a homosexual or "gay" identity—but that it brings into Moroccan literature and literature set in Morocco something he had not previously encountered. To be sure, expressions of love between men and sometimes of sexual intimacy between them have long been prevalent in French and American literature written and set in Morocco and the greater Maghreb, from André Gide's *L'Immoraliste* (1902) to Jean Genet's and Roland Barthes's Morocco journals and writings to the fiction of American expatriates such as William Burroughs and Alfred Chester. Taïa has spoken and written positively of the work of Genet and of the American expatriate writer Paul Bowles, who did not represent sexual love between men in his published fiction but was widely reputed in Morocco to have had intimate relationships with Moroccan men (Bowles himself consistently rejected identification as "gay" or "homosexual," but not, I think, because he was "closeted").[51] Taïa renders homage to Bowles in one of the pieces in his first book, *Mon Maroc*, where he calls him "the greatest Moroccan writer of today."[52] He has given Jean Genet still more attention, editing an entire collection in his honor and naming him a Moroccan saint. In *Le rouge du tarbouche*, the young Abdellah pays a visit to Genet's tomb in Larache (a coastal town in northern Morocco) and plays with the name Moroccans called him by—"Jinih"—which Taïa says sounds more Moroccan, "closer to me."[53] Roland Barthes's time in Morocco is also memorialized in *Le rouge du tarbouche*.[54] And of course writers of Moroccan nationality, including Mohamed Choukri and Rachid O. (the author of a sexually explicit autobiographical trilogy appearing between

1995 and 1998), had depicted male–male intimacy in the first person, and Bahaa Trabelsi had written in the third person about a male couple in her novel *Une vie à trois* (A life as three, 2000), which begins with a preface in which the female narrator says she met the men in a Casablanca bar.[55]

So what is it that Taïa thinks he was giving to Moroccan literature that hadn't been there before? There was something about the two aspects he conjoined in his comment: representing a social reality and offering something new to literature of Morocco. (I write "the literature of Morocco" rather than "Moroccan literature" to maintain the ambiguity of the writer's nationality; Taïa teaches us to see the work of Genet and Bowles, for instance, as a part of Moroccan literature.)[56] Taïa had championed the work of Mohamed Choukri, in particular—the Tangier writer who first came to prominence when his autobiographical novel *al-Khubz al-hafi* (Dry bread [i.e., bread with no sauce], 1982) appeared in Paul Bowles's English translation, with Bowles's poetic title *For Bread Alone* (1973), and who later wrote a book about Jean Genet (also translated by Paul Bowles as *Jean Genet in Tangier* [1974]). In Choukri's first book, sex acts are portrayed vividly. For Taïa, Choukri described poverty and despair in a way that few others had. He calls *For Bread Alone* an "extraordinary" book, one that spoke of a "world ignored and scorned by Moroccan intellectuals."[57]

So what did Taïa mean by his claim that his work was "the revelation of a reality of Moroccan society that [he] never came across in any literature"? The implication—at least as framed by *TelQuel*—was that Taïa offered a new *identity* to Moroccan literature, which is a lazy formulation that assumes no difference or distance between author and narrator, between life and art. I argue that Taïa means something about his particular literary form, neither realist nor closed. The openness of Taïa's sentences—the space within them so gracefully and evocatively suggested in his grammar, his ellipses, his form—is what he meant.

Taïa's public declaration of his homosexuality is, to be sure, courageous in a country where homosexual acts are illegal and homosexual identities are socially condemned. As *TelQuel* itself had reported in a 2004 cover story that made no mention of Taïa: "Homosexuality in Morocco is hit with a double H: *hshuma* (shame) and *haram* (sin). Only a year ago, Mohamed

Asseban, member of the Council of Ulama of Rabat-Salé, declared to the press 'burn gays at the stake.' Like its religion and its law, Moroccan society is uncontestably homophobic."[58]

Though Taïa surely wasn't hiding from identifying his sexuality, neither was he rushing to name it or delimit it. Yet if he rejected labels, *TelQuel* surely did not. The following summer, June 2007, the magazine depicted him on its cover with the word *homosexual* in large type above his face (figure 4.4). Framed across top and bottom horizontal axes of the cover by typescript and on the vertical axes by curtains decorated with the familiar eight-point star (or *sabniyyah*) readily identified as a Moroccan pattern, Taïa was walled in by the graphic design, a metaphor for the text of the article itself. For *TelQuel*, the story about Taïa was clearly a part of a larger editorial mission to open the discussion of sexuality to the nation and followed not only the earlier interview with him from the previous year but also the cover story from 2004. Both covers were provocative. If in 2004 the men on the cover of *TelQuel* turned their backs to the camera (figure 4.5), in 2007 Taïa faced directly into the lens. Although Taïa may have been captured by *TelQuel*'s designers, reporters, and editorial mission, he was gazing directly into the *TelQuel*'s readers' eyes—and gaining readers of his own in so doing.

Valérie Orlando has written about *TelQuel* in the context of a number of magazines founded since the death of King Hassan II in 1999. She argues that from its founding in 2000 *TelQuel* has been "dedicated to bringing Morocco's repressed memory and history to the [Moroccan] public's attention in order to cultivate productive debate in a communicative public space."[59] A *TelQuel* journalist, Nadia Lamlili, told Orlando in January 2007 that the magazine was then focusing on three specific subjects:

- The role of the monarchy in the future
- Sexuality, including gender, homosexuality, and premarital sexuality
- Religion and its place in civil society

Orlando remarks that the "young journalists believe that their abrasive, 'in your face' style is necessary in order to shock readers, waking them up to the reality of their country,"[60] a point borne out by the magazine's coverage of

FIGURE 4.4 Abdellah Taïa on the cover of *Tel Quel*, June 9–15, 2007.
(Reproduced with permission of TelQuel Media)

Taïa, which of course extended beyond cover design. The 2007 cover story goes so far as to predict or imagine future conflicts for Taïa himself: "The PJD is perfectly capable of posing, tomorrow, an oral question in Parliament to ask for a judgment or prohibition of the writer. The offensive directed, on another plane, by the party of Saad-Eddine El Othmani against the film *Marock* risks being repeated, this time against a person: Abdellah Taïa."[61]

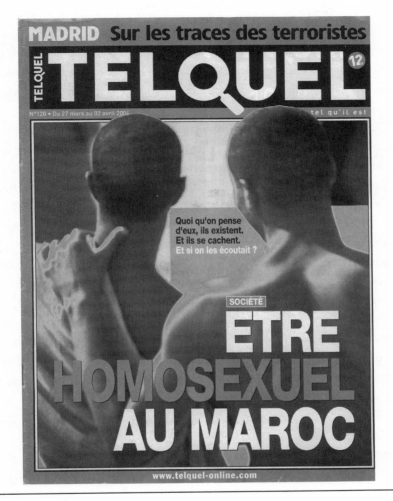

FIGURE 4.5 The over of *TelQuel*, March 27–April 2, 2004.
(Reproduced with permission of TelQuel Media)

Diverging from retrospective coverage, the reporting here takes on the future tense—indeed, the future conditional. The PJD *might* decide to replicate the logic it used in arguing for the censorship of the film *Marock* and prohibit the writer Taïa himself. Now, I am not suggesting that it was so far-fetched to imagine that the PJD would object to Taïa's public declaration of his homosexuality but rather pointing out that it was *TelQuel* itself that was raising the question. In making the link to Marrakchi's film *Marock* and the debate about her film from the previous year, *TelQuel* was pushing the debate. Marrakchi and Taïa, despite the differences of their themes, were linked in *TelQuel*'s editorial eye. The "scandal" was created by that same editorial vision.

Taïa has not objected to this linkage, except subtly in the 2009 interview I quoted earlier when he remarked that after *TelQuel*'s coverage he was no longer the "new hip Moroccan writer" but now always the "new hip *gay* Moroccan writer." We can say, then, that *TelQuel* limited Taïa's circulation even while launching it. In other words, *TelQuel*'s coverage of Taïa as a "hip *gay* Moroccan writer" made him a celebrity but also limited that celebrity to its own terms and to advance its own editorial project. One need not take a side on the magazine's mission to open up the discussion of Moroccan sexuality to note that it reduced the means of the author's circulation to his sexuality. What could the author do to escape this cycle?

Before attempting to develop the answer, there is one more strand to this story: YouTube. YouTube, the famous video-sharing website, was founded in the United States in 2005 and debuted in November of that year. During the following year, its use grew exponentially, and Google purchased the company in November 2006. In 2007, it quickly became clear that YouTube had the potential to affect Moroccan society. In July 2007, a Moroccan who identified himself only as the "sniper of Targuist," a town in northern Morocco, posted the first of a series of videos on YouTube that showed Moroccan gendarmes accepting bribes from drivers on the highway (figure 4.6). Police corruption was something that Moroccans knew to be a fact of daily life, even if it was officially denied. The videos posted by the so-called sniper—he shot from a distance and hit his target—quickly gained millions of views (the three primary postings by TarSniper—one has been removed— were viewed approximately 1.7 million times and rebroadcast or reposted by others). The videos shot and posted by the sniper of Targuist shocked Morocco profoundly.[62]

In the immediate wake of the Targuist sniper's videos, another video posted to YouTube by a Moroccan would have major repercussions. A gay

FIGURE 4.6 Still from the first of the Targuist Sniper's videos, posted July 8, 2007.

Moroccan couple living in the northern city of Ksar el Kebir, who were well known locally because one was a reputed smuggler of alcohol, held a private party on November 18 and 19, 2007. During the party, the two men staged a traditional Moroccan wedding for themselves, with one wearing the traditional clothing worn by Moroccan women during marriage. A guest at the party took amateur video of the celebration on his phone, which circulated locally for a day or two until an anonymous individual posted it on YouTube on November 21. Daily newspapers—including the popular Arabic-language papers *al Massae*, *Assabahia*, and *Attajdid*—reported on the event. By November 23, thousands of enraged Moroccans had gathered outside the door of the wealthy couple, threatening violence and reminding observers of a lynch mob. More Moroccan media descended on the small city. A national crisis was at hand.

Among the coverage conducted by socially liberal publications, *Le Journal Hebdomadaire* and *TelQuel* dedicated their covers to the Ksar el Kebir

FIGURE 4.7 The cover of *Le Journal Hebdomadaire*, December 1–7, 2007.

affair. *TelQuel*'s cover headline, "La Chasse aux homos" (Hunting gays), ran across a news photo of the menacing crowds. *Le Journal* took a different tack with its cover and made reference to Steven Soderbergh's film *Sex, Lies, and Videotape* (1989): its headline was "Homos, mensonges, et videos" (Gays, lies, and videos) (figure 4.7). Reproducing a still from the notorious YouTube video itself, *Le Journal*'s cover suggested neatly the ways in which the new technology coming from the West might be allied with the cultural products that earlier stood for a style now identifiable as from the West.

In this case, the video was shot by a Moroccan, and the subject was Moroccan. What the reference to *Sex, Lies, and Videotape* neatly suggested, however, was that the form of an individually shot and distributed video had come in from the outside and disrupted the social fabric of Morocco. For *Le Journal*, as for *TelQuel*, this intrusive upsetting of the Moroccan cultural balance was welcome. And to be sure, the issue was not that the event itself was unknown or unheard of—as noted, the Moroccan couple was well known—but that the "media fury" in response to the posting on YouTube turned the northern city of Ksar el Kebir into a cultural and almost physical battleground.

Taïa took a stand. *Le Journal* published a brief interview with him, included his photo, and described him as follows: "Abdellah Taïa: Écrivain et homosexuel assumé" (writer and admitted homosexual). Choosing the most sensational statement from his interview as its pull quote—"je ne suis pas une sale pédé" (I am not a dirty faggot)—*Le Journal* quoted Taïa as commenting:

It's still very bizarre, this negative, exaggerated reaction by Moroccan society as soon as one speaks of homosexuality, which has existed everywhere, in all social milieu, in Marrakech just as in Sidi Slimane. Morocco, a paternalistic society, macho, wants to believe and to make people believe that virility is possible only within the framework of heterosexuality. Homosexuality would be, of course, a Western vice. We are the pure, the others are the unbelievers, the sinners, and they will go to hell, while we, of course, will go to heaven. . . . Morocco is at base and despite its so-called legendary hospitality a closed country. The country is still a gigantic prison for both its homosexual and heterosexual citizens.[63]

What Taïa suggests is that the framework—the "cadre"—is constricted or forced by the question of West versus "East." YouTube intrudes here—as medium but also as form that layers the depiction of something thoroughly and profoundly Moroccan now as "foreign" or "Western." The technology and the expression of sexuality are inextricable. In an interview in 2009, Taïa looked back and confirmed this point: "For me, what happened at Ksar el Kebir was the Moroccan equivalent of Stonewall." If the reference to Stonewall when speaking to a Western journalist was distracting, Taïa continued: "Something historic happened there, in the interior of Morocco, between Moroccans, and the West had nothing to do with it."[64] The technology might have come from the West, but the West had nothing to do with the video or the events and discussions it provoked in Morocco. YouTube had jumped publics. The Ksar el Kebir "wedding" video makes no sense in the United States except as a "gay marriage," which it is not.

So is there a way out of this apparent contradiction? Earlier I discussed Taïa's literary form as akin to cinema, distinct from therapy or testimony, on the one hand, and from realism or "gay fiction" on the other. Taïa, of course, had a biographical connection to cinema. It was what he first wanted to do as an artist (although the first chapter of *Mon Maroc* describes a formative year in the Bibliotheque nationale of Rabat), and he has since directed a film adaptation of his novel *Salvation Army*, which premiered in 2013. But there is more. In *Le rouge du tarbouche*, Taïa offers a lesson:

> An eternity ago, my older brother Abdelkebir showed us, to little Mustapha and me, an unforgettable film by Alfred Hitchcock, a film that circulates still in the alleys of my memory, even though I only saw it once and only once: *Rear Window*. When my brain comes to think of that fat filmmaker, who would have been superb in a white *Fassi djellaba*, it is this feature film that surges and projects itself immediately upon the screen of my eyes. James Stewart, his leg in a cast, immobile, elegant, on the *point de croquet* as always, facing a window that looks out on a courtyard. He can see everything. Several stories at once. Serialized stories. He gets a lot out of it. He is aided by his maid, then by his fiancée, the beautiful blonde Grace Kelly (and her haute couture dresses and her pearls that sparkled . . .). As usual in Hitchcock, there will be a crime, a conjugal crime. *Rear Window* came into me *at the moment when I began to take cinema seriously*—it was not just an amusement, it was something else: an art! Since then, this art follows me every day. I see with cinema permanently.

I live with cinema constantly. I see with *Rear Window*. I am a voyeur. (emphasis added)[65]

The cinematic aspects of Taïa's literary writing emerge from the voyeurism he associates with cinema and with Hitchcock in particular. Taïa's Hitchcock always places a conjugal crime at the center, which is both an interpretation of Hitchcock and (more) a reflection of the way in which Taïa's life and literary career are oriented around the conjugal crime he describes so powerfully and poignantly in *Une mélancholie arabe*: his family sleeping together, too intimately, the father in one room, his older brother in another, and Abdellah, his mother, and six other siblings in a third. Once a week, his father appears and lures his mother away from Abdellah and his sisters for sex. An incestuous family from the start. And later, Abdellah sleeps with his older brother, next to him, his hero, the brother who shows him *Rear Window* in *Le rouge du tarbouche*.

What makes Taïa so interesting is how he embraces the Hitchcock film and takes it on as his own. He is not struggling with postcolonial anxiety against the literary aura of Jean Genet or Paul Bowles or Alfred Hitchcock, as Tahar Ben Jelloun does with Bowles in *Partir* (Leaving Tangier).[66] Hitchcock is Taïa's to do with what he will, an affair for Moroccans from which Hitchcock is isolated. Taïa gives us example after example in his fiction of ways he can incorporate a foreign author or text into his own work and for his own local (Moroccan) purposes.

In a 2009 interview with Brian Whitaker, Taïa provides yet another example of how American texts circulate into his work and appear there without anxiety—but detached from their U.S. referent. Here we have another remarkable memory about cinema. Discussing the time after he was "outed" by *TelQuel*, he reflects:

[A]fter a few days I realized that no one called me to ask me how I was, how I had managed to live all these years with the fact that I am homosexual. . . . No one cared. I realized that, again, it was about them, about their names and reputations, not about me. It was about what my sister's colleagues would say, what the neighbors would say. And, I remembered

Douglas Sirk's masterpiece film, *All That Heaven Allows*, and how he shows that society tries to destroy the love between the characters played by Jane Wyman and Rock Hudson. So, during those two weeks of feeling completely naked, I bought the DVD of this film and watched it several times, maybe ten times. And it helped me a lot to become strong again. To be free without tears. Again: cinema saved me as it did when I was a child and had no place to go and cry, except the cheap movie theatres in my poor town, Salé.[67]

Douglas Sirk is an icon of queer sensibility in the United States. Just at the moment when *TelQuel* recasts Taïa as a "gay writer," Taïa takes up Sirk. It is as if he is performing the translation of an unlabeled or unmarked identity into an identity that would resonate as a headline. The digital copy of *All That Heaven Allows* (the DVD) comes to his rescue, saves him from the social nakedness of his exposure by *TelQuel*—and by "exposure" I don't mean his "coming out" but rather the way in which *TelQuel* reduced his sexuality to a stark and recognizable model of sexual identity (recognizable within the Western framework that *TelQuel* was adopting), which may have boxed him in as much as it liberated him. Repeated viewings of the Sirk film open up a space and give Taïa a place to go, just as Hitchcock gave him a way to be a voyeur. He can then remake himself in the gaps—in the disjuncture of *décalage*—that the Sirk DVD permits him. This remaking is in the context of a familiar Western icon (Sirk), but it will lead to a kind of freedom—without tears—that detaches from the source. And these repeated viewings, this cinematic voyeurism, give him a language that is not quite the language of *TelQuel*—though it will be propelled forward by *TelQuel*— to bring back to Moroccan literature something that was not there before.

ENVOI

This chapter has focused on three episodes from the middle and later years of the first decade of the 2000s: the Miloudi video products made by Hamada from 2003 to 2005; the scandal around Laïla Marrakchi's film *Marock* in 2006; and the response and debate around Abdellah Taïa's fiction in 2006 and 2007. Much has changed in the meantime, of course, and through the years that passed while I did the research for this book, I spent extensive time in Morocco and kept up with new cinema and fiction through at least December 2012, when I returned to the Festival International du Film de Marrakech. In December 2012, I watched eight new Moroccan films, mostly by younger directors, including Faouzi Bensaidi (b. 1967), Leïla Kilani (b. 1970), Brahim Chkiri (b. 1969), Nour-Eddine Lakhmari (b. 1964), and Nabil Ayouch (b. 1969). In 2012 and then again in 2014, when I returned to do further research beyond the purview of this chapter, I interviewed younger writers who follow Taïa—some of whom he has promoted, including several of the younger contributors to *Lettres à un jeune marocain*, such as Fadwa Islah (b. 1979) and Hicham Tahir (b. 1989), who write in French, and Sanaa Elaji (b. 1977), a bold journalist, columnist, and novelist who writes in Arabic. Tahir's first book, *Jaabouq* (The joint), was published in 2013 and brings Moroccan fiction forward into yet another stage with a frankness about sexuality that might not have been possible without Taïa. Beyond writers and journalists, a new generation of Moroccan activists—who overlap with several of the writers and filmmakers named here—is using social networking software both to magnify the impact of their brave protests for lesbian, gay, bisexual, transgender, and queer rights and as a forum for protest and activism in itself. All of this new activity in the Moroccan cultural sphere is exciting and deserves careful attention.

I decided to focus this chapter on the years 2003 to 2008, however, because they seem to me a key turning point to understand first. The new crop of Moroccan films exhibited over and again the influence of what I call a Hollywood "look," now taken in multiple directions. And to read the fiction or blogs of Hicham Tahir or to encounter the presence of Fadwa Islah—whom I interviewed in August 2014 as she finished the editing of her bold new novel—on the page or to follow the columns and jokes of Sanaa Elaji is to witness new strategies and new voices that define themselves within a Moroccan context even while conversant and cosmopolitan in their engagement with global culture. I mean, of course, not to privilege either the local or the global because it came first but to focus on transitional moments and texts and the debates that surround them as a critical strategy. Developing reading and interpretive strategies is my goal here, but in the digital age analyzing forms of circulation—or forms in circulation—may be in itself an end.

EPILOGUE

Embracing Orientalism in the Homeland

O NE OF THE ASSUMPTIONS about globalization in the realm of culture is that there is endless circulation, that the technologies of the digital age that have brought so many cultural products from the United States to the Middle East and North Africa might bring them back home to Americans after their journey abroad—safe and sound, as it were. In our technocentric moment, digital technologies and circulation are imagined as intertwined, with everything propelled seamlessly via the former and nothing outside the reach of the latter. If my discussion of some of the ways in which American cultural forms have been altered, localized, and disoriented in their Egyptian, Iranian, and Moroccan adaptions is accurate, we should wonder if perhaps in their return to the United States they might become repatriated. With a little debriefing, maybe they can teach us something about ourselves we didn't know.

Yes, you can find some clips of *Shrek* dubbed into Persian on YouTube if you take a look. You can order online some of the Egyptian and Moroccan literary works or perhaps a couple of the films I have discussed and get them shipped directly to your front door. (Too few are translated into English, though, and several are not available online—imagine that!—and the DVDs have the wrong region code.) To be sure, very little of the material I have discussed in this book circulates back to the United States in any substantial quantity or with much impact. Abdellah Taïa's novels are slowly but surely being translated into English, but the public who will read them in the United States is very limited. Iranian new wave filmmakers such as Kiarostami, the Makhmalbafs, Panahi, and Farhadi may have been the darlings of the film festival set in New York, Chicago, and Los Angeles, but that counterpublic, too, was small, and many of its members already had knowledge of Iranian society. The Arab uprisings of 2010–2011 riveted American attention for months, and commercial book publishers briefly tried to capitalize on the attention that U.S. media lavished on Egypt, Tunisia, and Libya. But Magdy El Shafee's graphic novel *Metro*, which was published by a major New York commercial house sixteen months after the Tahrir uprisings, did not get much attention, and two years after its release, as I write this epilogue, the New York edition of *Metro* languishes, with an Amazon sales rank well higher than 1 million. Hardly a best seller, despite the return of the brutal police state he describes.

That these texts from the Middle East and North Africa reach limited audiences in the United States should not be surprising. I have argued in this book that the ways in which American cultural products and forms are altered as they jump publics make it impossible to translate them back, except laboriously, and that they lose their humor or critical edge in the process. The situation is reminiscent of the case of Mark Twain's "Celebrated Jumping Frog of Calaveras County," the wildly popular story of 1865. Decades after its initial publication, Twain encountered a French translation published in Paris. Twain, in turn, translated this French version of his story back into English. His goal, he wrote in 1903, was to demonstrate that the French translator "has not translated it at all; he has simply mixed it all up; it is no more like the Jumping Frog when he gets through with it than I am like a meridian of longitude."[1] Twain had an enormous amount of fun translating the French translation of his work into English, of course, and his grammar in the second English version is heavily French inflected; it reads like what you would get with early versions of Google translate! Yet there is a serious point embedded in Twain's fun. The jumping frog jumped publics, and like the frog in the original—surreptitiously loaded with quail shot so that it could not jump—the translation is heavy. If the French appreciated something different in Twain's tale from what American audiences got from it, then the clunky third version of the story shows something important: a story may be able to move across publics (once, at least), but it is difficult for the *uptake* in its new public to move again to yet another public.[2] In other words, as the French took up Twain's tale and made it their own, it was entextualized in such a way that the uptake itself became embedded in the translation, and *that* uptake evaded further circulation. Twain turned the French uptake into an object of humor, which highlights the process. Enjoying Twain's English translation of the French translation requires a sense of how French operates; otherwise, the linguistic jokes fall flat.

If circulation is not an *aller-retour* trip, there is, however, another alternative. After all, doesn't circulation work in the other direction, too? There have been flows of people from the Middle East and North Africa westward to the United States for longer than the American century, encompassing the first wave of large-scale migration of Lebanese to the United States in the nineteenth and early twentieth centuries and later flows of Arabs and Iranians to North America. These people came for a range of reasons, including to escape a political situation (Iranians after the 1979 revolution), to find refuge (Palestinians, Iraqis, Syrians), and to seek economic opportunities (greater chances for employment for young Moroccans), and they did not of course leave their love for and attachment to their cultures of origin at Ellis Island or at passport control at Los Angeles International Airport. The technologies of the digital age, especially satellite television and the Internet, have for decades brought cultural products from the Middle East to the United States for those who know where to look for them, and the diasporas of the Middle East and North Africa have maintained cultural ties accordingly. Hamid Naficy's classic work *The Making of Exile Culture* drew attention to the diasporic communities in Los Angeles that cohered around watching Iranian television and found that some such communities affiliated across national and ethnic lines and often had only ancestry in the Middle East region in common: "Shared cultures and history allow cross-viewing among not only Iranian subethnics but also other Middle Eastern populations in diaspora." Naficy tells the story of an elderly Jewish émigré from Palestine who watched Iranian programs even though she didn't understand the Persian: "The nostalgic music and visuals of exile music videos remind her of her own childhood and homeland."[3] But again, these diasporic communities engage with most of the works from the Middle East–North Africa region that make it to the United States.

These diasporic communities lead us to wonder: perhaps the circulation of cultural artifacts from the Middle East and North Africa to the United States at large might provide an antidote to older traditions of Orientalism. Perhaps greater access to those cultural products might bring Americans into more direct contact with creative people from the region and open up otherwise binary perspectives. In the long and painful years since September 11, 2001, the media obsession with the Middle East and North Africa has of course had an impact on nearly every category of contemporary cultural production in the United States. As noted in a previous chapter, more than two decades ago Edward Said quipped: "American attention works in spurts; great masses of rhetoric and huge resources are lavished somewhere (Vietnam, Libya, Iraq, Panama) followed by virtual silence."[4] Those from the region with a story to tell or a creative work to show have a greater possibility to share or present their work in the U.S. market during such moments—and we are in one now—than at any other time.

So what does make it back to the United States? What works do U.S. publishers and distributors circulate? The sad truth is that when creative works by authors from the Middle East and North Africa *have* reached larger audiences in the United States during the first decade and a half of the twenty-first century, they have tended to confirm prevailing and debilitating stereotypes about the region. As noted in earlier chapters, Ali Behdad and Juliet Williams identify a recent phenomenon they call "neo-Orientalism": texts about the Middle East published in English by writers with origins in the region whose "self-proclaimed authenticity sanctions and authorizes their discourse."[5] In their important essay, Behdad and Williams focus on the high number of memoirs by Iranian women published in English in the first decade of the twenty-first century, such as the best-selling *Reading Lolita in Tehran* (2003) by Azar Nafisi and *Journey from the Land of No: A Girlhood Caught in Revolutionary Iran* (2004) by Roya Hakakian. Such works are explicitly political in their intent and either explicitly or implicitly justify U.S. intervention in the region through what Behdad and Williams call their "ahistorical historicism." Namely, these authors purport to teach American readers the history of some aspect of the region that has gone wrong while at the same time making historical errors or misleading statements—say, Nafisi's inaccurate history of veiling in Iran before the revolution—and suggest that outside assistance is required to set Iran back on its correct course.

For Behdad and Williams, Marjane Satrapi's wonderful graphic novel *Persepolis*—written and first published in Paris in 2000—was the exception that proved the rule in large part (in their analysis) because of the ways in which Satrapi refused a *New York Times* reporter's attempt to essentialize her as a Muslim invested in "denounc[ing] Islamic fanaticism." (In her interview with Deborah Solomon in the *New York Times Magazine*, Satrapi turned Solomon's questions on themselves. Solomon disagreed with Satrapi when the latter claimed that Iranian veiling and Western unveiling of women are "equally reductive" of women. Satrapi then called out the Western hypocrisy around body image and plastic surgery: "If in Muslim countries they try to cover the woman, in America they try to make them look like a piece of meat.")[6] One might go further and note that within her comics themselves, Satrapi is able efficiently to critique both Iranian contradictions in the obsession with the dangers of American culture and the shallow ways in which the West regards Iran. Her simple, even naive style of drawing allows her, via her autobiographical character Marji, to reveal the paradoxes inherent in both Iran's and the West's regard of each other.

Nonetheless, the ways in which *Persepolis* was read in the United States and adopted in schools tended to focus more on the perfidious nature of Iran than on Satrapi's critique of the limitations of the West. As Satrapi commented on the U.S. publication of the second volume of *Persepolis* in 2004 (the original French edition appeared in four volumes, whereas the American edition was divided into two, appearing in 2003 and 2004, respectively), in the first book she had "the benefit of being cute, and not really responsible for the world around me. In the second book, I'm absolutely not cute anymore."[7] For schools, the first volume offered a user-friendly approach to teaching the Iranian Revolution, and the younger Marji in *Persepolis: The Story of a Childhood* offered a more charismatic hero than the older Marji in *Persepolis 2: The Story of a Return*, which begins when a fifteen-year-old Marji emigrates from Iran to Vienna. In 2013, the Chicago Public School system pulled its copies of the graphic novel from school libraries and restricted access for students in grade 11 and lower.[8] Barbara Byrd-Bennett, the CEO of Chicago Public Schools, named the book's "graphic language and images" as the reason; by "graphic," Byrd-Bennett was not referring to the fact that the book was a graphic novel, of course, but rather to the frames that rendered scenes of torture, apparently too vividly.[9] The paradox was apparent. As the manager of Chicago's feminist bookstore Women & Children First commented, it was "'shocking and ironic' that a book about freedom and freedom of expression would itself be restricted by [Chicago Public Schools]."[10] Satrapi herself responded: "[T]his whole story in Chicago was absolutely shocking to me. They're saying it's inappropriate for kids because of the scenes of torture that were in just a couple of frames—in a book that is 200 pages long! It's as if children never killed anybody in their video games, or as if they had never seen any films that contain violence. As you know, in America, kids can watch violent movies, and it's not a problem, but if you say the word 'fuck,' that is unacceptable. Children are exposed to violence. But if it's the violence of guns on TV, that is accepted."[11]

Despite their differences, what authors such as Satrapi, Nafisi, and Hakakian have in common is that they are, as Behdad and Williams put it, "Middle Eastern women and men who use their native subjectivity and newfound agency in the West to render otherwise biased accounts of the region . . . more authoritative and objective."[12] Nafisi and Hakakian play on this assigned authority or representativeness, and Satrapi finds it difficult to escape. Either way, the alchemy happens in the U.S. marketplace, whether in the worlds of publishing or in the mediascape populated by talking heads, both of which desire "native informants." Now, I would be the last critic to argue that people with origins or heritage in the Middle East region should not comment on that region for viewers and readers in the United States, but the point is that biases are of course carried over with the experience of exile or diaspora (quite notably in the case of Iran) and that these biases are often effaced via the logic that the native informant is necessarily unbiased and objective because of his or her heritage. Neo-Orientalism therefore may have continuities with the past, but, as Behdad and Williams argue, it also is a "supplement to enduring modes of Orientalist representation."[13] Such memoirs proliferate in what seems to have become an entire genre—the memoir by the previously unknown figure, who serves as native informant to a little-known part of the world. This proliferation of memoirs in turn limits other Iranians' or Egyptians' or Moroccans' ability to publish in different genres in the United States. The market expects new titles to follow in the preestablished niche.

The Iranian memoir is only a part of the terrain in the new fascination with the Middle East. In the wake of the Tahrir uprisings, for example, as I discussed in chapter 2, the work of Alaa Al Aswany stood in for a much more complicated group of writers working in Cairo. For many, Al Aswany's melodramatic novel *The Yacoubian Building* confirmed the Orientalist perspective on Egypt that was being revised in Cairo by writers of the next generation. Based on the ways that Al Aswany's novel was translated and circulated in the United States in 2011 and after, therefore, he can be grouped with those whom Behdad and Williams call the neo-Orientalists. Within neo-Orientalism, as I am describing it, both the author and the U.S. marketplace (publishing world plus media outlets) work together, creating and sustaining the writer's authority to represent his or her region—to be its representative. The author writes and speaks; the U.S. marketplace publishes and publicizes and effectively filters out competing voices that might challenge the perspective of the chosen representative.

Neo-Orientalism does not replace Orientalism, however; it supplements it. Beyond the popular Iranian memoirists and those representative Arab "native informants" propelled by the U.S. marketplace, can we claim that classic Orientalism endures in the twenty-first century? If so, does Orientalism operate differently in the digital age?

The persistence of Orientalist patterns of representing the Middle East and North Africa is visible in a staggering quantity of representations of the region in contemporary U.S. literature, television serials, comedy, and consumer culture—works that cross the highbrow–lowbrow divide. That which Edward Said predicted twenty years ago, alas, remains true, but with a twist. Since September 2001, the United States has been in a perpetual state of war or troop deployment to sustain the military occupation of two nation-states in the Middle East; we have been in an extended version of that Saidian "spurt" of attention. American Orientalism has been not only renewed but also extended and exaggerated.

It bears recalling that by "Orientalism," Said meant something a bit more nuanced than the common (mis)usage of the term. His three-part definition noted that Orientalism was, first, an academic field of inquiry that studied, cataloged, and archived a part of the world it referred to as "the Orient."[14] For the most part, we have given up the term *Orient* to designate the area of study and adopted other denominations, but Orientalism itself is enduring. The academic and scholarly landscape has been transformed by the military invasion and occupation, with massive new resources and interest by government funding agencies and private donors alike available to develop programs and academic departments. This transformation comes with a level of attention to Middle East studies that can at times be intense. Scholars in the field have had to tread carefully and to face pressures from groups outside the university who can mobilize resources and attention that can be overwhelming or at times intimidating to those who diverge from mainstream or traditionally dominant positions. In this sense, the enduring aspects of American Orientalism make the numerous contests over the field itself in the past decade and a half—from political accusations of radical politics on both congressional and state levels in the wake of September 11, 2001, to the fights over the Boycott, Divest, Sanction movement in the present moment—quite important.

Second, Said defined Orientalism as a "style of thought" based on a distinction between Orient and Occident, imagined as an "ontological and epistemological distinction"—in other words, a way of understanding the world as binary.[15] There are still those who maintain these binaries, though the term *Orient* has been replaced by the phrase "the Muslim world" or "the Arab world" or "the Middle East," all constructs that collapse internal differences and diversity in place of an imagined totality.[16] In such designations, distinctions between Arab countries or Muslim societies across the world are minimized so that they remain lumped together in a different universe from the United States. A remainder of Orientalism is left over in the twenty-first century: anxieties over the ways in which globalization links these apparently disparate or cut-off parts of the world. But the process of what Said called the third aspect of Orientalism, a "corporate institution for *dealing with* the Orient,"[17] remains continuous. In Said's account, Europeans needed Orientalism as a way to understand the lands being occupied by France and Britain and to justify to themselves how they could tolerate such explicit aggression. Here is where the new American Orientalism—and the embrace of it—serves its cultural purpose, where it does cultural "work."

One would think that globalization and the digital age would put unbearable pressure on Orientalism, especially since the digital age collapses those distances on which Orientalism relies. How can one maintain a binarism when the points of connection and the means by which the worlds connect are ubiquitous and undeniable?

And yet the persistence and renewal of Orientalism in the past five years are notable. The tone of major and popular works such as Craig Thompson's epic graphic novel *Habibi* (2011), the Showtime television serial *Homeland* (2011–), the FX television series *Tyrant* (2014–), literary novels such as *The Yellow Birds* (2012) by Kevin Powers and *A Hologram for the King* (2012) by Dave Eggers—both finalists for the National Book Award—and even the massive popularity of Moroccan style in fashion, beauty, and home-design consumer culture in the past decade (and the way Morocco is described within those marketing mechanisms) go beyond mere persistence of Orientalism to at times the outright embrace of it. To be sure, each of these representations handles its subject differently, with authors or creative teams holding political positions that range from the liberal (Eggers) to the neoconservative (*Tyrant* producer-creators Howard Gordon and Gideon Raff), but there is definitely a new and quickly deepening archive of twenty-first-century American Orientalism.

All of these representations appear in a context where Said's critique is well known and studied in the universities that educated many of the authors of these representations. The term *Orientalism* itself is a part of the cultural landscape. When asked directly whether he distinguished between using Orientalism as a "playground" and reproducing it in his graphic novel *Habibi*, Craig Thompson responded: "As for the charge of Orientalism, I knew it was going to come up no matter what, so why not embrace it?"[18]

Given that the recurrence of Orientalism takes place within the context of continued—even expanded—U.S. political and military presence in the region and that all the examples I have given (except perhaps the fashion) are explicitly political, either in authorial intent or content, we can recognize a continuity in the tradition of American Orientalism that goes back as least as far as the 1942 military landings at Casablanca (and the Warner Bros. film of the same name). In the 1940s and 1950s, as I argue in my book *Morocco Bound*, American Orientalist texts represented a part of the world generally considered exotic to Americans even as the United States was emerging as a global superpower with increasing interests around the world. In that period, as opposed to our own, U.S. cultural producers recognized that European colonialism preceded American presence. As a result, such artists, filmmakers, and writers were as interested in attending to French and British models of internationalism as they were caught up in portraying Arab exoticism. That interest changed progressively after 1973, when the domestic impact of U.S. presence in the Middle East became increasingly fraught, after which American representations of the Middle East and North Africa, especially in fiction and film, took on a different tenor.

In the post-2001 period, there has been a crucial twist. Unlike the neo-Orientalism of the Iranian memoirists or of American Orientalists of the twentieth century, the twenty-first-century Orientalists are aware of and sometimes fascinated by the question of circulation. It is the specter that haunts this body of work—sometimes even its provocation. Alternatively a theme inscribed in the work and a shadow cast over it, circulation and the anxiety it provokes run through the works of the new American Orientalists. To note this is both to offer a rubric by which to make sense of a diverse body of contemporary work and to suggest that the disconnect between the Iranian, Egyptian, and Moroccan works I have discussed and those works produced in the United States during the same time period may occur precisely in the realm where they might have crossed. The circulation that fuels cultural production and creativity in the Middle East–North Africa region in the period after the American century—and that is their distinguishing characteristic—is something that the American texts do not quite know how to handle. The anxiety over circulation does not delimit the success of such works; indeed, it makes for entertaining dramas. The works I discuss next have been critically acclaimed and sold well. Perhaps the anxiety over circulation is the reason for their success; they channel a more common concern in the age of globalization.

In Showtime's blockbuster series *Homeland*, which broadcast its fourth season from October through December 2014, there is an aggressive, if implicit, justification for maintaining the so-called war on terror and, more specifically, for a hard-line approach to dealing with Iran. In that sense, *Homeland*, before all else, manages for its American viewers their discomfort about the U.S. military's presence in the region via a thrilling and ever complex and twisting plot. This might come as little surprise because the series was developed by producers Howard Gordon and Alex Gansa—the team behind the Fox series *24*—based on an Israeli miniseries developed by Gideon Raff. As viewers watch the travails of CIA agents chasing down an international network of al-Qaʾida-inspired terrorists, the fictional narrative helps illuminate the masterful opening credits that open each episode. In the first three seasons, the opening credits juxtaposed documentary footage of Presidents Ronald Reagan, George H. W. Bush, Bill Clinton, and Barack Obama making statements within the long-lasting war against terrorism in the Middle East. We are in it for the long haul, the montage suggests week after week. The credits make a historical point—and a controversial one at that—by connecting the dots between events in the region; in quick succession, we hear four presidents and snippets of actual news broadcasts make reference to U.S. strikes on terrorist facilities in Libya in 1986; the bombing of Pan American flight 103 over Lockerbie, Scotland, in 1988; Iraq's invasion of Kuwait in 1990; the attack on the U.S.S. *Cole* in 2000; the attack on the Twin Towers in 2001; and the assassination of Osama bin Laden. In turn, the credits connect the fictional characters and plot of *Homeland* with the nonfiction individuals and events. The last of the nonfiction clips is a phrase drawn from President Obama's speech after the capture of bin Laden, a sentence that might characterize the series' political message: "We must, and we will, remain vigilant at home and abroad." Thus, the series' fictional aspects are intertwined with the long U.S. presence in the Middle East and justify continued sustenance of that presence—a way of dealing with the Middle East, to paraphrase Said.

Beyond such first-level Orientalism, we can note that the central problem of the plot revolves around circulation. When Marine sergeant Nicholas Brody (played by British actor Damian Lewis) is rescued in Iraq after eight years of captivity, the premise of the series, he is hailed as a hero by a naive American public, which includes a media that lionizes him and a political establishment that sees his return as a victory within the unending war on terror. The dramatic tension is twofold. First, his family hardly knows how to receive him. In the long years of his captivity, during which he was assumed dead, his wife, Jessica (played by Italian Brazilian actress Morena Baccarin) has become involved with Brody's best friend, a fellow marine who has become a sort of surrogate father to their children. Second, CIA analyst Carrie Mathison (played by Claire Danes) is convinced that Brody has been "turned" during his time in the hands of a terrorist organization clearly modeled on al-Qa'ida. The dramatic tension is that few believe her, including her CIA colleagues and supervisors, whereas the audience of the show is given clues that her hunches are correct (figure E.1), all while Brody capitalizes on his celebrity by catapulting quickly to the highest levels of political access.

Transnational circulation is at the heart of the danger imagined in the series: al Jazeera journalists who secretly work for al-Qa'ida, Muslim professors at American universities who are operatives for the terrorist network, and Brody's own secret conversion to Islam (he sneaks into his suburban garage to pray) are key elements in the first season. As the seasons continue, the fictional version of al-Qa'ida turns out to have alliances and networks that go beyond the believable, at least for those with knowledge of Middle East politics (e.g., the series turns to Iran). Meanwhile, the romantic subplot is so thoroughly intertwined with the geopolitical one—Sergeant Brody and Agent Mathison become romantically and sexually involved—that it

FIGURE E.1 Sergeant Nicholas Brody (Damian Lewis) dons a suicide vest in the finale of *Homeland*, season 1.

does not seem a stretch to call the adulterous affairs (including that of Jessica Brody with Captain Mike Faber, played by Diego Klattenhoff) examples of illicit circulation, too, especially since in the case of Carrie and Brody it will eventually require her to follow him to Iran. The age-old problem of soldiers returning home to find transition difficult, a popular subject for Hollywood during and after previous wars (e.g., the 1946 Academy Award winner *The Best Years of Our Lives* [William Wyler]), is here in the twenty-first century a problem of not being able to leave the other continent behind. One is never outside the immediate reach of the Middle East in the United States, as this series imagines vividly across a number of story lines.

In *Homeland*, the Orientalism is yet more entrenched when we consider two metatextual aspects of the series: one, its relationship to ongoing geopolitics, and two, its origins as an Israeli miniseries and its afterlife as a new series in the United States: *Tyrant*.[19] In the first case, the series has an eerie relationship to Obama administration politics, as Joseph Massad has argued.

Noting that Barack Obama welcomed star Damien Lewis to the White House in March 2012 and that the president is apparently a big fan of the series, Massad sees the show's unexpected narrative diversion toward Iran as a means by which to prepare a viewing public for an Israeli bombing campaign. To support this obviously bold claim, Massad reads much into the report of a conversation between Damian Lewis and Barack Obama. He quotes *TV Guide*'s account of the actor's visit to the White House, when Lewis "did sort of joke with [Obama] that the creators of the show had asked him [Obama] to give us a heads up on any foreign policy moves so that we could just stay current with Season 2. And he looked me straight in the eye and said, 'I'll be sure to do that.' "[20] As it turned out, season 3 of the series (2013) suggested that improvement of U.S.–Iran political relations would come not from military strikes but by CIA manipulation inside Iran (specifically the "flipping" and political elevation of a high-level Iranian). Massad's general point still holds true: that the divergence of *Homeland*'s plot from geopolitical realities has the potential to have a political impact on American audiences by "teaching" its audience how to think about U.S.–Iranian relations (and in season 4 about U.S.–Pakistani relations) and by inventing political alliances between forces in the Middle East. To be sure, the narrative association of al-Qaʾida with Iran in the series is startling. The figurehead of the fictional terrorist organization in *Homeland* is Abu Nazir, an Arab according to the script (though played by Navid Negahban, who was born and raised in Iran). *Homeland*'s chief terrorist is connected implausibly first to Hezbollah and then to Iran, both of which are antipathetic to al-Qaʾida in real-world politics. Thus, part of what *Homeland* teaches its audiences is to make connections between real-world entities based on fictional plot twists. Because I am arguing that the series manages and justifies continued American military, political, and covert presence in the region, these connections are troubling.

Homeland is already a text in circulation. The American series is based on an Israeli series titled *Hatufim* (Prisoners of war), which has been a critical and popular success in Israel since its 2010 premiere. The Israeli series imagines the return of three Israeli soldiers who have been held captive by Palestinian forces for seventeen years when their release is brokered. The core theme that carries over from the original Israeli series to the American one is the idea of the difficulties of returning home after captivity, and yet a comparison of the two series demonstrates the ways each is tailored for its own domestic public. Gideon Raff, the producer of *Prisoners of War* and *Homeland*, is himself an intriguing transnational figure. A former paratrooper in the Israeli army, he not only created the original Israeli miniseries, then sold and adapted it with Howard Gordon for Showtime, but also went on to create a second series for the U.S. market: *Tyrant*. The latter series is tailored to a perhaps less-sophisticated audience (moving networks from Showtime to FX). But its success demonstrates both Raff's and Gordon's marketing acumen, the ways in which Orientalism is adaptable across publics, and the continuing obsession with—perhaps anxiety over—circulation.

Tyrant premiered in the summer of 2014, and the network announced that it would be renewed for a second season. It, too, is aggressively Orientalist and haunted by transnational circulation, in perhaps more basic ways. The plot of the first season is based on the idea that an apparently "normal" American pediatrician in Pasadena, Barry Al-Fayeed (Adam Rayner)— married to an Anglo-American woman, Molly (Jennifer Finnigan), and the father of two teenage children (Noah Silver and Anne Winters)—is in fact the second son of a repressive dictator in a fictional Middle Eastern country. Though Barry has lived in the United States for twenty years, during which time he refused to return "home," it takes only one family trip back to his native Abbudin—the fictional country whose invented name suggests the Arabic words for "Father of Religion"—to draw him back into the complex atmosphere of his treacherous family and the repressive nation they rule over with astounding violence and brutality.

With Howard Gordon as executive producer, Gideon Raff as creator, and Avi Nir as an executive producer,[21] *Tyrant* transposes the anxiety about circulation from *Homeland* onto this new and bolder representation of an irredeemably violent Arab Middle East. The very whiteness of Barry's nuclear family and the portrayal of his wife's startling naïveté—she seems unable to fathom why Barry might be hesitant about returning to Abbudin or why, once he arrives to find things as bad as ever, he is eager to leave— suggest a portrayal of American innocence that one might think impossible in U.S. popular culture after 2001. *Tyrant* further plays on the possibility that the family next door in the United States might in fact be linked to Middle East terror abroad, a fantasy of the most culturally conservative variety. *Tyrant* proposes that travel to the Middle East can pull one into a world that is at such a remove from American democracy and innocence that the best one can do is stay far away. Here, children are gun-wielding terrorists dealt with by assassination (episode 2), and Barry's (Arab) American responsibility is to moderate or soften the repression while maintaining order. Circulation in *Tyrant* is centrifugal. The Middle East is a vortex that sucks America and Americans back in.

Despite the popularity of such series as *Homeland* and *Tyrant* and the way they double down on Orientalism, television, even putatively serious television, might seem an easy target for discussions of how contemporary American artists are haunted by questions of circulation. After all, transnational circulation is at the heart of twenty-first-century TV with its massive audiences, rebroadcasts, and reruns. So let us take a quick and final detour through recent fiction to see if it is haunted by these questions as well.

Fiction, both graphic fiction and old-fashioned prose narrative, is supposed to be an endangered category in the digital age. And yet a number of critically and popularly acclaimed works have taken up the same obsessions that run through *Homeland* and *Tyrant* alike, though in more subtle ways. In novels such as Dave Eggers's *A Hologram for the King* (2012), set in Saudi Arabia, and U.S. Army veteran Kevin Powers's *The Yellow Birds* (2012), set in Iraq, as well as in Craig Thompson's epic graphic novel *Habibi* (2011), set in an invented Middle Eastern nation, the region is understood as a central setting for the American novel in the second decade of the twenty-first century. Eggers explores the odd juxtapositions of aging American business models and the new wealth and ambitions to be found on the Arabian Peninsula with a sense of precision that comes with an awareness of the historical or geopolitical proximity of Saudi Arabia and the United States. Powers recrafts the U.S. war novel as the poetic *Yellow Birds* alternates between Iraq in 2004 and Richmond, Virginia, in 2005 (and elsewhere in the United States later in the decade) in the soldier-writer's perpetual attempt to bridge two worlds that are kept ever apart for those who were not in Iraq but that haunt each other through the decade and beyond. And Thompson sets out to create an epic that might itself open up U.S. culture to question the debilitating Islamophobia that is so prevalent, while embracing that which is beautiful in Arab and Islamic culture, religion, and art.

Habibi is perhaps the most interesting of the three because its author is so ambitious in his effort to counteract misapprehension about Islam in the United States even while he embraces Orientalism. In *Habibi*, Thompson, a Michigan-born graphic novelist, crafts an enormous and lushly drawn novel set in a timeless Middle East. The author-artist juxtaposes throughout the novel gorgeous Arabic calligraphy and the geometric patterns of Islamic art and architecture alongside a fictional narrative about two orphan refugees and their desperation as they move through treacherous and violent worlds in a desert kingdom. (The characters are Dodola, an adolescent girl, and Zam, otherwise referred to as "Habibi," a child who becomes at once Dodola's adoptive son and her brother.) As critics who championed *Habibi* pointed out, one of the intriguing features of *Habibi* is Thompson's almost scholarly exploration of the proximity of the Qur'an and the Bible, and there are many occasions when he takes pains to compare biblical and Quranic stories, demonstrating their similarities but also their differences, as if to show how intertwined West and East are. Thompson was raised by fundamentalist Christian parents, which he explores autobiographically at length in his first graphic novel, the blockbuster *Blankets* (2003), and is fascinated by religion in his work.

The premise of *Habibi*, however, is problematic in its implicit assumption of the binary that haunts Orientalism and maintains the distance that Thompson would seem to want to bridge through his work. He apparently doesn't recognize this problem: his timeless desert is a world apart. The fictional city/kingdom of Wanatolia is a place where a lecherous and murderous sultan seems to come directly from the medieval worlds of the *Arabian Nights* even while the city outside the palace has advertisements for Pepsi and American consumer culture (thereby suggesting that the tale is set in the present). As Thompson's critics pointed out, despite the author's effort to open up American attitudes, his embrace of a sumptuous Orient laced through by dramatically retrograde gender and racial politics renders *Habibi* a familiar example of old-fashioned Orientalism, albeit in a new medium. Robyn Creswell wrote in the *New York Times Book Review*, "Thompson the illustrator is in the same situation as Zam: both are prisoners of their own fantasies, apparently unable to think of Dodola without disrobing her."[22] Demonstrating his admitted embrace of visual Orientalism, Thompson went so far as to redraw scenes from classic European Orientalist paintings. Jean-Auguste-Dominique Ingres's famous bathhouse scenes, for example, appear in *Habibi*, redrawn in Thompson's own hand. But here they are neither parody nor pastiche and instead mingle the artist's pleasure in gazing at Muslim women's bodies and his apparent pride in finding an occasion for the new form (the graphic novel) to encompass the older one (painting).

How does circulation operate in *Habibi*? First, on the level of plot: the two characters at the heart of this 670-page epic are lost and always attempting to find each other. Their fates are intertwined, and just as the Qur'an and the Bible diverge from the same source, in Thompson's vision Dodola and Zam's reunion will be both inevitable and forever impossible. Zam's desire for Dodola—along with his earlier pain in having to witness her prostitute herself to save them both—is so great that he allows himself to be castrated: a eunuch. Thompson traffics in the classic Western obsession with "Oriental" sexual deviance and in so doing finds a figure—the eunuch—by which to represent the inability to connect the disparate worlds he is trying to bridge in graphic narrative.

Thompson tried to connect to Arabs during the period he was working on *Habibi*—to find a way to draw the worlds he was trying (he claimed) to open up to American eyes—by traveling through contemporary Morocco. There he found numerous visual motifs he would employ in *Habibi*. But based on his own testimony about his trip to Morocco, he failed to bridge the cultural gap that might have been predicted by his embrace of Orientalism. Thompson published his journals and sketchbooks from the period when he was working on *Habibi* in the small-format book *Carnet de voyage* (2004). There he depicts himself as an artist trying to connect with Moroccans while traveling solo in North Africa and admittedly getting caught in the tourist circuits. Travelers' sickness, loneliness, the impossibility of escaping the tourism mill confronted Thompson in Morocco, according to his own graphic account, and I think this account helps to explain the way the Orientalism of *Habibi* ultimately reinscribes the very distance he wanted to break down. Thompson himself suggests that *Carnet de voyage* should be read in connection with *Habibi*: in his opening disclaimer, he states that *Carnet de voyage* was "not 'the Next Book,'"[23] and so I read it as an artist's study for the graphic novel that would follow.

Circulation is everywhere, and yet it does not allow American characters in the new Orientalism to bridge the gap. In Dave Eggers's novel *A Hologram for the King*, there is a sense of the passing of a torch from the United States to China and the end of an American century. Eggers puts his protagonist in an empty tent at the King Abdullah Economic City in Saudi Arabia, ever ready to make a sales presentation to the Saudi king using the latest in American digital novelties, though the meeting is ever deferred. The opportunity to renew the glories of the American century—here represented by the Chicago-based bicycle company Schwinn, whose corporate dissolution haunts the protagonist—by using the newest innovations in U.S. technology will not present itself. Eggers has in the past several years written two novels and a work of narrative nonfiction—*Zeitoun* (2009), *A Hologram for the King* (2012), and *The Circle* (2013)—that together help explain the way circulation and the fate of the United States in the Middle East are associated for him. Eggers has not called these works a trilogy, but a series of associated tragedies and paradigm shifts is explored in them. First, in *Zeitoun* Eggers exposes the failure of American institutions—especially the Federal Emergency Management Agency (FEMA)—during the cataclysmic tragedy of Hurricane Katrina in 2005. In *A Hologram for the King*, he represents the loss of American economic hegemony and corporate breakdown in the global shift toward the Persian Gulf states, which recognize a different set of economic ties and cultural affiliations. And, finally, in *The Circle*, taking on an area where the United States is still dominant, Silicon Valley, he forecasts the threat to private life and individuality as we know it by imagining the logical extension of the digital revolution. For my purposes, these three books serve as a trilogy documenting the various "ends" of the American century. In *Zeitoun*, Syrian-born character

Abdulrahman Zeitoun finds in his confinement, as FEMA agents spit at him and randomly and painfully call him "Taliban" and "al-Qa'ida," that the United States will jail him rather than celebrate his embrace of ur-American values of hard work and community. *A Hologram for the King* recalls the greatness of an era in American manufacturing and civic pride that is now lost and associates its demise with the personal and professional failures of the novel's middle-aged protagonist and his inability to thrive in Saudi Arabia. *The Circle* imagines that a piece of software that links one's "true," real-world identity with one's digital identity will eventually end privacy and individual subjectivity itself, and it thereby sees that the end of the digital revolution as driven by U.S. culture will be a form of totalitarianism.

Circulation remains a useful rubric for thinking through the persistence of Orientalism in the second decade of the twenty-first century, wherein many cultural producers are rethinking the national narrative itself. If discussion of circulation reflects the anxieties of Americans as they contemplate the world around them, it too holds the potential to show us the world in a way that may free us from the debilitating logics of the American century.

But anxieties over circulation can provoke nightmares for Americans, too. As I wrote this epilogue, a brief but intense fear of the arrival of the Ebola virus flared up in the United States, fueled by media coverage and running across both broadcast and social media platforms with a speed far greater than the actual incubation period of the virus itself. (The virus seems to have died out as a news story and was replaced on the front pages by the midterm elections in November 2014 and then later in the month by the devastating events in Ferguson, Missouri, following a police shooting of an unarmed black teenager.) For so long during the past century, Americans felt at a geographical remove from the rest of the world, which perhaps kept the United States from experiencing that sense of empire and Orientalism that Said describes for British and French subjects living in the nineteenth and early twentieth centuries. But now, in the period after the American century, anxieties run deep about the ways digital connectivity and the interconnectedness of the transnational grid make "domestic America"—that still sacred space in *Homeland*, *Tyrant*, *The Yellow Birds*, and so on—an ever-fractured fantasy. Thinking through these anxieties is a way of grappling with a logic that no longer makes sense for the contemporary period. In this regard, examples of American cultural production—such as *Habibi*—are still caught in the earlier paradigm. Eggers's trilogy knows how to represent that paradigm but cannot break free from it. Meanwhile, new creative work in Cairo, Casablanca, and Tehran has already moved beyond American century logics of how culture moves through the world and has found ways to shift the center of gravity away from New York and Hollywood in ways that frequently defy American expectations—when these works are noticed at all. It is about time we paid attention to such innovations and caught up with the logics of a new century well under way.

ACKNOWLEDGMENTS

I HAVE RECEIVED favors great and small while working on this book. Scholarship is an extended conversation, and it happens both inside and outside the pages of a book. To those who made the effort to ask a question when I presented parts of this work publicly, those who read and commented on a portion of it, and those who helped me during almost uncountable trips to the Middle East and North Africa or when I was back at home over the past ten years since I began this project, I send my thanks. Those whom I have forgotten here should know that they are named between the lines and have my gratitude as well.

I thank, in Morocco, Jamal Bahmad, Hakim Belabbes, Khalid Bekkaoui, Taieb Belghazi, Sanaa Elaji, Fadwa Islah, Abdelatif Khayati, Driss Ksikes, Hosna Lebaddy, Mostafa Ouajjani, Hicham Tahir, and Abdellah Taïa as well as students at the Moroccan Cultural Studies Center at Sidi Mohammed Ben Abdellah University in Fes, where I led graduate seminars and presented some of this material. Sadik Rddad and Ouafae Elattaoui have opened their home in Fes for me—and my family—time and again, and over the course of nearly two decades of friendship Sadik has been one of my closest interlocutors and taught me so much about Morocco. I also thank, in Egypt, Muhammad Aladdin, Ahmed Alaidy, Humphrey Davies, Ira Dworkin, Ibrahim El Batout, Nadia El Kholy, Magdy El Shafee,

Manar El Shorbagy, Mansoura Ez Eldin, Walid El Hamamsy, Mohammed Hashem, Osama Madany, Weaam Mokhtar, Leri Price, Mounira Soliman, and Bahaa Taher. And I am grateful, in Iran, to Saied Ameli, Ghazileh Behdad, Fatima Kamali Chirani, Azadeh Ghahghaei, and numerous students and faculty at the Institute for North American and European Studies at the University of Tehran, where I taught on two different occasions as I did the research for this book. Ehsan Khoshbakht has been especially generous, sending me articles, answering questions about film, and introducing me to numerous people in the worlds of Iranian cinema. Pejman Danaei provided me the opportunity to view a huge amount of new Iranian cinema when he invited me to serve on the selection committee of the London Iranian Film Festival.

I was helped by Waleed Hazbun, Samir Khalaf, Wahib Maalouf, and Patrick McGreevy in Beirut; by Faouzi Bensaidi, Jocelyne Dakhlia, Pap Ndiaye, Kapil Raj, and Moumen Smihi in Paris; by Everette Dennis, Joe Khalil, and Firat Oruc in Doha; by Kim Fortuny, Meltem Gürle, Sibel Irzik, Gönül Pultar, and Cevza Sevgen in Istanbul; by Lawrence Raw, Tanfer Tunc, and Üfük Özdağ in Ankara; by Catherine Carey and Liam Kennedy in Dublin; and by Gianna Fusco, Fiorenzo Iuliano, Donatella Izzo, and Giorgio Mariani in Naples and Rome.

I have been fortunate to have the opportunity to present portions of this work as it developed at a number of universities in the United States, including Chicago, Cornell, Dartmouth, Illinois, Indiana, Iowa, New York, Oklahoma State, Princeton, Rutgers, Stanford, California at Berkeley and Los Angeles, Williams College, Wisconsin, and Yale. In every case, I have learned from my interlocutors and appreciated the opportunity to try out new material in progress. I thank friends and colleagues in the United States who have invited me or engaged with my work during such visits or both, including Hussein Agrama, Moustafa Bayoumi, Ali Behdad, Russ Castronovo, Deborah Cohn, Jennifer Cole, Julian Dibbell, Wai Chee Dimock, Douglas Doetsch, Amina El-Annan, Brad Evans, Jonathan Freedman, Nouri Gana, Leela Gandhi, Zareena Grewal, Allen Hibbard, Gordon Hutner, Brian Larkin, Peter Limbrick, Françoise Lionnet, Saba Mahmood, Timothy Marr, Mark McGurl, Alan Nadel, Jonathan Nashel,

Crystal Parikh, Donald Pease, Katarzyna Pieprzak, Elizabeth Povinelli, Sangeeta Ray, Larry Rothfield, Leyla Rouhi, Nancy Ruttenburg, Richard Jean So, Harry Stecopoulos, Dominic Thomas, Michael Warner, and Renée Zuckerbrot.

Several colleagues went above and beyond the call of collegiality. The following read the manuscript at various stages and provided useful advice for its revision: Kate Baldwin, Ali Behdad, Tarek El-Ariss, Susan Manning, Hamid Naficy, Donald Pease, Andrew Wachtel, and two anonymous readers for Columbia University Press. I have benefitted from their advice and am deeply appreciative that they took time out of their busy schedules to help me.

My colleagues at Northwestern have made life at my home institution consistently stimulating, especially in my four primary affiliations: English, comparative literary studies, American studies, and Middle East and North African studies. Among so many great colleagues, I want to thank in particular Mohammad Abdeljaber, Chris Bush, Jorge Coronado, Holly Clayson, Scott Durham, Stuart Dybek, Betsy Erkkila, Harris Feinsod, Reginald Gibbons, Katherine Hoffman, Elizabeth Shakman Hurd, Rebecca Johnson, Henri Lauzière, Andrew Leong, Susan Manning, Hamid Naficy, Inna Naroditskaya, Carl Petry, Jan Radway, Laurie Shannon, Carl Smith, Wendy Wall, Ivy Wilson, and Jessica Winegar. The English Department staff has been exceptional—Kathy Daniels, Dave Kuzel, Nathan Mead, and Jennifer Britton—as have Tim Garrett, Lexy Gore, and Katie Rashid in the MENA Program. I also thank the Buffett Institute for Global Studies, which has provided support and venues to present some of this work, and especially Bruce Carruthers, Brian Hanson, Rita Koryan, Krzysztof Kozubski, Hendrik Spruyt, and Andrew Wachtel.

At Northwestern, my students at both the undergraduate and graduate levels have taught me much. I owe thanks to a number of excellent research assistants: Aretha Chakraborti, Farah Chami, Maziyar Faridi, Wahib Maalouf, and Marjan Mohammadi.

The Northwestern administration has been generous with research support, leave time, and flexible teaching arrangements. At Weinberg College of Arts and Sciences, former dean Sarah Mangelsdorf and associate deans

John Franks, Simon Greenwold, and Marie Jones were greatly supportive. Daniel Linzer was my dean when the project began and my provost when it was completed, and he has my great appreciation. Henry Bienen, former president of Northwestern, had a significant role in this project, first by nominating me to be a Carnegie Scholar and then by standing by my work throughout. I would also like to express my sincere thanks to Northwestern's Office of Foundation Relations, especially Sarah Fodor and Susan Fisher Miller, and to Storer Rowley and Pat Vaughan Tremmel in Media Relations.

I benefitted from the exceptionally generous support of two foundations without which this book would never have come to be. The Carnegie Corporation of New York, which named me a Class of 2005 Carnegie Scholar, launched this project and allowed me to imagine a comparative study on a scale that seemed nearly impossible when I first proposed it. My special thanks to Patricia Rosenfield and Hillary Wiesner, program directors of Carnegie Scholars and the Islam Initiative, respectively. Two years later, the Andrew W. Mellon Foundation named me a New Directions Fellow, which allowed me the unimaginable pleasure to take a year's leave to train in a new discipline, which I did in 2008/2009 in the Department of Anthropology at the University of Chicago, an academic experience that significantly changed the conception of my research. The Mellon Foundation then awarded me a second major grant: a New Directions Post Fellowship Award in 2012/2013 to complete the writing of this book manuscript. I thank Joseph Meisel, Nora Lambert, Philip Lewis, Martha Sullivan, and Harriet Zuckerman at the Mellon Foundation. I also thank colleagues at Chicago for opening their graduate classrooms to me as a student, especially Jean Comaroff, John Comaroff, Judith Farquhar, John Kelly, and Joe Masco in anthropology as well as Amina Mohamed and the late Farouk Mustafa in the Center for Middle East Studies.

I thank the Fulbright program for awarding me two Senior Specialists grants to teach and interact with faculty at Cairo University in Giza and at Università degli Studi di Napoli "L'Orientale" in Italy, both of which helped me make progress on this book. My thanks to the Binational Fulbright Commission in Cairo, especially Maggie Nassif and Nevine Gad El Mawla. Various institutions have invited me to be visiting faculty, where I worked out some of these ideas with an international body of students and colleagues: the Clinton Institute for American Studies at University College, Dublin; the École des Hautes Études en Sciences Sociales in Paris; and the Institute of North American and European Studies at the University of Tehran.

Earlier versions of some parts of the manuscript have appeared in print elsewhere. A portion of chapter 1 was published as "The World, the Text, and the Americanist," *American Literary History* 25, no. 1 (2013): 231–246. A few paragraphs of chapter 2 are included in "Tahrir: Ends of Circulation," *Public Culture* 23, no. 3 (2011): 493–504. Another section of that chapter appeared as "Jumping Publics: Magdy el Shafee's Cairo Comics," *NOVEL: A Forum on Fiction* 47, no. 1 (2014): 67–89. A portion of chapter 3 was printed as "Watching *Shrek* in Tehran," *The Believer* 8, no. 3 (2010): 5–11. And one section of chapter 4 appeared as "*Marock* in Morocco: Reading Moroccan Films in the Age of Circulation," *Journal of North African Studies* 12, no. 3 (2007): 287–307. I am grateful to these journals for publishing my work and for allowing me to incorporate it here. Most of all, I thank the editors with whom I worked on those pieces for their engagement, intelligence, and advice: Plaegian Alexander, Nancy Armstrong, Brigid Hughes, Gordon Hutner, Heidi Julavits, Eric Klinenberg, Andrew Leland, Nancy Ruttenburg, and Stephen Twilley.

For permission to reprint his comics in chapter 2, I thank Magdy El Shafee. Thanks to Fantagraphics for permission to use the drawing by Joe Sacco. My appreciation also goes to Abdellah Tourabi, editor of *TelQuel*, for permission to reprint the covers of *TelQuel* in chapter 4.

At Columbia University Press, Philip Leventhal has been a remarkably enthusiastic advocate for the book, offered great advice on its structure, and been especially patient in waiting for the manuscript. Whitney Johnson answered numerous questions with professionalism and efficiency and was a pleasure to work with. Irene Pavitt guided the manuscript through production brilliantly. Annie Barva's excellent work as a copy editor improved the manuscript from close-up, and Bob Schwarz completed the book's index.

Finally, my family has endured both the most and the least pleasant aspects of this book, and I hope in the end the balance tips in the positive direction. My children—Oliver, Pia, Theo, and Charlotte—have literally grown up with this book. What that means in practice is that they have endured my absence from them too frequently. The few occasions when they could accompany me to Morocco, Cairo, Istanbul, and Paris have been some of the most pleasurable times of the past years, and their presence—and their questions—have frequently opened up my understanding of aspects of the region I thought I understood. Kate Baldwin is my partner in life and has not only thrived in her own career as a scholar, teacher, and writer while raising four children but also done so with my extended absences abroad to work on this book. She also made time to read a late draft of this manuscript and to offer advice and encouragement. To say I am in her debt is an understatement.

NOTES

PREFACE

1. In 2008, the Hamra branch of Café Younes expanded and added a second space a few steps from the roaster. The additional space includes indoor seating, a sidewalk terrace, a food menu, and souvenirs. The roaster remains open in the original space, though the counter has been removed.

2. Quoted in James Di Properzio, "Hamra, Beirut, Lebanon: Café Younes," *Fresh Cup Magazine*, June 2008, formerly available at http://www.freshcup.com/featured-article.php ?id=42&phpMyAdmin=JlgiooVFyONF9tSXMEc7CXjMqNb (accessed April 15, 2014).

3. Despite the iconic status of Smihi's first feature film, *El Chergui* (1976), his later work has been ignored or given short shrift by those few works on Moroccan cinema, according to Peter Limbrick, "Moumen Smihi's Tanjawi/Tangérois/Tangerian Cinema," *Third Text* 26, no. 4 (2012): 443–454.

1. AFTER THE AMERICAN CENTURY

1. I develop the idea of the American autumn, which engages with the work of world-systems theorists Giovanni Arrighi and Beverly Silver, in "After the American Century," in "States of Emergency—States of Crisis," ed. Winfried Fluck, Katharina Motyl, Donald E. Pease, and Christoph Raetzsch, special issue, *REAL: Yearbook of Research in English and American Literature* 27 (2011): 57–72. See also Beverly J. Silver and Giovanni Arrighi, "The End of the Long Twentieth Century," in *Business as Usual: The Roots of the Global Financial Meltdown*, ed. Craig Calhoun and Georgi Derluguian (New York: Social Science Research Council and New York University Press, 2011), 53–68.

2. Brian T. Edwards, "American Orientalism: Taking Casablanca," in *Morocco Bound: Disorienting America's Maghreb, from Casablanca to the Marrakech Express* (Durham, N.C.: Duke University Press, 2005), 29–77.

3. Michael Hardt and Antonio Negri associate Occupy Wall Street and the Tahrir Square uprisings with several other "encampments" of the previous year, which they find "permutations" of similar political demands ("The Fight for 'Real Democracy' at the Heart of Occupy Wall Street," *Foreign Affairs*, October 11, 2011).

4. Nakoula Basseley Nakoula, a Coptic Christian born in Egypt in 1957, had a string of convictions on his record, including an arrest for possession and intent to manufacture methamphetamines, for which he served a year in the Los Angeles County jail in 1997. American director Alan Roberts's film credits include soft-core films such as *Young Lady Chatterley* (1977) and *The Happy Hooker Goes Hollywood* (1980) as well as the action film *Karate Cop* (1991). See the *Innocence of Muslims* entry at imdb.com; and Ben Piven, "Who Is Nakoula Basseley Nakoula?" al Jazeera, September 15, 2012, http://www.aljazeera.com/indepth/features/2012/09/2012915181925528211.html (accessed March 28, 2014).

5. " 'Innocence of Muslims' Actress Demands Google Be Sanctioned," *Hollywood Reporter*, March 25, 2014, http://www.hollywoodreporter.com/thr-esq/innocence-muslims-actress-demands-google-691182 (accessed March 29, 2014). The motion reads:

> As of this morning, at 7:55 A.M. EST, a version of *Innocence of Muslims* that includes Ms. Garcia's performance is still available on Google's Worldwide Platform and also viewable in Egypt, the nation in which the fatwa was issued for Ms. Garcia's execution. All a viewer needs to do to view a copy of the video that contains the infringing material from any computer in the world and within YouTube's global platform—and therefore is governed by the takedown order—is to change his or her settings to any country platform, such as "Egypt."

6. Eriq Gardner, "Second Actor Sues Google over 'Innocence of Muslims,'" *Hollywood Reporter*, September 15, 2014, http://www.hollywoodreporter.com/thr-esq/second-actor-sues-google-innocence-732849 (accessed October 18, 2014).

7. Robert Mackey and Liam Stack, "Obscure Film Mocking Muslim Prophet Sparks Anti-U.S. Protests in Egypt and Libya," *New York Times* blogs, September 11, 2012, 7:25 P.M., http://thelede.blogs.nytimes.com/2012/09/11/obscure-film-mocking-muslim-prophet-sparks-anti-u-s-protests-in-egypt-and-libya/ (accessed March 28, 2014).

8. David D. Kirkpatrick and Steven Lee Myers, "Libya Attack Brings Challenges for U.S.," *New York Times*, September 12, 2012, http://www.nytimes.com/2012/09/13/world/middleeast/us-envoy-to-libya-is-reported-killed.html (accessed March 28, 2014). The original statement has since been deleted from U.S. Embassy pages, but a screen shot can be found via Twitter, https://twitter.com/USEmbassyCairo/status/245481070101929984 (accessed March 28, 2014). The statement reads: "We firmly reject the actions by those who abuse the universal right of free speech to hurt the religious beliefs of others."

9. Here the overwhelming point was that the United States was the origin of the film and that its actors were American, but in form, too, the film's style resonated with bad Ameri-

can television series (which are shown on Moroccan television) and its look with cheap porn minus the sex.

10. In *The Net Delusion: The Dark Side of Internet Freedom* (New York: PublicAffairs, 2011), Evgeny Morozov argues that the Internet and platforms such as Twitter, Facebook, and YouTube tend toward surveillance more than toward freedom. He has, in turn, criticized the cyberutopianism of authors such as Clay Shirky. I take up this argument further in chapter 2.

11. Adam Horowitz, in the blog *Mondoweiss*, quotes unnamed Occupy Wall Street material: "'We are using the revolutionary Arab Spring tactic to achieve our ends and encourage the use of nonviolence to maximize the safety of all participants'" ("'Ready for Tahrir Moment': Occupy Wall Street, the Arab Spring, and Israel/Palestine," *Mondoweiss*, post, October 4, 2011, http://mondoweiss.net/2011/10/ready-for-a-tahrir-moment-occupy-wall -street-the-arab-spring-and-israelpalestine.html [accessed July 12, 2012]). See also an Occupy Wall Street blog at Adbusters (http://www.adbusters.org/blogs/adbusters-blog /occupywallstreet.html [accessed July 12, 2012]), where the connection is explicit. After discussing Tahrir Square, the blog entry states explicitly that Occupy Wall Street is "following this model." The graphic asks: "Are you ready for a Tahrir moment?"

12. Internet World Stats, http://www.internetworldstats.com (accessed July 9, 2015); see also Annabelle Sreberny and Gholam Khiabany, *Blogistan: The Internet and Politics in Iran* (London: Tauris, 2010). The number in Iran represents the second highest number of Internet users in the Middle East. Egypt recently overtook Iran, with 48 million users as of December 31, 2014, the latest figure available as this book goes to press. Internet penetration in the United States, with 277 million users, is 86.9 percent. The world average is 42.4 percent.

13. India's 243 million users (June 2014 figure) represent 19.7 percent of its population. China, with 642 million users in June 2014, is at 47.4 percent penetration (Internet World Stats, http://www.internetworldstats.com [accessed July 9, 2015]).

14. Several authors have in various ways written this history: Victoria de Grazia, *Irresistible Empire: America's Advance Through Twentieth-Century Europe* (Cambridge, Mass.: Harvard University Press, 2005); Penny Von Eschen, *Satchmo Blows Up the World: Jazz Ambassadors Play the Cold War* (Cambridge, Mass.: Harvard University Press, 2006); Kristin Ross, *Fast Cars, Clean Bodies: Decolonization and the Reordering of French Culture* (Cambridge, Mass.: MIT Press, 1996); and Uta G. Poiger, *Jazz, Rock, and Rebels: Cold War Politics and American Culture in a Divided Germany* (Berkeley: University of California Press, 2000). Brian Larkin discusses the panic caused in British India by the arrival of Hollywood films in the 1930s in "Circulating Empires: Colonial Authority and the Immoral, Subversive Problem of American Film"; and Elizabeth F. Thompson considers the response to *Gone with the Wind* in 1940s Damascus, Cairo, and Beirut in "Scarlett O'Hara in Damascus: Hollywood, Colonial Politics, and Arab Spectatorship during World War II," both in *Globalizing American Studies*, ed. Brian T. Edwards and Dilip Parameshwar Gaonkar (Chicago: University of Chicago Press, 2010), 155–183, 184–208. These essays provide more models for this earlier history and, of course, have informed

my work. Miriam Bratu Hansen's work on Hollywood traveling as a global film vernacular is particularly important to my work; see, for instance, "The Mass Production of the Senses: Classical Cinema as Vernacular Modernism," *Modernism/Modernity* 6, no. 2 (1999): 59–77.

15. Richard F. Kuisel, *Seducing the French: The Dilemma of Americanization* (Berkeley: University of California Press, 1997), 38; Roger Cohen, "France and Spain Impose Quotas," *New York Times*, December 22, 1993. Cohen quotes Daniel Toscan de Plantier, the president of Unifrance, the French film industry association, as saying at the time, "There is a sudden realization in Europe now that a country or continent with a strong movie and broadcasting industry will be strong in the next century, and those without these industries will be weak."

16. Quoted in Hishaam Aidi, "The Grand (Hip-Hop) Chessboard: Race, Rap, and Raison d'Etat," *Middle East Report* 260 (2011): 36. See also "The Cauldron: Islam and Hip-Hop in Europe," *Hip Hop Diplomacy*, June 25, 2012, http://hiphopdiplomacy.org/category /us-state-department/ (accessed October 18, 2014).

17. Quoted in Hishaam Aidi, "Leveraging Hip Hop in US Foreign Policy," al Jazeera, November 7, 2011, http://www.aljazeera.com/indepth/opinion/2011/10/201110309101829992 4.html (accessed October 18, 2014).

18. Ibid.

19. In the case of jazz, see, in particular, Kate A. Baldwin, "Black Shadows across the Iron Curtain: Robeson's Stance between Cold War Cultures," on Paul Robeson, in *Beyond the Color Line and the Iron Curtain: Reading Encounters Between Black and Red, 1922–1963* (Durham, N.C.: Duke University Press, 2002), 202–252. In the case of commodities, see her essay "Cold War Hot Kitchen," in *Globalizing American Studies*, ed. Edwards and Gaonkar, 135–152, and her fascinating discussion of Soviet responses to the American National Exhibition in her book *The Racial Imaginary of the Cold War Kitchen: From Sokol'niki Park to Chicago's South Side* (Hanover, N.H.: Dartmouth College Press, 2016).

20. Von Eschen, *Satchmo Blows Up the World*.

21. Though one can of course learn from surveys and audience studies, I have not employed them while doing this project. My reluctance to use such research methods—or to attempt to pursue my own polling or audience surveys—is based on a mixture of skepticism about polling and an underlying belief that you can derive a more sophisticated sense of the relationship between a text and its public by examining rich moments of uptake. To be clear, I have been engaged in research that combines techniques in the humanities with strategies derived from sociocultural anthropology, which I took a year off to study more formally during the process of writing this book. But for those who are attracted to survey data, one can turn to polls by Zogby Research Service (http://www .zogbyanalytics.com/) and the Pew Global Attitudes Project (http://www.pewglobal .org/topics/middle-east-and-north-africa/) or, more interesting still, to John L. Esposito and Dalia Mogahed, *Who Speaks for Islam? What a Billion Muslims Really Think* (New York: Gallup Press, 2007), which interprets the large-scale Gallup Poll.

22. "Reading in the Digital Age," in "The Changing Profession," special issue, *PMLA* 128, no. 1 (2013): 193–243.

23. Brian T. Edwards and Dilip Parameshwar Gaonkar, "Introduction: Globalizing American Studies," in *Globalizing American Studies*, ed. Edwards and Gaonkar, 1–44; Brian T. Edwards, "Fragments of America: Response to Marius Jucan," *American, British, and Canadian Studies* 14 (2010): 96–103.

24. The classic definition of the uses and meanings of the word *culture* remains Raymond Williams, *Keywords: A Vocabulary of Culture and Society*, rev. ed. (New York: Oxford University Press, 1985).

25. I am alluding to Fredric Jameson's famous (and in some circles notorious) essay "Third-World Literature in the Era of Multinational Capitalism," *Social Text* 15 (1986): 65–88. For a powerful account of the ways that literary and anthropological texts about sub-Saharan Africa have informed each other, see also Christopher Miller, *Theories of Africans: Francophone Literature and Anthropology in Africa* (Chicago: University of Chicago Press, 1993).

26. Samuel P. Huntington, "The Clash of Civilizations?" *Foreign Affairs* 72, no. 3 (1993): 22–49.

27. Arjun Appadurai, "Introduction: Commodities and the Politics of Value," in *The Social Life of Things: Commodities in Cultural Perspective*, ed. Arjun Appadurai (New York: Cambridge University Press, 1986), 3–63. Subsequent references are cited in the text.

28. Henry R. Luce, "The American Century," *Life*, February 17, 1941.

29. Stephen J. Whitfield, "The American Century of Henry R. Luce," in *Americanism: New Perspectives on the History of an Ideal*, ed. Michael Kazin and Joseph A. McCartin (Chapel Hill: University of North Carolina Press, 2006), 90–107.

30. Ibid.

31. Walter LaFeber provides a vivid account of the complexities of this marriage of commerce, culture, and capitalism in the case of Michael Jordan's professional relationship with Nike, in *Michael Jordan and the New Global Capitalism*, rev. ed. (1999; reprint, New York: Norton, 2002).

32. There are many examples of this association of globalization and Americanization. The prominent Moroccan sociologist and economist Mahdi Elmandjra, whose numerous books have been ubiquitous in Moroccan bookstores in the past few decades, made this equation starkly in several of his publications in the 1990s, including *Première guerre civilisationnelle* (First civilizational war) (Casablanca: 'Ouyoun, 1991; Casablanca: Toubkal, 1992). Elmandjra makes the point most explicitly in his long essay "La mondialisation c'est tout simplement l'américanisation" (Globalization is quite simply Americanization), *al Alam* (Rabat), January 24, 1999.

33. Mahdi Elmandjra pursues this argument in *La décolonisation culturelle: Défi majeur du 21ème siècle* (Cultural decolonization: Major challenge of the twenty-first century) (Marrakech: Editions Walili; Paris: Futuribles, 1996). But waves of similar books hit the shelves through the 1990s and 2000s.

34. Faisal Devji is the most convincing in his argument that we see the movement to Islamic jihad as an alternative globalism, in *Landscapes of the Jihad: Militancy, Morality, Modernity*

(Ithaca, N.Y.: Cornell University Press, 2005), and *The Terrorist in Search of Humanity: Militant Islam and Global Politics* (New York: Columbia University Press, 2009).

35. Daniel T. Rodgers argues for the year 1981 as a turning point based on a greater focus on rhetoric and changing structures of language that emerged with Ronald Reagan's presidency and rhetorical strategies, which Rodgers documents in stunning fashion in *Age of Fracture* (Cambridge, Mass.: Harvard University Press, 2011).

36. An extended argument about these forces is given in Edwards and Gaonkar, "Introduction."

37. In this goal, I am greatly inspired by the work of Donald E. Pease, especially *The New American Exceptionalism* (Minneapolis: University of Minnesota Press, 2009), and "American Studies After American Exceptionalism? Toward a Comparative Analysis of Imperial State Exceptionalisms," in *Globalizing American Studies*, ed. Edwards and Gaonkar, 47–83.

38. Edward W. Said, "The World, the Text, and the Critic," in *The World, the Text, and the Critic* (Cambridge, Mass.: Harvard University Press, 1983), 35. Subsequent references are cited in the text.

39. Edwards and Gaonkar, "Introduction."

40. Michael Warner, "Publics and Counterpublics," *Public Culture* 14, no. 1 (2002): 49, 82. Warner's sixth axiom is also important for my purposes: "A public seems to be self-organized by discourse," Warner writes, "but in fact requires preexisting forms and channels of circulation. It appears to be open to indefinite strangers, but in fact selects participants by criteria of shared social space (though not necessarily territorial space), habitus, topical concerns, intergeneric references, and circulating intelligible forms (including idiolects or speech genres)" (75); "the projection of a public is a new, creative, and distinctively modern mode of power" (75).

41. Paul Giles, *The Global Remapping of American Literature* (Princeton, N.J.: Princeton University Press, 2011), 15, 21.

42. Rodgers has called this transitional period an "age of fracture." In *Age of Fracture*, he makes a compelling argument for the ways in which the 1970s and 1980s—across a variety of fields of discourse, from Ronald Reagan's rhetoric to shifts in the field of economics, where an abstracted idea of "market" as derived from conservative monetarists such as Milton Friedman and the Chicago Gang displaces a Keynesian model of economic projects—allow us to see the sweep of the shift Giles alludes to and Rodgers charts.

43. Giles, *Global Remapping of American Literature*, 16.

44. Wai Chee Dimock, *Through Other Continents: American Literature Across Deep Time* (Princeton, N.J.: Princeton University Press, 2006).

45. Edward W. Said, "Traveling Theory," in *The World, the Text, and the Critic*, 226–247.

46. Ibid., 241.

47. Alan Riding, "Rerun Our Cold War Cultural Diplomacy," *New York Times*, October 27, 2005.

48. On the Soviet response to *Porgy and Bess*, see Baldwin, *Beyond the Color Line and the Iron Curtain*; on the Friendship Fest, see Samuel Loewenberg, "Christian Rock for Muslims," *New York Times*, May 10, 2005.

49. Neil MacFarquhar, "An Anti-American Boycott Is Growing in the Arab World," *New York Times*, May 10, 2002.

50. Michael Silverstein and Greg Urban, "The Natural History of Discourse," in *Natural Histories of Discourse*, ed. Michael Silverstein and Greg Urban (Chicago: University of Chicago Press, 1996), 1–17.

51. Marc Lynch brilliantly shows how changing forms in Arab media—such as the call-in program—have had a profound effect on politics through the creation of new publics, in *Voices of the New Arab Public: Iraq, al-Jazeera, and Middle East Politics Today* (New York: Columbia University Press, 2006).

2. JUMPING PUBLICS

1. Richard Jacquemond, *Conscience of the Nation: Writers, State, and Society in Modern Egypt*, trans. David Tresilian (2002; Cairo: American University in Cairo Press, 2008).

2. Quoted in Caroline Rooney, "Egyptian Literary Culture and Egyptian Modernity: Introduction," *Journal of Postcolonial Writing* 47, no. 4 (2011): 369.

3. Taher's own novels—such as *Qalat Duha* (As Doha said, 1985), about workers in an Egyptian ministry during Nasser's presidency, and *al-Hubb fi al-Manfa* (Love in exile, 1995), which portrays the massacre of Palestinian refugees in the Sabra and Shatila camps and fictional journalists' debates over how to report the tragedy—and Taher's own public comments during the Arab uprisings of 2011 help us to flesh out his meaning here. On March 18, 2011, Taher published a full-page editorial in the Egyptian daily *al-Shuruq* in which he addressed the #Jan25 movement directly ("Akemlaou Thaourakum" [Complete your revolution], *al-Shuruq* [Cairo], March 18, 2011; see also an interview with Taher in Karen Krüger, "Modern Egypt Was Built on the Shoulders of Intellectuals," *Qantara*, May 24, 2012, http://en.qantara.de/content/interview-with-the-egyptian-writer-baha-taher-modern-egypt-was-built-on-the-shoulders-of [accessed October 30, 2012]).

4. Rooney argues that literary culture itself is "at the vanguard of any democracy" and turns for support to Ahdaf Soueif (b. 1950), the London-based Egyptian author who writes primarily in English. For Soueif, explains Rooney, the novel is "a polyvocal form of writing . . . that enables different points of view to be aired alongside each other, thereby allowing for our self-doubts and undermining our self-certainties" ("Egyptian Literary Culture and Egyptian Modernity," 369).

5. Benjamin Lee and Edward LiPuma, "Cultures of Circulation: The Imaginations of Modernity," *Public Culture* 14, no. 1 (2002): 191–213. See also Brian T. Edwards, "Logics and Contexts of Circulation," in *A Companion to Comparative Literature*, ed. Ali Behdad and Dominic Thomas (Oxford: Blackwell, 2011), 454–472.

6. A number of texts have debated the appropriate term, which itself has a politics, as my reference to the term *diffusion*, with its Cold War resonance, suggests. Here, rather than dedicate space to discussing the benefits and shortcomings of these various terms

(*appropriation*, *hybridity*, *diffusion*, etc.), let me point to some of the strongest works that explore alternatives in the case of Middle Eastern literatures and cultures: Jessica Winegar, *Creative Reckonings: The Politics of Art and Culture in Contemporary Egypt* (Stanford, Calif.: Stanford University Press, 2006); Tarik Sabry, *Cultural Encounters in the Arab World: On Media, the Modern, and the Everyday* (New York: Tauris, 2010); and Kamran Rastegar, *Literary Modernity Between the Middle East and Europe: Transactions in Nineteenth-Century Arabic, Persian, and English Literatures* (London: Routledge, 2007). Rastegar as well as other young scholars such as Shaden Tageldin and Rebecca Johnson have been forcing us to reconsider Egyptian literature of the nineteenth and twentieth centuries and to think in terms of the encounter, the transactional, and so on, demonstrating that this model is of course not limited to the episteme of globalization. Most recently, Tarek El-Ariss engages and extends the revision of the account of Arab modernity in *Trials of Arab Modernity: Literary Affects and the New Political* (New York: Fordham University Press, 2013). For El-Ariss, modernity should be seen not as a belated encounter with the Western Enlightenment but as a series of trials, accidents, and affects—"a somatic condition, which takes shape through accidents and events (*ahdath*) emerging in and between Europe and the Arab world, the literary text and political discourse" (3). I discuss later in this chapter El-Ariss's reading of Ahmed Alaidy's novel, in which he argues for a sensitivity to "hacking" as a mode of engagement. Margaret Litvin's wonderful book *Hamlet's Arab Journey: Shakespeare's Prince and Nasser's Ghost* (Princeton, N.J.: Princeton University Press, 2011) offers what may be, for me, the most compelling model emerging from Middle East studies by which to interpret the ways in which Arabic-language literature has productively engaged with "foreign" literatures. She argues that Arab dramatists and authors who adapted Shakespeare's *Hamlet* were not simply derivative or exhibiting the symptoms of postcolonial anxiety but were in fact exercising a productive form of cultural engagement. Showing the way that Shakespeare's work has filtered through Egyptian literature and culture, Litvin provides the metaphor of a "global kaleidoscope" as a model for thinking through what happens when a foreign text finds its way into a second, distant literature. As she describes this process, individual writers do not necessarily respond to a major text such as *Hamlet* in a one-on-one, binary manner. Rather, they respond to a range of possible aspects, meanings, and interpretations of the text, from previous productions of a play to competing translations and from contemporary political pressures to directors' and actors' unique artistic temperaments and training. Shakespeare's *Hamlet* may be a play for the ages, but it has meant radically different things in different national and historical contexts, and its translations into Arabic have been filtered through competing pressures, affiliations, and politics.

7. Samia Mehrez, *Egypt's Culture Wars: Politics and Practice* (Cairo: American University in Cairo Press, 2010), 125.

8. Arjun Appadurai, "Disjuncture and Difference in the Global Cultural Economy," *Theory, Culture & Society* 7 (1990): 299.

9. The original news item appeared on page 2 of *al Ahram* on February 18, 2011, and then was quickly picked up in news sources from CNN News, ABC News, and the *Village*

Voice to *PC Mag* and even *New Parent*. See "Yutlaqu mawludatihi 'ism 'Facebook'" (Man names his newborn girl "Facebook"), *al Ahram*, February 18, 2001, http://www .ahram.org.eg/pdf/Zoom_1500/Index.aspx?ID=45365 (scan of article) (accessed October 30, 2012). It is perhaps not surprising that social media such as Facebook would be a venue for spreading the story about Facebook. For example, see Catharine Smith, "Egyptian Father Names Baby 'Facebook,'" *Huffington Post*, February 21, 2011, http:// www.huffingtonpost.com/2011/02/21/baby-named-facebook-egypt_n_825934.html (accessed October 30, 2012); and Catharine Smith, "Richard Engel Tweets Photo of Egyptian Protestors with 'Thank You Facebook' Sign," *Huffington Post*, February 4, 2011, http:// www.huffingtonpost.com/2011/02/04/egypt-protesters-thank-you-facebook_n_818745 .html (accessed October 30, 2012). An intriguing follow-up piece noted other occasions when the Internet had inspired baby names, such as "Google," "Hashtag," and "Like": Samantha Rollins, "4 Internet Inspired Baby Names," *Week*, n.d., http://theweek.com /article/index/236939/4-internet-inspired-baby-names (accessed October 30, 2012). Even a year later, the *New York Times* was willing to attribute authorship of the revolution to Facebook in a review of Wael Ghonim's book *Revolution 2.0*: Jose Antonio Vargas, "Spring Awakening: How an Egyptian Revolution Began on Facebook," *New York Times Book Review*, February 19, 2012.

10. As I mentioned earlier, in *The Net Delusion: The Dark Side of Internet Freedom* (New York: PublicAffairs, 2011), Evgeny Morozov argues against what he calls "cyberutopianism" and discusses a number of moments when Western journalists have given far too much credit to social-networking software as an agent of change, from the so-called Twitter revolution in Moldova to the failed Green Movement in Iran in 2009.

11. The work of several of these writers is included in Brian T. Edwards, ed., "Cairo 2010: After Kefaya," *Public Space*, no. 9 (2009): 127–175.

12. The latter position is advanced most forcefully in Dilip Parameshwar Gaonkar and Elizabeth A. Povinelli, "Technologies of Public Forms: Circulation, Transfiguration, Recognition," *Public Culture* 15, no. 3 (2003): 385. I discuss the debate around it in "Logics and Contexts of Circulation."

13. This theme is apparent even in accounts that did not emphasize the digital aspects of the revolution. Wendell Steavenson focused on the role of the army and the respect it garnered among protestors, suggesting its major role in post-Mubarak Egypt, in "On the Square," *New Yorker*, February 28, 2011. Her long, well-reported piece was published shortly after Mubarak's departure on February 11. Despite the article's focus on the military, the two large images the *New Yorker* ran in full color were of Egyptian youth in Tahrir. One of the captions underlines the focus on youth in the images: "It struck me that these kids now finally believe in the ownership of their country." But Steavenson's very long essay is not the kind of piece I am focusing on here. The attention needed to read it and the socially rarified audience of the *New Yorker* already differentiate it from the rapidly circulating, small-bite narratives of the emerging revolution in other venues. And although I do find traces of the pattern I am describing in the reporting from Cairo by the *New York Times*, particularly in David Kirkpatrick's early writing, the number of

journalists working in Cairo for that paper and their experience as journalists (Michael Slackman, Nadim Audi, Mona El-Naggar, Liam Stack, Nazila Fathi, and Anthony Shadid in particular) show through the strong reporting there. What I want to point out here, rather, is the nonexpert coverage of the events in Egypt in the hundreds of other venues, especially broadcast venues. Ironically, detecting an overarching "narrative" in an event means that the long-form journalism of the *New Yorker*, the *New York Times*, and the *Los Angeles Times* is a bit different.

14. Ali Behdad and Juliet Williams, "Neo-Orientalism," in *Globalizing American Studies*, ed. Brian T. Edwards and Dilip Parameshwar Gaonkar (Chicago: University of Chicago Press, 2010), 283–284.

15. Thomas Friedman, interview, Meet the Press, January 30, 2011, http://www.nytimes.com /video/opinion/1248069599421/thomas-friedman-on-meet-the-press.html (accessed January 21, 2013).

16. My colleagues Jessica Winegar, a cultural anthropologist, and Wendy Pearlman, a political scientist, have been exploring ways in which attention to affect opens up discussions of the Arab uprisings of 2010/2011. See Jessica Winegar, "Fed-up and Bored: Affect and Political Action in Revolutionary Egypt," and Wendy Pearlman, "An Emotional Lens on the 2011 Arab Uprisings," both in *On the Ground: New Directions in Middle East and North African Studies*, ed. Brian T. Edwards (Doha: Northwestern University in Qatar, 2013), 23–30, 31–38 (also available at http://www.ontheground.qatar.northwestern.edu).

17. For more on Eurasia Group, see http://eurasiagroup.net/about-eurasia-group (accessed January 21, 2013).

18. Martha Raddatz and Kristina Wong, "Egypt, Yemen Protests Unnerve U.S. Officials," ABC News, January 27, 2011, http://abcnews.go.com/WN/egypt-yemen-protests-spark -fears-us-officials/story?id=12780724 (accessed January 21, 2013).

19. For an intriguing argument about what moves culture through the world, see Greg Urban, *Metaculture: How Culture Moves Through the World* (Minneapolis: University of Minnesota Press, 2001).

20. For such reflections on AJE, see Sam Gustin, "Al Jazeera's Spring," *Time*, October 26, 2011, http://www.time.com/time/specials/packages/article/0,28804,2091589_2091591 _2097895,00.html (accessed January 21, 2013); Aram Bakashian, "The Unlikely Rise of al Jazeera," *Atlantic*, January 10, 2012, http://www.theatlantic.com/international/archive /2012/01/the-unlikely-rise-of-al-jazeera/251112/ (accessed January 21, 2013); and David Zurawik, "It's Outrageous That Al Jazeera English Is Not on Cable in Most US Cities," *Baltimore Sun*, August 21, 2012, http://articles.baltimoresun.com/2012-08-21/entertain ment/bal-al-jazeera-english-cable-baltimore-20120821_1_al-jazeera-english-cable-balti more-viewers (accessed January 21, 2013).

21. For some of the glamour that Anderson Cooper's "undisclosed location" drew to him, see Mark Joyella, "Undisclosed Locations and Low-Light Live Shots: Reporters Adapt to Risks in Egypt," *Mediaite*, February 3, 2011, http://www.mediaite.com/tv/security -teams-undisclosed-locations-and-low-light-liveshots-reporters-adust-to-risks-in -egypt/ (accessed January 21, 2013).

22. For a brief account of the assault on Logan, which launched a torrent of discussion and debate in itself, see Brian Stelter, "CBS Says Lara Logan Suffered Brutal Attack in Cairo," *Media Decoder*, February 15, 2011, http://mediadecoder.blogs.nytimes.com/2011 /02/15/cbs-lara-logan-suffered-brutal-attack-in-cairo/?scp=5&sq=Lara+Logan&st=nyt (accessed January 21, 2013); for links to Egyptian journalist Mona Eltahawy's interviews, go to her website at http://www.monaeltahawy.com. Eltahawy was assaulted by Egyptian riot police in November 2011.

23. Edward W. Said, *Culture and Imperialism* (New York: Vintage, 1993), 289.

24. In *Politics of Piety: The Islamic Revival and the Feminist Subject* (Princeton, N.J.: Princeton University Press, 2005), Saba Mahmood provides a way of thinking about the agency of pious women, those whom Western feminists had overlooked as subjects of their own fate. Mahmood added a new preface to the 2012 reprint that addresses the question of religion and the Egyptian revolution. A nuanced account of how an older auditory technology—the cassette tape and the analog recordings of Islamic sermons, long for sale in Cairo and elsewhere—punctuates daily life is Charles Hirschkind, *The Ethical Soundscape: Cassette Sermons and Islamic Counterpublics* (New York: Columbia University Press, 2006). More recently, Hussein Ali Agrama's account of fatwas, court cases, and Islamic authority in *Questioning Secularism: Islam, Sovereignty, and the Rule of Law in Modern Egypt* (Chicago: University of Chicago Press, 2012) has shown the ways in which secularism and religion are constantly shifting and self-questioning categories. Agrama did the research for his book before Mubarak fell but completed the book afterward, which allowed him to make provisional comments on linkages between religion and the uprisings.

25. Thus making ironic Obama's statements such as "I am convinced that in order to move forward, we must say openly the things we hold in our hearts, and that too often are said only behind closed doors." Juan Cole summarized several such critiques of Obama's speech in Arab media in his posting "Reactions to Obama's Speech," *Informed Comment*, June 5, 2009, http://www.juancole.com/2009/06/reactions-to-obamas-speech.html (accessed November 6, 2012).

26. Omar Taher, "*Looks Like It's Falling Apart*: An Introduction," trans. Brian T. Edwards, *Public Space*, no. 9 (2009): 138. Subsequent references are cited in the text.

27. Omar Taher, *Kabitan Masr* (Captain Egypt) (Cairo: Atlas, 2007).

28. Michael Warner, "Publics and Counterpublics," *Public Culture* 14, no. 1 (2002): 75.

29. Ibid., 82.

30. Brian T. Edwards, "Tahrir: Ends of Circulation," *Public Culture* 23, no. 3 (2011): 493–504.

31. Robin Wright, *Rock the Casbah: Rage and Rebellion Across the Islamic World* (New York: Simon & Schuster, 2011).

32. Barbara Becker, "Near Forgotten MLK Comic Gains Fans in the Middle East," *Huffington Post*, January 18, 2011, http://www.huffingtonpost.com/barbara-becker/near -forgotten-mlk-comic-_b_808995.html (accessed October 30, 2012).

33. Michael Cavna, "Amid Revolution, Arab Cartoonists Draw Attention to Their Causes," *Washington Post*, March 7, 2011, http://www.washingtonpost.com/blogs/comic-riffs

/post/amid-revolution-arab-cartoonists-draw-attention-to-their-causes/2011/03/11/
ABlIBaR_blog.html (accessed October 30, 2012).

34. Brian T. Edwards, *Morocco Bound: Disorienting America's Maghreb, from Casablanca to the
Marrakech Express* (Durham, N.C.: Duke University Press, 2005), chap. 1.

35. *Metro* was not noticed despite the publication of Magdy El Shafee's short graphic fiction in the New York literary journal *A Public Space* in 2009, the AJE feature on his trial
in Cairo for publishing something that "infringed on public decency," as well as the
publication of an excerpt of *Metro* on the website Words Without Borders in February
2008.

36. Magdy El Shafee, interview with the author, Cairo, March 2011.

37. Magdy El Shafee, "About Me," Magdy El Shafee Comics, http://magdycomics.com
(accessed November 9, 2012).

38. Joe Sacco, *Palestine* (1996; reprint, Seattle: Fantagraphics, 2001).

39. I discuss *zahma* as a metaphor for contemporary Egypt (before the Tahrir uprisings) in
my introduction to the portfolio "Cairo 2010: After Kefaya," 128–133.

40. Edward Said, introduction to Sacco, *Palestine*, i–v.

41. Alan Moore, *Writing for Comics* (1985; reprint, Rantoul, Ill.: Avatar Press, 2003), 6.

42. Manar El Shorbagy, "The Egyptian Movement for Change—Kefaya: Redefining Politics in Egypt," *Public Culture* 19, no. 1 (2007): 175–196.

43. Magdy El Shafee, *Metro*, trans. Chip Rossetti (2008; reprint, New York: Metropolitan Books, 2012), 4. Subsequent references are cited in the text.

44. Scott McCloud, *Understanding Comics: The Invisible Art* (New York: Morrow, 1994), 66.

45. Magdy El Shafee and Ahmed Alaidy, "The Parkour War," trans. Brian T. Edwards,
Public Space, no. 9 (2009): 161–166.

46. In "Logics and Contexts of Circulation," I discuss texts that resist globalization's imperative to make the foreign a translatable value—in other words, economically fungible—
and survey critical discussions on this question.

47. MLynxQualey, "In Praise of . . . Mohamed Hashem, Force of Literary Freedom," *Arabic
Literature* blog (in English), *Word Press*, December 19, 2011, https://arablit.wordpress.
com/2011/12/19/in-praise-of-mohamed-hashem-force-of-literary-freedom/ (accessed October 30, 2012).

48. As Richard Jacquemond points out, "The opaque conditions that prevail in the publishing business, in Egypt more than elsewhere, make it a hard task to try to figure out the
actual sales [of the Arabic edition]" ("*The Yacoubian Building* and Its Sisters: Reflections
on Readership and Written Culture in Modern Egypt," in *Popular Culture in the Middle
East and North Africa: A Postcolonial Outlook*, ed. Walid El Hamamsy and Mounira Soliman [New York: Routledge, 2013], 144). He conservatively estimates 200,000 copies of
the Arabic edition of *The Yacoubian Building*. In 2009, Alaa Al Aswany announced that 1
million copies of the novel had been sold worldwide (cited in Jacquemond, "*The Yacoubian Building* and Its Sisters," 144).

49. Pankaj Mishra, "Where Alaa Al Aswany Is Writing From," *New York Times Magazine*,
April 27, 2008. After the revolution, the *New Yorker* called Al Aswany "Egypt's leading

novelist" (Wendell Steavenson, "Writing the Revolution," *New Yorker*, January 16, 2012).

50. See, for example, Marilyn Booth, "House as Novel, Novel as House: The Global, the Intimate, and the Terrifying in Contemporary Egyptian Literature," *Journal of Postcolonial Writing* 47, no. 4 (2011): 377–390; Jacquemond, "*The Yacoubian Building* and Its Sisters"; and the discussion of *The Yacoubian Building* in Joseph A. Massad, *Desiring Arabs* (Chicago: University of Chicago Press, 2007), 388–411.

51. Mehrez, *Egypt's Culture Wars*, 56.

52. Ibid., 56, 57.

53. Pascale Casanova, *The World Republic of Letters*, trans. M. B. DeBevoise (Cambridge, Mass.: Harvard University Press, 2007).

54. Mishra, "Where Alaa Al Aswany Is Writing From"; Steavenson, "Writing the Revolution." Robyn Creswell, the poetry editor at the *Paris Review* and a scholar of modern Arabic literature at Yale University, is the exception that proves the rule. Creswell took advantage of his relatively unique position to write a blog in the online edition of the *New Yorker* that discussed Sonallah Ibrahim as a visionary Egyptian writer ("Sonallah Ibrahim: Egypt's Oracular Novelist," Newyorker.com, August 20, 2013, http://www.newyorker.com/books/page-turner/sonallah-ibrahim-egypts-oracular-novelist [accessed November 13, 2013]). Creswell in turn retranslated Ibrahim's great first novel, *Tilk al-Ra'iha* (1966) (see note 56).

55. Ahmed Alaidy, *Being Abbas el Abd*, trans. Humphrey Davies (Cairo: American University in Cairo Press, 2006), 36 (original novel, *An Takun 'Abbas al-'Abd*, 2003). Subsequent references are cited in the text.

56. Sonallah Ibrahim, *That Smell and Notes from Prison*, ed. and trans. Robyn Creswell (New York: New Directions, 2013), and *The Committee*, trans. Mary St. Germain and Charlene Constable (Syracuse, N.Y.: Syracuse University Press, 2001).

57. Muhsin J. al-Musawi, "Engaging Globalization in Modern Arabic Literature: Appropriation and Resistance," *Modern Language Quarterly* 68, no. 2 (2007): 316.

58. Ibrahim, *Committee*, 16. Subsequent references are cited in the text.

59. Al-Musawi, "Engaging Globalization in Modern Arabic Literature," 315.

60. Mehrez, "The Value of Freedom: The Writer Against the Establishment," in *Egypt's Culture Wars*, 72–88.

61. Marilyn Booth, "Introduction: On the Fringes of Cities (Cairo) and Languages (Arabic)," in Hamdi Abu Golayyel, *Thieves in Retirement*, trans. Marilyn Booth (Syracuse, N.Y.: Syracuse University Press, 2006), xi–xviii.

62. Tarek El-Ariss, "Hacking the Modern: Arabic Writing in the Virtual Age," *Comparative Literature Studies* 47, no. 4 (2010): 534, 538, 543.

63. Chuck Palahniuk, *Fight Club* (1996; reprint, New York: Norton, 2005), 210. Subsequent references are cited in the text; inserted ellipses indicated by square brackets.

64. Miriam Bratu Hansen, "The Mass Production of the Senses: Classical Cinema as Vernacular Modernism," *Modernism/Modernity* 6, no. 2 (1999): 59–77. I discuss Hansen further in chapter 4.

3. "ARGO FUCK YOURSELF"

1. This rapprochement may have receded later. A ceremony to honor Asghar Farhadi in Iran was called off, as reported in Dave Itzkoff, "Iranian Ceremony to Honor 'Separation' Director Is Canceled," *New York Times*, ArtsBeat, March 12, 2012.

2. "Hollywoodism" is an annual conference held to coincide with the Fajr Film Festival; it was in its third year in 2013, though it seems not to have been repeated in 2014 or 2015. "The Hoax of Hollywood" was a one-day affair staged on March 11, 2013, at the Palestine Cinema in Tehran. See Saeed Kamali Dehghan, "Iran to Sue Hollywood over a Series of Films, Including the Oscar-Winning *Argo*," *Guardian,* March 12, 2013; and Thomas Erdbrink, "Stung by 'Argo,' Iran Backs Conference Denouncing 'Hollywoodism,'" *New York Times*, February 18, 2013, http://www.nytimes.com/2013/02/19/world/middleeast /stung-by-argo-iran-backs-conference-decrying-hollywoodism.html (accessed March 15, 2013). According to organizers, "the conference is set to concentrate on 'the aim of producing anti-Iranian and anti-Islamic films,' 'strategies to encounter the domination Cinema' and 'Hollywood and Zionism Cinema'" (http://www.fajrfilmfestival.com/en /index.php/first/36-the-third-international-conference-on-hollywoodism-will-be-held-in-tehran-on-the-sidelines-of-fajr-film-festival [accessed March 15, 2013]; although the main festival website is still available, the specific link given here is not).

3. The fuller language is as follows: "In 1950, the people of Iran elected Mohammad Mossadegh, a secular democrat, as Prime Minister. He nationalized British and US petroleum holdings, returning Iran's oil to its people. But in 1953, the US and Great Britain engineered a *coup d'état*, that deposed Mossadegh and installed Reza Pahlavi as Shah. The young Shah was known for opulence and excess. . . . The people starved. The Shah kept power through his ruthless internal police, the Savak. An era of torture and fear began" (Ben Affleck, dir., *Argo* [Warner Bros. Pictures, 2012]).

4. Secretary of State Madeleine Albright, remarks before the American-Iranian Council, March 17, 2000, Washington, D.C., http://www.fas.org/news/iran/2000/000317.htm (accessed March 21, 2013). While commentary at the time debated whether these remarks constituted a formal apology or not, Albright did officially acknowledge mistakes made:

> But that common ground has sometimes been shaken by other factors. In 1953 the United States played a significant role in orchestrating the overthrow of Iran's popular Prime Minister, Mohammed Mossadegh. The Eisenhower Administration believed its actions were justified for strategic reasons; but the coup was clearly a setback for Iran's political development. And it is easy to see now why many Iranians continue to resent this intervention by America in their internal affairs. Moreover, during the next quarter century, the United States and the West gave sustained backing to the Shah's regime. Although it did much to develop the country economically, the Shah's government also brutally repressed political dissent. As President Clinton has said, the United States must bear its fair share of responsibility for the problems that have arisen in U.S.–Iranian relations.

5. Hamid Naficy, *A Social History of Iranian Cinema*, 4 vols. (Durham, N.C.: Duke University Press, 2011–2012); Saeed Zeydabadi-Nejad, *The Politics of Iranian Cinema: Film and Society in the Islamic Republic* (New York: Routledge, 2010); Hamid Dabashi, *Close Up: Iranian Cinema, Past, Present, and Future* (London: Verso, 2001); Negar Mottahedeh, *Displaced Allegories: Post-revolutionary Iranian Cinema* (Durham, N.C.: Duke University Press, 2008). See also some of the essays in Richard Tapper, ed., *The New Iranian Cinema: Politics, Representation, and Identity* (London: Tauris, 2004).

6. Zeydabadi-Nejad, *Politics of Iranian Cinema*, 2.

7. Franco Moretti, *Distant Reading* (London: Verso, 2013); Dilip Parameshwar Gaonkar and Elizabeth A. Povinelli, "Technologies of Public Forms: Circulation, Transfiguration, Recognition," *Public Culture* 15, no. 3 (2003): 385–397.

8. Thomas Erdbrink, "Film to Present Iran's View of 'Argo' Events," *New York Times*, January 11, 2013.

9. Erdbrink joined the *New York Times* after a decade in Tehran as a correspondent for the *Washington Post*. He was still at the *Post* for the previous Academy Awards, when Asghar Farhadi won the Best Foreign Film Award in 2012. Erdbrink covered that award a bit differently, as reported in "'A Separation' Oscar Win Heralded by Iranians," *Washington Post*, February 27, 2012.

10. When I say a larger discussion of Iranian art cinema had "made its way" into Erdbrink's article, I am indicating the way in which the discussion of circulation works. On this point, I have been inspired by Greg Urban's powerful discussion in *Metaculture: How Culture Moves Through the World* (Minneapolis: University of Minnesota Press, 2001).

11. I thank Hamid Naficy for helping me to make this point more clearly.

12. Thomas Erdbrink, "As Iran's Currency Keeps Tumbling, Anxiety Is Rising," *New York Times*, October 5, 2012.

13. I was in Iran in December 2005 when President Ahmadinejad made his infamous speech denying the Holocaust (I was in Kashan at the time and then returned to Tehran). What was being discussed domestically was not the speech but rather a terrible pollution crisis.

14. Sarah Gillespie, "'Argo' and the Iranian Savage—a Film Review," *Palestine Chronicle*, November 27, 2012, http://www.palestinechronicle.com/argo-and-the-iranian-savage-a-film-review/ (accessed March 11, 2013).

15. Brian T. Edwards, "American Studies in Motion: Tehran, Hyderabad, Cairo," in *Globalizing American Studies*, ed. Brian T. Edwards and Dilip Parameshwar Gaonkar (Chicago: University of Chicago Press, 2010), 319.

16. Mohsen Milani, "Scholar of Iran Hostage Crisis Puts 'Argo' in Historical Context," *al-Monitor*, November 2, 2012, http://www.al-monitor.com/pulse/originals/2012/al-monitor/argo-obscures-hostage-crisis.html (accessed April 5, 2013).

17. "'Argo': Former Ambassador Ken Taylor Sets the Record Straight," *Star* (Toronto), October 7, 2012, http://www.thestar.com/news/canada/2012/10/07/argo_former_ambassador_ken_taylor_sets_the_record_straight.html (accessed April 5, 2013).

18. According to a PBS documentary, *Canadian Caper* (1980), a Filipino housekeeper named Lolita worked for John Sheardown, the Canadian deputy chief of mission, and

his wife, Zena. It was at Sheardown's house that four of the six "houseguests" actually lived (Sheardown and his wife are not characters in *Argo*). The website History vs Hollywood calls Lolita the original for Sahar because she knew but did not reveal the true identity of the Americans. See *"Argo* (2012)," History vs Hollywood, n.d., http://www .historyvshollywood.com/reelfaces/argo.php (accessed November 27, 2013). Notable, of course, is that Lolita was not Iranian.

19. Farhang Rajaee, ed., *The Iran–Iraq War: The Politics of Aggression* (Gainesville: University Press of Florida, 1993).

20. Eric Volmers, *"Argo* Takes Entertaining Liberties with Canadian Legend: Ben Affleck Invites Former Canadian Ambassador to Iran to Change Postscript of Film *Argo*," *Calgary Herald*, October 12, 2013.

21. *"Argo*: Absolute Authenticity," on Ben Affleck, dir., *Argo*, BluRay DVD (Warner Brothers, 2013).

22. For a Canadian press view of *Argo*, see Jian Ghomeshi, *"Argo* Is Crowd-Pleasing, Entertaining—and Unfair to Iranians," *Globe and Mail* (Toronto), November 2, 2012. Iranian sources picked up on the Canadian criticism.

23. Erdbrink, "Film to Present Iran's View of 'Argo' Events."

24. Erdbrink had been the *New York Times* Tehran bureau chief for less than a year, although he had lived in Tehran, by his account, for the previous decade and was a reporter for the *Washington Post* through much of that time. A powerful example of this manner of reporting on Iran took place prior to Erdbrink's tenure at the *Times* when President Ahmadinejad approached the United States during the Bush administration in an attempt to reopen dialogue between the two nations. The *New York Times* gave a psychological reading of the Iranian president and covered the story as an "interesting window into the mentality and thinking of Iran," particularly because "it seemed to reflect a[n] inclination to dwell on myriad grievances of the past rather than on the problem at hand, namely Iran's suspected nuclear weapons program" (Christine Hauser, "Iranian President's Letter to Bush Emerges," *New York Times,* May 9, 2006). For an argument about how journalism can act as a reasoning institution, see James Ettema: "Journalism should be asked to participate not merely by presiding over an uncritical forum for reason-giving but by acting as a reasoning institution that aggressively pursues and compellingly renders reasons satisfying the criterion" ("Journalism as Reason-Giving: Deliberative Democracy, Institutional Accountability, and the News Media's Mission," *Political Communication* 24, no. 2 [2007]: 143).

25. Quoted in Charles Laurence, "Silicon and World Domination," *Daily Telegraph* (London), reprinted in *The Nation* (Bangkok), April 23, 1997. Laurence quotes David Hasselhoff as saying:

> *Baywatch* is a cultural revolution. It affects the whole world. All these people—200 million of them in China alone—watch our show and get a little bit of California; the beautiful people, the freedom, the weather. And they want it, they want to live like us. . . . Listen, in Iran, this show is leading the people away from the Ayatollahs. Just the other day, I was at this dinner, and there was the Shah of Iran's

widow at the next table. She comes over and she hugs me. And she tells me that over there, the counter-revolution has started, that people gather in households with satellite television to come together and watch. And when the women lift their veils—what's underneath? Blonde hair! They dye their hair to be like *Baywatch*!

26. In 1987, Mark Gasiorowski published "The 1953 Coup d'Etat in Iran," *International Journal of Middle East Studies* 19, no. 3: 261–286. But it was not until 2000 that the documentation of the coup was made public. In 1998, CIA director George Tenet reneged on a pledge that he and his predecessors had made to declassify material relating to the 1953 coup. In 1999, the National Security Archive filed a lawsuit for the release of two reports believed to give details of CIA activity. The *New York Times* received a leaked copy of the report and published large sections of it in the April 16 and June 18, 2000, editions and posted them on its website at http://www.nytimes.com/library/world/mideast/041600iran-cia-index.html (accessed March 20, 2013). For a full account of the history of this disclosure, see Malcolm Byrne, ed., *The Secret History of the Iran Coup, 1953*, National Security Archive Electronic Briefing Book no. 28 (Washington, D.C.: National Security Archive, November 29, 2000), http://www.gwu.edu/~nsarchiv/NSAEBB/NSAEBB28/ (accessed March 20, 2013). For Albright's remarks before the American-Iranian Council on March 17, 2000, see note 4.

27. Stephen Kinzer, *All the Shah's Men: An American Coup and the Roots of Middle East Terror* (Hoboken, N.J.: Wiley, 2003).

28. This was a major bone of contention regarding the film for Canadians, especially Ken Taylor:

> Mr. Taylor applauded former U.S. president Jimmy Carter for appearing on CNN on Thursday night to assert that "90 per cent of the contributions to the ideas and the consummation of the plan was Canadian." "I think it was pretty well clarified by President Carter's remarks," Mr. Taylor said Sunday. Mr. Taylor said that, while the CIA did contribute significantly to the rescue, history must reflect that it was overwhelmingly a Canadian mission. "I wouldn't want to leave it with young Canadians that we were sort of carried along by the CIA," he said. "It was a cooperative venture and the two countries worked very well together." (Kirk Makin and Steven Chase, "Oscar Win for *Argo* Highlights Canada's Role in Iran Hostage Rescue," *Globe and Mail*, February 25, 2013)

Ben Affleck was apparently eager to convert Taylor and flew him to Los Angeles. As reported by the *Globe and Mail*, "Mr. Affleck later assuaged much of Mr. Taylor's anger by flying him to Los Angeles and allowing him to write a new postscript that more accurately reflected Canada's role."

A Canadian friend I spoke to about this refashioning of history in *Argo* reminded me, "I don't go to the movies expecting authenticity." True enough. But the BluRay release goes to great lengths to assure viewers of the film's authenticity. In an interview included on the BluRay DVD, Affleck claims to have been a Middle Eastern studies major (he appears to have dropped out of college after a semester or a year; he does not mention this detail in the interview) and asserts an almost scholarly pedigree, saying that he had read everything and seen everything about the hostage crisis. So even if my friend from Canada didn't expect historical authenticity, the film hits you over the head with its attempt at authenticity.

29. Rebecca Ford, "Alan Arkin on the Studio Exec Who Inspired His 'Argo' Character," *Hollywood Reporter*, October 12, 2012, http://www.hollywoodreporter.com/news/argos -alan-arkin-his-character-378391 (accessed July 15, 2013).

30. Tom Junod, "The Lethal Presidency of Barack Obama," *Esquire*, August 2012.

31. The Taylors were the Canadian ambassador and his wife. John Sheardown was the second-ranking member of the Canadian Embassy in Iran who in reality hid four of the Americans in his home for four months. The remaining two Americans stayed in Ambassador Taylor's house.

32. This scene at the Oscars puts me in mind of the argument made by Jodi Dean and what she calls the fantasies of communicative capitalism, in *Democracy and Other Neoliberal Fantasies: Communicative Capitalism and Left Politics* (Durham, N.C.: Duke University Press, 2009). See also Evgeny Morozov, *To Save Everything, Click Here: The Folly of Technological Solutionism* (Philadelphia: PublicAffairs, 2013).

33. Ramin Mostaghim, "Tehran Film Conference Denounces 'Cultural Assault' of Hollywood," *Los Angeles Times*, February 5, 2013, http://articles.latimes.com/2013/feb/05/world /la-fg-wn-tehran-conference-denounces-cultural-assault-of-hollywood-20130205 (accessed March 26, 2013).

34. Mike Gravel, "On Balancing Personal Freedom with Its Responsibilities," abstract for a presentation in February 2013, reprinted at http://www.hollywoodism.org (accessed May 10, 2013, but no longer available).

35. "Speakers at Iranian Conference Decry 'Zionist' Influence on Hollywood," *Adl*, February 5, 2013, http://www.adl.org/press-center/press-releases/anti-semitism-international/speakers -at-iranian-conference-decry-zionist-influence-hollywood.html (accessed April 20, 2013).

36. Omid Hoseini, "Is *Argo* More Dangerous Than Our Hibernation?" (in Persian), *Ahestan*, March 1, 2013, http://www.ahestan.ir (accessed April 10, 2013) (trans. Marjan Mohammadi). I thank Marjan Mohammadi for the translations she provided for this chapter.

37. "The Film 'Argo' from an Iranian Perspective" (in Persian), BBC Persian, October 25, 2012, http://www.bbc.co.uk/persian/arts/2012/10/121025_argo_tamasha.shtml (accessed April 22, 2013) (trans. Marjan Mohammadi).

38. Tahmineh Milani, "'Argo' Is Made to Normalize Relations Between the Two Countries" (in Persian), *Cinemaema*, 11 Esfand 1391 (March 1, 2013), http://www.cinemaema .com/module-pagesetter-viewpub-tid-26-pid-8389.html (accessed April 26, 2013) (trans. Marjan Mohammadi). I thank Ehsan Khoshbakht for pointing me to this article.

39. Gisu Faghfuri, "An Interview with Asghar Farhadi: Impossible to Rest" (in Persian), *Bahar Newspaper*, February 26, 2013, http://www.baharnewspaper.com/News /91/12/08/6582.html, (accessed April 26, 2013) (trans. Marjan Mohammadi). I thank Ehsan Khoshbakht for pointing me to this article.

40. Richard Corliss, "Asghar Farhadi," *Time*, April 18, 2012.

41. Massoud Mehrabi, "An Interview with Asghar Farhadi," *Film International: Iranian Film Quarterly* 17, nos. 1–2 (2011): 110, 109, 127.

42. Quoted in Erdbrink, "'A Separation' Oscar Win Heralded by Iranians."

43. I thank Russ Castronovo for pushing me to think further about the role of the judge and for his insightful remarks after he heard a portion of this chapter at the Futures of American Studies Institute, Dartmouth College, Hanover, New Hampshire, June 2013.

44. Asghar Farhadi, dir., *A Separation* (Filmiran and Sony Pictures Classics, 2011).

45. Hamid Dabashi's takedown of Jafar Panahi is in "The Tragic Endings of Iranian Cinema," al Jazeera, March 21, 2013, http://www.aljazeera.com/indepth/opinion/2013/03 /201332017573910035z.html (accessed April 26, 2013).

46. Aram, "Who Represents What in *A Separation*?" (in Persian), http://www.scenario.ir /thread-396.html (accessed April 10, 2013) (trans. Marjan Mohammadi). Thanks to Marjan Mohammadi also for locating this passage.

47. Jean-Luc Nancy, *L'Évidence du film: Abbas Kiarostami = The Evidence of Film: Abbas Kiarostami* (Brussels: Yves Gevaert, 2001).

48. Ezatolah Zarghami, *Hozeh News*, 14 Shahrivar 1390 (September 5, 2011); Jamal Shourjeh, *Tehran Today*, 26 Mordad 1390 (August 17, 2011), quoted in "A Literal Disagreement in Viewpoint: Controversies over Selecting This Year's Iranian Representative in the Oscars" (in Persian), *Bistochahar* (Twenty-Four), no. 85, 1 Aban 1390 (October 23, 2011): 88–89 (trans. Marjan Mohammadi).

49. All the names in this section have been changed, except for those of public figures.

50. In his four-volume *Social History of Iranian Cinema*, Naficy makes a number of remarks about the history of Iranian dubbing that allow avenues into further research on this topic.

51. Deborah Solomon, "Tales from Tehran: Questions for Abbas Kiarostami," *New York Times Magazine*, March 11, 2007.

52. Joan Copjec, "The Object-Gaze: Shame, Hejab, Cinema," *Filozofski Vestnik* 27, no. 2 (2006): 11. Subsequent references are cited in the text.

53. See, especially, Hamid Naficy, "Under Cover, on Screen: Women's Representation and Women's Cinema," in *The Globalizing Era, 1984–2010*, vol. 4 of *A Social History of Iranian Cinema* (Durham, N.C.: Duke University Press, 2012), 92–174.

54. Ali Khamenei, *Farhang va tahajom-e farhangi* (Culture and cultural invasion) (Tehran: Sazman-e Farhangi-ye Enqelab-e Eslami, 1994), 163, quoted in ibid., 252.

55. Ali Behdad and Juliet Williams, "Neo-Orientalism," in *Globalizing American Studies*, ed. Edwards and Gaonkar, 284–285; Hamid Dabashi, "Native Informers and the Making of the American Empire," *Ahram*, June 1–7, 2006, http://weekly.ahram.org.eg/2006 /797/special.htm (accessed January 26, 2010), and *Brown Skin, White Masks* (New York: Pluto Press, 2011).

56. Hamid Naficy, *An Accented Cinema: Exhilic and Diasporic Filmmaking* (Princeton, N.J.: Princeton University Press, 2001), and *Iran: A People Interrupted* (New York: New Press, 2008).

57. Michael M. J. Fisher, *Mute Dreams, Blind Owls, and Dispersed Knowledges: Persian Poesis in the Transnational Circuitry* (Durham, N.C.: Duke University Press, 2004), x.

58. Saeed Kamali Dehghan, "Iran Jails Director Jafar Panahi and Stops Him Making Films for 20 Years," *Guardian*, December 20, 2011, http://www.theguardian.com/world /2010/dec/20/iran-jails-jafar-panahi-films (accessed May 11, 2013).

59. Ben Child, "Jafar Panahi Loses Appeal Against Six-Year Prison Sentence," *Guardian*, October 18, 2011, http://www.theguardian.com/film/2011/oct/18/jafar-panahi-loses-ap peal-prison (accessed May 11, 2013).

60. Hamid Dabashi, "The Tragic Endings of Iranian Cinema," al Jazeera, March 21, 2013, http://www.aljazeera.com/indepth/opinion/2013/03/201320175739100357.html (accessed April 26, 2013).

61. Ehsan Khoshbakht, dir., *A Journey Through Iranian Cinema with Mark Cousins* (Type-cast Films, 2012).

62. Abbas Kiarostami, "An Unfinished Cinema" (text written for the Centenary of Cinema, Paris, 1995, and distributed at the Odeon Theatre), reprinted in the DVD release of Abbas Kiarostami, dir., *The Wind Will Carry Us* (MK2 Productions, 1999).

63. Mehrnaz Saeedvafa, *Jerry & Me* (Typecast Films, 2012).

64. I thank Ehsan Khoshbakht for this detail and for discussing with me the particulars of the Iranian dubbing of this scene. At the time of writing, Doostdar maintained a Wikipedia entry in Farsi with samples of his dubbing of John Wayne (http://fa.wikipedia .org/wiki, accessed July 15, 2013).

65. Ehsan Khoshbakht, e-mail to the author, May 19, 2013.

66. Ehsan Khoshbakht, "Survival of the Unfit: On Mehrnaz Saeed-Vafa's *Jerry & Me*," *Mubi*, June 10, 2013, https://mubi.com/notebook/posts/survival-of-the-unfit-on-meh rnaz-saeed-vafas-jerry-me (accessed July 15, 2013).

67. Hakim Belabbes is not identified in the film itself, but his voice is immediately recognizable to me, and he is thanked in the credits. I confirmed with Saeedvafa that Belabbes indeed posed this question in 1996.

4. COMING OUT IN CASABLANCA

1. The picnickers are known as MALI (Mouvement alternatif pour les libertés individuelles). On Taïa's coming out, see Karim Boukhari, "Abdellah Taïa, homosexuel envers et contre tous" (Abdellah Taïa, homosexual against all opposition), *TelQuel*, June 9–15, 2007, 82–88, http://www.telquel-online.com/277/couverture_277.shtml (accessed February 27, 2012).

2. I refer to Gerald Graff's classic book *Beyond the Culture Wars: How Teaching the Conflicts Can Revitalize American Education* (New York: Norton, 1993).

3. Alexander R. Galloway, *The Interface Effect* (Malden, Mass.: Polity, 2012).

4. For arguments pointing toward a new Morocco, see Marvine Howe, *Morocco: The Islamist Awakening and Other Challenges* (New York: Oxford University Press, 2005). More

thoughtful are Valérie K. Orlando, *Francophone Voices of the "New" Morocco in Film and Print: (Re)presenting a Society in Transition* (New York: Palgrave Macmillan, 2009), and *Screening Morocco: Contemporary Film in a Changing Society* (Athens: Ohio University Press, 2011).

5. Joshua Asen and Jennifer Needleman's documentary *I Love Hip Hop in Morocco* (Rizz Productions, 2007) provides a good introduction to the Moroccan hip-hop scene and some valuable interviews that demonstrate how Moroccan rap artists variously interpret the meanings of American rap as an art form and its relationship to African America as representative of (alternatively) an oppressed minority or wealthy consumerist society.

6. For several years, I engaged with Moroccan graduate students at the Moroccan Cultural Studies Center at Sidi Mohammed Ben Abdellah University in Fes, leading seminars on theories of globalization and circulation and sometimes co-supervising or advising graduate student projects. With the help of research assistant Aretha Chakraborti, I created a website on the theme of the effect of aspects of globalization on Fes. The projects that emerged from the Fes center were inevitably creative and taught me the range of changes that young Moroccans felt were impacting their daily lives, including American-style cosmetics, shopping centers, film styles, music, and tourism, among many others.

7. Miriam Bratu Hansen, "The Mass Production of the Senses: Classical Cinema as Vernacular Modernism," *Modernism/Modernity* 6, no. 2 (1999): 59–77.

8. Brian T. Edwards, "Preposterous Encounters: Interrupting American Studies with the (Post)colonial, or *Casablanca* in the American Century," *Comparative Studies of South Asia, Africa, and the Middle East* 23, nos. 1–2 (2003): 70–86.

9. Maria Daïf, "VCD: Doublages à la marocaine" (VCD: Dubbing, Moroccan style), *TelQuel*, May 8–14, 2004, http://www.telquel-online.com/archives/126/sujet6.shtml (accessed December 19, 2012), now at http://w.telquel-online.com/archives/126/sujet6.shtml (accessed March 28, 2015) (my translation).

10. Ibid. Original quote: "Que font les jeunes quand ils ne se reconnaissent pas dans les images que leur renvoient téléfilms, films marocains et télévision marocaine? Ils s'approprient des images d'ailleurs et les adaptent à leur quotidian et à leur langage."

11. Ibid. Original quote: "Celle que vous n'entendrez pas à la télévision marocaine parce que trop politically not correct (ça jure, ça parle de filles, de haschisch, d'argent et de chômage, la vie des jeunes de quartiers, en somme).Voilà pourquoi ces doublages ont du succès, en plus du fait, bien entendu, que le décalage (Matrix parlant marrakchia, par exemple) est hilarant."

12. Brent Hayes Edwards, "The Uses of *Diaspora*," *Social Text* 19, no. 1 (2001): 65.

13. Ranajit Guha, *Dominance Without Hegemony: History and Power in Colonial India* (Cambridge, Mass.: Harvard University Press, 1997), 13, 157, quoted in ibid., 73, 60.

14. I thank Sadik Rddad for transliterating and helping me understand the lyrics. Mostafa Ouajjani further discussed their meaning with me.

15. Later in 2006, new legal restrictions against the piracy of Moroccan films made it harder to obtain *Marock* in this way. But in the winter of 2007, it was still possible to obtain contraband copies of Hollywood and other foreign films openly on Moroccan sidewalks.

16. For example, the director and actor Nabil Lahlou, a harsh critic of *Marock*, stated simply that neither the film nor its director was Moroccan at all, in "Tanger accueille le huitième Festival du film national: 'Marock' fait scandale" (Tangier hosts the eighth national film festival: "Marock" scandalizes), Maghreb Arabe Presse, December 6, 2005. Others called for a demand for reimbursement of Centre Cinématographique Marocain (CCM) funds on similar grounds. Nourredine Sail, director of CCM, the national film agency—which authorizes, promotes, and helps fund Moroccan films—defended the film and its Moroccanness.

17. Laïla Marrakchi, *Marock* (Pan Européene Distribution, 2005).

18. In addition to traditional research methods, my research for this essay includes a wide range of websites, chat rooms, blogs, and Internet reviews. In addition, I opened an online, password-protected discussion of *Marock* with graduate students in cultural studies at Sidi Mohammed Ben Abdellah University, Dhar Mahrez, Fes, where I am an affiliate. I thank participants for sharing a diverse range of views on the film and its controversies.

19. "'Marock' Sparked Clash in Tangiers," *Morocco Times*, December 19, 2005. In February 2006, an Islamist website, Mejliss al Kalam, further discredited the director by highlighting Laïla Marrakchi's apparent support for cartoons representing the Prophet. See Mejliss al Kalam, February 14, 2006, http://www.mejliss.com/showthread.php?s=a0c1b 0269e7766387faede413d33a917&t=227880 (accessed February 10, 2007). Magoo 57 (a contributor) rails against Marrakchi for saying that she is in favor of freedom of expression: "Leila Marrakchi [sur le programme de canal+ 'LA MATINALE*'] se dit '*au nom de la liberté d'expression*' à la diffusion des caricatures de sidna mohamed [alih salt]" (Leila Marrakchi [on the Canal+ program "Morning"] says that "in the name of freedom of expression" [she defends] the diffusion of caricatures of our prophet Mohamed [peace be upon him]).

20. Mohamed Dahan, letter to Sawt Annass, *Attajdid*, May 21–27, 2006.

21. Shana Cohen and Larabi Jaidi, *Morocco: Globalization and Its Consequences* (New York: Routledge, 2006).

22. Susan Ossman, *Three Faces of Beauty: Casablanca, Paris, Cairo* (Durham, N.C.: Duke University Press, 2002).

23. Valérie Orlando employs a rubric with respect to understanding Maghribi literature that does not fit within the familiar terms of "postcolonial" literary studies in "To Be Singularly Nomadic or a Terrorized National: At the Crossroads of Francophone Women's Writing of the Maghreb," *Meridians: Feminism, Race, Transnationalism* 6, no. 2 (2006): 33–53. But the tensions between "nationalist" and "nomadic" that animate her compelling discussion seem relevant to this argument.

24. I discuss Franklin Roosevelt's famous conversation with Sultan Mohammed in terms of racial time and deferral of Moroccan rights in *Morocco Bound: Disorienting America's Maghreb, from Casablanca to the Marrakech Express* (Durham, N.C.: Duke University Press, 2005), chap. 1. For a discussion of the flood of commodities that followed the arrival of American troops in World War II as well as of some Moroccan responses to that

flood (such as those by Fatima Mernissi and Houcine Slaoui), see *Morocco Bound*, chap. 2. By "promise/threat," I am alluding to Jacques Derrida's formulation in *Monolingualism of the Other: Or, The Prosthesis of Origin*, trans. Patrick Mensah (Stanford, Calif.: Stanford University Press, 1998), in which he suggests that a promise is a threat risked.

25. Said Graiouid, *Social Exile and Virtual H'rig: Computer-Mediated Interaction and Cyber-café Culture in Morocco* (London: Idea Group, 2005), 57–92.

26. Benjamin Lee and Edward LiPuma express this idea efficiently: "The contemporary decline of the nation-state as the relevant unit of analysis for global capitalism is reflected in two distinct circulatory movements; the increasingly transnational character of labor and the global mobility of finance capital" ("Cultures of Circulation: The Imaginations of Modernity," *Public Culture* 14, no. 1 [2002]: 208). See also Arjun Appadurai, *Fear of Small Numbers: An Essay on the Geography of Anger* (Durham, N.C.: Duke University Press, 2006).

27. The idea that contemporary Moroccan cultural production should not be caught forever in the logic of postcolonialism is not a unique position, but I want to attribute it to Mohammed Dahan, who stated it eloquently at an academic conference at Mohammed V University, Rabat, on October 3, 2004. The setting was an open session following the conference "Urban Generations: Post-colonial Cities," at which Dahan had spoken on "cinéma et culture urbaine." I attended the meeting as well, and so here I draw on my notes. The minutes of the meeting, with Dahan's comment, may be viewed online at http://www.open.ac.uk/Arts/ferguson-centre/AfricaNetwork/Documents/minso3oc tober2004tb2.pdf (accessed February 10, 2007).

28. Hicham Houdaifa and Fedoua Tounassi, "Marock: Le vrai débat" (Marock: The real debate), *Le Journal Hebdomadaire*, May 27–June 2, 2006, 18–25.

29. Ibid., 20–21.

30. Ibid., 20.

31. See, for example, the photos of Marrakchi posted in her profile at IMDB.com.

32. Some of Fatima Mernissi's pieces for *Femmes du Maroc* were later collected in *Êtes-vous vacciné contre le "harem"?* (Are you vaccinated against the "harem"?) (Casablanca: Editions le Fennec, 2008).

33. Hansen, "Mass Production of the Senses," 60. Subsequent references are cited in the text.

34. Lee and LiPuma, "Cultures of Circulation"; Dilip Parameshwar Gaonkar and Elizabeth A. Povinelli, "Technologies of Public Forms: Circulation, Transfiguration, Recognition," *Public Culture* 15, no. 3 (2003): 385–397.

35. Edwards, "Preposterous Encounters."

36. Patrick Antona, "Interview: Laila Marrakchi & Morjana El Alaoui (*Marock*)," *Ecranlarge*, February 15, 2006, http://www.ecranlarge.com/interview-252.php (accessed February 10, 2007).

37. Ibid.

38. Ronald A. T. Judy, "On the Politics of Global Language, or Unfungible Local Value," *Boundary 2* 24, no. 2 (1997): 101–143; Gayatri Chakravorty Spivak, *Death of a Discipline* (New York: Columbia University Press, 2003).

39. On incorporating the regular breakdown of technology into the notion of circulation, see Brian Larkin's brilliant essay "Degraded Images, Distorted Sounds: Nigerian Video and the Infrastructure of Piracy," *Public Culture* 16, no. 2 (2004): 289–314.

40. Karim Boukhari, *"Marock*: Le film de tous les tabous" (Marock: The film of all the taboos), *TelQuel*, April 29–May 5, 2006, 40–47.

41. Joseph Massad, "Re-orienting Desire: The Gay International and the Arab World," *Public Culture* 14, no. 2 (2002): 362, 363. See also Joseph A. Massad, *Desiring Arabs* (Chicago: University of Chicago Press, 2007).

42. The wording is careful in the biography published on Taïa's most recent books published by Seuil. On the back cover of *Infidèles*, published in August 2012, he is described as follows: "Through his books and through the public positions he has taken, openly [literally, with an uncovered face], for defending homosexuality and the freedom of individuals in his country, he has become a sort of icon in Morocco and in Muslim countries, violently attacked by Islamists and praised by youth and modernists" (my translation).

43. Abdellah Taïa, "L'enfant endormi" (The sleeping child), in *Des nouvelles du Maroc* (Stories from Morocco), ed. Loïc Barrière (Paris: Paris–Méditerranée; Casablanca: Éditions EDDIF, 1999), 73–85.

44. I don't mean to suggest that Taïa did not garner any attention with the publication of *Mon Maroc*, which was reviewed in the Moroccan press. See, for example, Aziz Daki, "'Mon Maroc' de Abdellah Taia" ("Mon Maroc" by Abdellah Taïa), *Aujourd'hui le Maroc*, December 4, 2001, where it is given a positive review. In the film *Tarik el Hob* (Road to love, Rémi Lange [Les films de l'ange, 2001]), Taïa appears as himself in a documentary within the documentary, speaking of marriage between men and public acceptance of homosexuality in the oasis of Siwa (in Egypt near the Libyan border) until the mid-twentieth century.

45. Abdellah Taïa, *Mon Maroc* (Paris: Séguier, 2000), 45–49.

46. Chadwane Bensalmia, "J'ai été élevé dans la honte" (I was raised in shame), *TelQuel*, January 28–February 3, 2006, http://www.telquel-online.com/archives/210/arts2_210 .shtml (accessed July 7, 2013), now at http://ykzxlck.telquel-online.com/archives/210 /arts2_210.shtml (accessed March 28, 2015) (my translation). Original quote: "Au-dessus de ces petites obsessions, planaient deux ombres: son rêve enfantin de faire du cinéma et une peur profonde de la réaction de sa famille quand elle percerait le secret de son homosexualité."

47. Brian Whitaker, "Interview with Abdellah Taia," *Al-bab*, January 2009, http://www .al-bab.com/arab/articles/abdellah_taia_salvation_army.htm (accessed June 28, 2013).

48. Bensalmia, "J'ai été élevé dans la honte." Original quote: "Est-ce un témoignage, un testament, une thérapie? Abdellah Taïa refuse toute étiquette: 'C'est simplement la révélation d'une réalité de la société marocaine que je n'ai jamais croisée dans aucune littérature.'"

49. Abdellah Baïda, *Au fil des livres: Chroniques de literature marocaine de langue française* (About books: Chronicles of Moroccan literature in French) (Casablanca: Croisée des Chemins, 2011), 139–141 (my translation). Original quotes: "on entre dans *Le jour du roi*

comme on entre dans un songe, imperceptiblement"; "loin du ton sec et froid d'un discours sociologique, le récit opte pour la fluidité du temps et de l'espace."

50. Brian T. Edwards, review of *An Arab Melancholia*, by Abdellah Taïa, *Bookforum* 19, no. 1 (2012): 42–43.

51. I discuss Bowles in *Morocco Bound*, chap. 5, as well as in "The Worlds of Paul Bowles," *Tingis* 2, no. 2 (2005):14–22, and "The Moroccan Paul Bowles," *Michigan Quarterly Review* 50, no. 2 (2011): 191–209.

52. Taïa, *Mon Maroc*, 105. Taïa mentions Bowles again: "Paul Bowles is dead. Mohammed Mrabet guards his tomb which will one day perhaps be as mythic as that of Jean Genet in Larache: a Muslim tomb!" (*Le rouge du tarbouche* [Paris: Séguier, 2004], 113 [my translation]). This description corresponds to a conversation I had with Taïa on a train ride between Casablanca and Rabat, when he spoke positively to me about Bowles's work.

53. Taïa, *Le rouge du tarbouche*, 48.

54. Ibid., 51.

55. Rachid O.'s trilogy consists of *L'enfant ébloui* (Dazzled child) (Paris: Gallimard, 1995), *Plusieurs vies* (Many lives) (Paris: Gallimard, 1996), and *Chocolat chaud* (Hot chocolate) (Paris: Gallimard, 1998). Rachid O., who was born in Rabat in 1970 but has not divulged his full identity, later published *Ce qui reste* (That which remains) (Paris: Gallimard, 2002) and, most recently, *Analphabètes* (Illiterates) (Paris: Gallimard, 2013).

56. I agree with this categorization. I call Bowles a "Tangerian" writer in *Morocco Bound*, 86.

57. Quoted in Catherine Simon, "Abdellah Taïa, le vertige de la liberté" (Abdellah Taïa, the dizziness of freedom), *Le Monde des livres*, September 22, 2010 (my translation). Original quote: "monde ignoré et méprisé par les intellectuels marocains."

58. Laetitia Grotti and Maria Daïf, "Etre homo au Maroc" (To be homo in Morocco) (cover story), *TelQuel*, March 27–April 2, 2004, http://www.telquel.ma/archives/120/couverture_120_1 (accessed July 2, 2013), now at http://w.telquel.ma/archives/120/couverture_120_1 (accessed March 28, 2015) (my translation). Original quote: "L'homosexualité au Maroc est frappée d'un double H : Hchouma (honte) et Haram (péché). Il y a encore un an, Mohamed Asseban, membre du conseil des ouléma de Rabat-Salé déclarait à la presse : 'Le bûcher pour les homos.' À l'instar de sa religion et de sa loi, la société marocaine est incontestablement homophobe."

59. Orlando, *Francophone Voices of the "New" Morocco in Film and Print*, 137. In a different chapter, Orlando discusses Taïa in the context of what she calls "Moroccan libertine authors." I review Orlando's book in *Journal of North African Studies* 16, no. 3 (2011): 493–496.

60. Orlando, *Francophone Voices of the "New" Morocco in Film and Print*, 137.

61. Boukhari, "Abdellah Taïa, homosexuel envers et contre tous" (my translation). Original quote: "Le PJD est parfaitement capable de poser, demain, une question orale au Parlement, pour demander le jugement ou l'interdiction de l'écrivain. L'offensive menée, sur un autre plan, par le parti de Saâd-Eddine El Othmani, contre le film Marock risque de se reproduire, cette fois contre une personne: Abdellah Taïa."

62. For an update on the "sniper," who revealed his identity in early 2013, see "Corruption au Maroc: Le 'sniper de Targuist' poursuit son combat à visage découvert" (The "sniper of

Targuist" continues his fight with his face shown), *Jeune Afrique*, March 4, 2013, http://www.jeuneafrique.com/Article/ARTJAWEB20130304154535 (accessed June 27, 2013).

63. "Interview: Abdellah Taïa," *Le Journal Hebdomadaire*, December 1–7, 2007, 31 (my translation). Original quote:

> C'est quand même très bizarre, cette réaction toujours négative, toujours exagérée, de la société marocaine dès qu'on parle d'homosexualité qui existe pourtant partout, dans tous les milieux sociaux, à Marrakech comme à Sidi Slimane. Le Maroc, société paternaliste, machiste, veut croire, et faire croire, que la virilité n'est possible que dans le cadre de l'hétérosexualité. L'homosexualité serait, bien sûr, un vice occidental. Nous, nous serions les purs, les autres seraient les mécréants, les pécheurs et iront en enfer alors que nous irons, nous, bien évidemment au paradis. . . . Le Maroc, au fond, malgré sa soi-disant légendaire hospitalité, est un pays fermé. Le pays est encore une gigantesque prison pour ses "citoyens," qu'ils soient homosexuels ou hétérosexuels.

64. Marc Endeweld, "Abdellah Taïa, une colère marocaine" (Abdellah Taïa, a Moroccan anger), Minorites, November 16, 2009, http://www.minorites.org/index.php/2-la-revue/552-abdellah-taia-une-colere-marocaine-1.html (accessed July 7, 2013) (my translation). Original quotes: "Pour moi, ce qui s'est passé à Ksar El-Kebir est l'équivalent marocain de Stonewall"; "Quelque chose d'historique s'est passé là, à l'intérieur du Maroc, entre Marocains et l'Occident n'y était pour rien."

65. Taïa, *Le rouge du tarbouche*, 61–62 (my translation).

66. I make this argument in the final section of "Logics and Contexts of Circulation," in *A Companion to Comparative Literature*, ed. Ali Behdad and Dominic Thomas (Oxford: Blackwell, 2011), 454–472. I contrast a postcolonial approach to one that focuses on circulation in the reading of Tahar Ben Jelloun's continued critical engagement with the work of Paul Bowles, in particular the latter's translation projects with Mohammed Mrabet.

67. Whitaker, "Interview with Abdellah Taia."

EPILOGUE

1. Mark Twain, *The Jumping Frog: In English, Then in French, Then Clawed Back into a Civilized Language Once More by Patient, Unremunerated Toil* (New York: Harper, 1903), 3.

2. Twain's story was translated into French and embedded in a discussion of his and two other American humorists' work in the famous *Revue des Deux Mondes*. Twain complained that though the French critic "says all manner of kind and complimentary things about me," he "still he can't see why it [the story] should ever really convulse any one with laughter" (ibid., 3–4).

3. Hamid Naficy, *The Making of Exile Culture: Iranian Television in Los Angeles* (Minneapolis: University of Minnesota Press, 1993), 90.

4. Edward W. Said, *Culture and Imperialism* (1993; reprint, New York: Vintage, 1994), 289.

5. Ali Behdad and Juliet Williams, "Neo-Orientalism," in *Globalizing American Studies*, ed. Brian T. Edwards and Dilip Parameshwar Gaonkar (Chicago: University of Chicago Press, 2010), 284.

6. Deborah Solomon, "Revolutionary Spirit: Questions for Marjane Satrapi," *New York Times Magazine*, October 21, 2007, quoted in ibid., 296.

7. Quoted in Boris Kachka, "Pen International," *New York*, September 20, 2004, http://nymag.com/nymetro/arts/books/reviews/9870/ (accessed November 13, 2014).

8. Karyn M. Peterson, "'Persepolis' Restored to Chicago School Libraries; Classroom Access Still Restricted," *School Library Journal*, March 19, 2013, http://www.slj.com/2013/03/books-media/persepolis-restored-to-chicago-school-libraries-classroom-access-still-restricted/ (accessed November 8, 2014).

9. Patty Wetil, "'Persepolis' Ban by CPS Boosts Sales at Local Bookstores," March 18, 2013, http://www.dnainfo.com/chicago/20130318/lincoln-square/persepolis-ban-by-cps-boosts-sales-at-local-bookstores (accessed November 13, 2014).

10. Quoted in ibid.

11. Khury Petersen-Smith, "Who's Afraid of *Persepolis*?" (interview of Marjane Satrapi), SocialistWorker.org, April 9, 2013, http://socialistworker.org/2013/04/09/whos-afraid-of-persepolis (accessed February 12, 2015). See also Betsy Gomez, "Marjane Satrapi Wants to Know What CPS Fears About *Persepolis*," April 9, 2013, Comic Book Legal Defense Fund, http://cbldf.org/2013/04/marjane-satrapi-wants-to-know-what-cps-fears-about-persepolis/ (accessed November 13, 2014).

12. Behdad and Williams, "Neo-Orientalism," 285.

13. Ibid., 284.

14. Edward W. Said, *Orientalism* (New York: Vintage, 1979), 2–9.

15. Ibid., 3.

16. On the history of the discipline of Middle East studies in the United States, see Zachary Lockman, *Contending Visions of the Middle East: The History and Politics of Orientalism* (New York: Cambridge University Press, 2004).

17. Said, *Orientalism*, 3.

18. Nadim Damluji, "A Conversation About *Habibi*'s Orientalism with Craig Thompson," *Hooded Utilitarian*, November 16, 2011, http://www.hoodedutilitarian.com/2011/11/a-conversation-about-habibis-orientalism-with-craig-thompson/ (accessed November 12, 2014).

19. I thank Pamela Baldwin for alerting me to this new series as I was writing the epilogue and for discussing it with me.

20. Joseph Massad, "'Homeland,' Obama's Show," al Jazeera, October 25, 2012, http://www.aljazeera.com/indepth/opinion/2012/10/2012102591525809725.html (accessed November 12, 2014).

21. Avi Nir is the CEO of the Keshet Media Group in Israel, was also an executive producer of *Homeland*, and was named the most influential person in Israeli television in 2013 by the major Israeli newspaper *Haaretz*. See Ruta Kupfer, Gili Izikovich, and Liat

Elkayam, "Israeli Television's No. 1: Avi Nir," *Haaretz*, August 2, 2013, http://www .haaretz.com/life/culture/israeli-culture-s-100-most-influential-people/.premium -1.539468 (accessed November 16, 2014). The authors note that "Avi Nir . . . not only embodies, to a large extent, the values of local commercial television; he long ago achieved quasi-mythical status. Nir is regarded as the person who is able to predict what the viewing audience wants, satisfy their tastes precisely and, time after time, create shows that will keep them glued to the screen."

22. Robyn Creswell, "Alas, Babylon," *New York Times Book Review*, October 16, 2011, posted earlier with the title "The Graphic Novel as Orientalist Mash-Up," October 14, 2011, http://www.nytimes.com/2011/10/16/books/review/habibi-written-and-illustrated -by-craig-thompson-book-review.html?pagewanted=all&_r=0 (accessed November 12, 2014).

23. Craig Thompson, *Carnet de voyage* (Marietta, Ga.: Top Shelf, 2004), 5.

INDEX

Italicized numbers refer to pages on which illustrations appear.

Hollywood look, 144, 156, 162, 165–176, 197

Holocaust, denial of, 6. *See also* Jews

Hologram for the King, A (Eggers), 207, 214, 217–219

Homeland (television program), 207, 209–214, *211*

homosexuality, 140, 180–197, 250n44

Horizon perdu, L' (Lost horizon; film, 2000), 156

Horowitz, Adam, 229n11

Hosseini, Shahab, 110–111

Howe, Marvine, 246n4

al-Hubb fi al-Manfa (Love in exile, Taher), 233n3

al-Hubb fi Dar al-Baida (Love in Casablanca; film, 1991), 146, 162

Hudson, Rock, 196

humanism, 157

Huntington, Samuel, 17–18, 123

al Hurra (television station), 30

Hussein, Saddam, 143

hybridity, 38

Ibrahim, Sonallah, 38, 71, 75–76, 239n54

I Love Hip Hop in Morocco (film, 2007), 247n5

imagined public, 26

'Imarat Ya'qubian (*The Yacoubian Building*, Al Aswany), 70–72, 74, 205

Infidèles (Faithless, Taïa), 180

In film nist (This is not a film; film, 2011), 108, 129–131

Ingres, Jean-Auguste-Dominique, 216

Innocence of Muslims (film, 2012), 5–9, 31, 89, 137

interface effect, 142

International Monetary Fund, 144

Internet: and American cultural forms, 20; in Egypt, 69; hacking of, 61, 78–79, 81, 233n6; in Iran and India, 10; and media coverage of Arab uprisings, 46–47; in Morocco, 141–143, 151; and surveillance,

229n10; YouTube on, 158, 180, 190–194, 229n10. *See also* social networking

iPhones, 129, 132. *See also* technology

Iran: economic crisis in, 91–92; protests in, 9; relations of, with U.S., *14*, 84–86, 89–103, 116, 212

Iranian cinema: censorship and state control of, 86–87, 117–120, 245n49; and circulation, 114–115, 131–132; dubbing of, 8, 16, 117–118, 134–135, 199; and gender, 86; Western response to, 87–89, 103–104, 114–115, 123–124, 127. *See also specific films*

Iranian Revolution (1979), 202–205

Iran-Iraq War (1980–1988), 95

Iraq, invasion and occupation of, by U.S., 3, 50, 82, 143

Islah, Fadwa, 197

Islam: art and architecture of, 215; and globalization, 21; in *Homeland*, 210; and Islamophobia, 157, 215; and *Marock*, 156–157, 167–169; Qur'an, 3, 7, 77, 160, 215–216; and *A Separation*, 109; and women's agency, 237n24

Israel, 43–44, 212–213

It Takes a Village (Clinton), 51

I Want to Get Married (blog), 41

Jaabouq (The joint, Tahir), 197

Jacquemond, Richard, 36, 71, 238n48

Jadaliyya (website), 47–48

Jaidi, Larabi, 157

James, Henry, 17

Jameson, Fredric, 231n25

#Jan25 movement (Egypt), 39, 53, 61, 72, 233n3. *See also* Arab uprisings; Twitter

al Jazeera (television network), 46–47, 144

Al Jazeera English (AJE), 46. *See also* al Jazeera

jazz international tours, 10, 12–13, 20. *See also* cultural diplomacy (U.S.)

Jerry & Me (film, 2012), 133–137

Jews, 6, 101, 136, 157, 168, 177–178